Shakespeare's Arguments with History

Shakespeare's Arguments with History

Ronald Knowles

Reader in English Literature
University of Reading

palgrave

First published 2002 by
PALGRAVE
Houndmills, Basingstoke, Hampshire RG21 6XS and
175 Fifth Avenue, New York, N. Y. 10010
Companies and representatives throughout the world

PALGRAVE is the new global academic imprint of
St. Martin's Press LLC Scholarly and Reference Division and
Palgrave Publishers Ltd (formerly Macmillan Press Ltd).

ISBN 0–333–970217 hardback

This book is printed on paper suitable for recycling and
made from fully managed and sustained forest sources.

Library of Congress Cataloging-in-Publication Data

Knowles, Ronald, 1940–
Shakespeare's arguments with history / Ronald Knowles.
    p. cm.
    Includes bibliographical references (p.) and index.
    ISBN 0–333–97021–7 (cloth)
    1. Shakespeare, William, 1564–1616—Knowledge—History.
    2. Literature and history—Great Britain—History—16th century.
    3. Literature and history—Great Britain—History—17th century.
    4. Great Britain—History—1066–1687—Historiography. 5. Historical
    drama, English—History and criticism.   6. Shakespeare, William,
    1564–1616—Histories.   7. Shakespeare, William, 1564–1616
    —Technique.   8. Troy (Extinct city)—In literature.   9. Rome—In
    literature.   10. Rhetoric, Renaissance.   11. Persuasion (Rhetoric)   I. Title.

PR3014 .K58 2001
822.3'3—dc21
                                                            2001040660

10   9   8   7   6   5   4   3   2   1
11   10   09   08   07   06   05   04   03   02

Printed and bound in Great Britain by
Antony Rowe Ltd, Chippenham, Wiltshire

To the memory of Michael and Marian Butterworth

Contents

Acknowledgements

I am deeply grateful for a generous award from the Arts and Humanities Research Board which enabled me to finish this study. In this regard I am indebted to the support of Patricia Parker and Tom McAlindon. Agostino Lombardo and Pilar Zozaya are thanked for invitations to lecture on Shakespeare at, respectively, La Sapienza University, Rome, and Barcelona University, where I explored some of the ideas in this book. Some materials here derive from earlier publications. The discussion of *Henry IV Parts I and II* is an expanded version of what first appeared as 'Honour, Debt, the Rejection and St Paul' in my *Henry IV Parts I & II* 'The Critics Debate' (London: Macmillan, 1992). The chapter on *Coriolanus* is a much-developed enlargement of a short article, 'Action and Eloquence: Volumnia's Plea in *Coriolanus*' (*Shakespeare Bulletin*, vol. 14, no. 4, 1996, pp. 37–8). The section on *Henry VI Part II* focuses historical material researched for my edition of the play ('The Arden Shakespeare', Walton-on-Thames, Thomas Nelson and Sons, 1999).

For support from colleagues I thank Cedric Brown, Andrew Gurr, Christopher Hardman and Grace Ioppolo. Special thanks to the fifteenth-century historian Anne Curry who unfailingly answered my questions and provided references. As ever the Inter-library Loan department in Reading University Library has been a model of efficiency and courtesy. Throughout the production of this volume the enthusiastic support of Eleanor Birne at Palgrave has been very much appreciated. For several years my friends Neil Cornwell and Maggie Malone have taken a close interest in all my work – I look forward to continuing discussions. Once again Cheryl Foote is thanked for her word-processing skills.

Unless otherwise stated, the text quoted throughout this study is *The Riverside Shakespeare* edited by G. Blakemore Evans (Boston: Houghton Mifflin Company, 1974).

The dedication is to those with whom I shared house as a student many years ago. In return, I share their memory with this study.

RONALD KNOWLES
University of Reading

Introduction

The role of argument played a considerable part in the development of the western world. Arguments over Christian belief which were to establish religious practice were determining factors in the history of Europe. In turn, government of peoples and countries took shape over arguments concerning the relationship of secular and ecclesiastical powers. Legal right was determined by accommodating classical equity and Teutonic custom with faith. Thus religion, politics and law developed in the arguments of parliament and conclave, court and convocation. When words could no longer persuade, argument turned to action and finally, for some, to the suffering of martyrdom or the shame of execution. Such was the inheritance of the Tudor world of the Renaissance and the Reformation and it is reflected in Shakespeare's preoccupation with history.

This book is not a study of Shakespeare's use of historical sources. Investigation of that kind is found elsewhere, particularly in the now completed work of Geoffrey Bullough and in the scholarly, single-volume editions of Shakespeare's plays which provide learned commentary, notes and appendices.[1] Reference to use of historical materials will be made, however, in the wider purpose of this study which is to demonstrate the significance of argument in Shakespeare's dramatic art. Argument generates conflict and conflict generates action in the ensuing disjunction between words and deeds. Shakespeare's implicit theory and explicit practice as playwright draw on the centrality of argument in Renaissance culture and education and on the actuality of argument in the everyday world of human encounter, whether in council chamber or kitchen.

Shakespeare's characters speak and they act, they say things and they do things. Much of the speech is concerned with persuasion or dissuasion in one form or another, directly or indirectly, by reasoning or suggestion, command or plea. Even action itself was considered as a form of argument, as we shall see. The following chapters examine plays from English, Roman and Greek history in terms of the arguments they dramatise. Such a demonstration takes us to the heart of each play, even though a particular argument might seem, at first, incidental. This procedure offers a method of critical analysis, a mode of practical criticism, a technique of teaching and a revealing process of learning. Every writer on Shakespeare will stop to examine closely a passage of dialogue from time to time, and perhaps touch on argument, but usually in relation to something else – source, analogue, influence, etc. – which often leads away from the immediate dramatic moment. The pervasive practice of New Criticism, which laid the foundation for close textual analysis, usually concentrated on the interrelated patterns of organic imagery, converting poetic drama to dramatic poem. Only occasionally do we find discussion of any given argument which appraises intentional or unintentional tendentiousness as related to the character and play as a whole. More recent critical practice usually applies the various arguments of modern theorists to Shakespeare's plays. I wish to rediscover and re-examine the foundation of Shakespeare's art in the ramifications of argument without recourse to such rebarbative techniques as, for example, speech-act theory or discourse theory. Such criticism so often leaves the plays dead on the page. Consequently, I will keep specialist terminology to a minimum. Much can be gained from simple and direct questions. Chapter 1 will provide a sketch of Renaissance logic and rhetoric and, in the following chapters, such features will occasionally be identified. But at the outset what I propose can be immediately engaged with by any reader without any prior knowledge of early education or linguistic theory.

The demonstration of the efficacy of this approach is also the argument of this book. My thesis is that recognition of the function of argument at the heart of drama adds a huge dimension which, heretofore, has been overlooked or undervalued in Shakespeare criticism. This is not to imply that Shakespeare's theatre is a theatre of ideas, a drama of dry debate (though some might argue that this was true of *Troilus and Cressida*), with characters as merely vehicles for polemical positions. On the other hand, Shakespeare's plays are by no means devoid of ideas. His drama derives from ideas as concrete aspects of direct experience acted out in front of us, not from ideas as abstract concepts removed from life to books. Put another way, reason, meaning and motive are shown subjected to contingency and expedience. Conviction struggles with rationalisation, principle becomes pretext. By referring ideas to life rather than abstract thought, Shakespeare reveals meaning as more complex than the truisms of religion, politics and morality allow for in popular discourse of the day. In Shakespeare's presentation of human beings, in so far as individuals cannot have complete possession of truth or an entire grasp on circumstance, because of their essential fallibility and the ineffability of reality, what they say will often be coloured by bias, self-deception and special-pleading which are revealed by the partiality of their arguments. Shakespeare, like Machiavelli, is an empiricist by instinct and, like Falstaff, a sceptic when confronted with abstracts such as 'honour'. What Francis Bacon said of the Florentine Statesman could be emphatically said of his contemporary: 'We are much beholden to Machiavel and others, that write what men do and not what they ought to do.'[2]

Shakespeare's argument with history is threefold. Argument in the sense of plot is taken from the sources, but those sources have their own argument in the sense of the ideology which informs the presentation of history. Shakespeare's own argument arises in his reworking of both plot material and informing cultural beliefs in a critique which questions prevailing norms. Perhaps the most notorious example of this is the case of *Henry V*. Is it a play which celebrates nationalism and kingship, or a play which undermines the very celebration of English national heroism? The analysis of argument in the play is most revealing on this issue. The English chroniclers were strongly influenced by Christian providentialism and a didacticism tempered by rhetorical decorum (freely inventing speeches and such-like to agree with what was probable according to principles of stereotypical propriety).[3] Roman history, above all in Plutarch, freed Shakespeare from Christian teleology and nationalist propaganda, and laid bare the ethics of classical humanism confronted with the realities of politics and the individual. In a sense the story of Troy presented Shakespeare with his greatest challenge, since history and romance tradition had fostered both satirical and sentimental representations made complex by the medievalisation of Greek antiquity.[4]

The relative naturalism of late sixteen-century drama, an evolutionary jump away from the homiletics of morality play and interlude, allowed Shakespeare's imagination, influenced but not controlled by rhetoric and logic, to deconstruct and reconstruct his sources by re-enacting the process by which past experience becomes history. In the drama of the live theatre, as I discuss in the concluding chapter, Shakespeare not only recreated the empirical conditions of historian as witness, but also freed the past from the fixity of the page. The resurrected personages of history now spoke for themselves and the audience, free from the directives of a didactic narrator, could bear witness to the meaning of experience, rather than accept the truism of precept, by hearing and seeing arguments and actions, words and deeds. *Troilus and Cressida* is explicitly designed on this principle and our attention is drawn to it throughout performance: thus, as final chapter, it is placed as the summation of this aspect of Shakespeare's drama and the most demanding and fruitful challenge to this critical approach.

1
Shakespeare and Argument

The beginning of this chapter will survey Shakespeare's use of the word argument and the semantic range of the late sixteenth century. Then a most important meaning of the word, which is fundamental for this book as a whole, will be dwelt on, namely the argument of action. That is, argument often meant the 'proof' made manifest by an action – by an appearance, happening, incident, occasion, situation, gesture, and so on.[1] The physical action of argument has the constant potential of presenting a counter-argument. What takes place on stage, what we see, can confute what we hear said. In addition, action that we hear of can have various functions, as in *Antony and Cleopatra*, when Scarus bewails Antony's flight from the battle of Actium and spells out its significance. Antony

> Claps on his sea-wing, and (like a doting mallard),
> Leaving the fight in height, flies after her.
> I never saw an action of such shame;
> Experience, manhood, honor, ne'er before
> Did violate so itself.

>   (3.10.19–23)

The categorical dismay pre-empts any extenuation by the audience. Then a few examples of argument in the plays will be examined as illustration in preparation for the more extensive studies which follow.

Argument is related to rhetoric and logic in education and Renaissance humanism, and a brief sketch will evoke the particular cast of mind of Shakespeare's audience, or at least the educated part of it. If the reader finds this too technical he or she may turn directly to the chapters on the plays and only consult this section when a need arises.

Argument as evidence or proof is a common early meaning of the word (see *OED* 1) and in a particular instance, by use of a syntactic doublet Shakespeare reinforces this. In *1 Henry VI*, the king, accepting Lord Protector Gloucester's negotiations for a French marriage with Margaret, daughter of the Earl of Armagnac, instructs him: 'In argument and proof of which contract, / Bear her this jewel, pledge of my affection' (5.1.46–7). Argument as evidence is indicated by the word 'proof'. Thus evidence is what the jewel symbolises, to a lesser extent its value in itself, and implicitly the ceremonial embassy which will imbue the object with a further value. What the jewel symbolises will be put into courtly words by the Lord Protector. A comic counterpart to this, in *Love's Labours Lost*, Boyet reports of Moth, Armado's page, who is being instructed by King Ferdinand to lead his Russian 'embassage', 'Action and accent did they teach him there' (5.2.99). The argument of Henry's jewel consists, therefore, of the object, the action and speech, as evidence of royal intention. Again, when Gloucester dreams of the heads of Somerset and Suffolk on his broken staff, the Duchess peremptorily dismisses it:

> Tut, this was nothing but an argument
> That he that breaks a stick of Gloucester's grove
> Shall lose his head for his presumption.

> (*2 Henry VI* 1.2.32–4)

But the dream allegorises another argument for evidence of a political reality the truth of which Gloucester learns to his cost. At its simplest, argument can mean theme or subject as France reminds Lear of Cordelia '... she ... The argument of your praise' (*King Lear* 1.1.214–15). Or when, in *Troilus and Cressida*, Achilles' having taken over Ajax' fool Thersites is discussed:

Nestor Then will Ajax lack matter, if he have lost his argument.
Ulysses No, you see he is his argument that has his argument, Achilles.
(2.3.94–7)

The hapless Helena rebukes Hermia and Lysander for making her a theme for modesty:

> If you have any pity, grace, or manners,
> You would not make me such an argument.

> (*A Midsummer Night's Dream* 3.2.241–2)

Sometimes argument becomes something like business-in-hand, as in *Henry V* when Williams unknowingly argues with the king, the night before Agincourt, 'for how can they charitably dispose of any thing, when blood is their argument' (4.1.142–3), a context which will be looked at in greater detail later in this study. From another point of view, the cause rather than the effect, argument rather than action, can be stressed, as in *Hamlet*, 'Rightly to be great / Is not to stir without great argument' (4.4.53–4). Cause can be seen as the situation which gives rise to it, though the subtle inflections of the word are sometimes difficult to pin down.

Timon's steward warns him of the emptiness of fulsome gratitude, 'Ah, when the means are gone that buy this praise, / The breath is gone whereof this praise is made' (*Timon of Athens* 2.2.169–70), but Timon insists that if the situation were reversed, 'And try the arguments of hearts, by borrowing' (2.2.178), he would find a reciprocal generosity. Arguments here clearly allude to the preceding 'breath' of 'praise'. That is, Timon would test the avowals of his beneficiaries. However, when this situation arises out of necessity, at first urging that others are more indebted to Timon than himself and on hearing that he is the third to be asked, Sempronius rejects the approach for not having been first made to him on the pretext that it would 'prove an argument of laughter' (3.3.20). Argument here could be cause, occasion, theme, instance, topic or example. However, hovering in the background might be the technical literary meaning that Sempronius' situation could become an illustrative opening of the larger comedy of Timon's misfortune, as a synoptic argument often preceded the actual play. This metadramatic emphasis is made in *Love's Labours Lost*, in the context referred to above, when Boyet warns the ladies of the approach of the disguised 'Muscovites':

> Arm, wenches, arm! encounters mounted are
> Against your peace. Love doth approach disguis'd,
> Armed in arguments.

> (5.2.82–4)

Arguments are persuasions of love, arms in love's metaphorical war, but in addition there is much evidence to show the popularity of Russian masquers, a performance which would have been preceded by an argument. Though it should be stressed that this could be an action rather than speech as we see in watching the dumb show of 'The Mousetrap' in *Hamlet*. Ophelia comments, 'Belike this show imports the argument of the play' (3.2.139–46). King Claudius, in the course of the play itself sensing danger, wants to know if anyone has heard a more explicit argument, in words, 'Have you heard the argument? Is there no offense in't' (3.2.232–3). This fundamental duality between argument as speech and argument as action, is found in *Henry IV 1 & 2*. Falstaff asks 'shall we have a play extempore', to which Hal replies, 'Content, and the argument shall be thy running away' (*1 Henry IV*, 2.4.277–81). Subject as plot is clearly indicated here; however, in *2 Henry IV* there is a more complex instance. In Henry's well-known speech towards the end of the play – 'God knows, my son, / By what by-paths and indirect crook'd ways / I met the crown' – he reconsiders his life's struggle with the ideas and actions of usurpation, legitimacy, rebellion and succession, 'For all my reign hath been but as a scene / Acting that argument' (4.5.183–5, 197–8). This example is rather comprehensive in its inclusiveness: it is obviously metadramatic; it is literal, argument being the central argument of right in civil war; it is abstract and conceptual, involving political, legal and theological questions; and it is very concrete, involving action – force of arms, bloodshed and death.

Though arguments, debates, persuasions, etc., permeate Shakespeare's plays, the word 'argument' meaning 'a series of statements' or 'process of reasoning' (*OED* 4) rarely appears. Benedick is celebrated by Ursula, 'For shape, for bearing, argument, and valor' (*Much Ado About Nothing*, 3.1.96), and here intellectual wit is paralleled with chivalric action. Bringing to a halt a badinage sequence with obscene witty play debunking romantic love, Mercutio declares to Romeo and Benvolio that he 'meant indeed to occupy the argument no longer' (*Romeo and Juliet*, 2.4.100). He thereby graphically caps his argument by a *double entendre* offering the physical ('occupy' as coitus) to reject the ideal ('drivelling love' l.91), action subverting idea. Another more involved example shows Shakespeare's awareness of a distinction in scholastic logic.

In *The Merry Wives of Windsor*, citizen Ford, disguised as 'Master Brook', enlists the unwitting Falstaff into a stratagem to test his wife's faithfulness, considering that if Falstaff could discover any stain on her reputation it would further his illicit suit:

> Now, could I come to her with any detection in my hand, my desires had instance and argument to commend themselves.
>
> (2.2.232–4)

In the Oxford edition quoted here the editor astutely observes, '*instance and argument*. Both these are terms used in scholastic logic. An *instance*

(*OED sb*.5) is "a case adduced in objection to or disproof of a universal assertion", the assertion in this case being that Mistress Ford is always chaste. An *argument* (*OED sb*.3) is "a reason produced in support of a proposition".[2] Paradoxically, 'instance' could also mean the opposite to that cited here, *OED sb*.6 gives, 'A fact or example brought forward in support of a general assertion or an argument, or in illustration of a general truth'. So instance can both prove or disprove. Both meanings were current in Shakespeare's time, and both illuminate a major passage in *Troilus and Cressida*, Troilus' witness of Cressida's betrayal in act 5, scene 2. This scene is discussed more widely in a later chapter, but note here how Troilus insists, against the principle of contradiction, that 'This is, and is not, Cressid!' (l.146). Troilus cannot accept that the faithful Cressida has become unfaithful Cressida. The latter is 'Diomed's Cressida', the former is his. The irrationality of this is ratified by a neologism in an appeal to 'Bifold authority' (l.143). Troilus is disavowing what the rhetoricians called the 'inartistic' testimony of witness (which the audience has shared), and is trying to find some paradoxical authority. Having seen and heard the act of betrayal, empirical evidence has to be acknowledged and, in doing so, Troilus resolves his sophistry by seizing on the paradoxical meanings of 'instance':

> Instance, O instance, strong as Pluto's gates,
> Cressid is mine, tied with the bonds of heaven;
> Instance, O instance, strong as heaven itself,
> The bonds of heaven are slipp'd, dissolv'd and loos'd,
> And with another knot, [five]-finger-tied,
> The fractions of her faith, orts of her love,
> The fragments, scraps, the bits and greasy relics
> Of her o'er-eaten faith, are given to Diomed.

> (ll.153–60)

In the first 'instance' Cressida is a particular example as evidence of a general proposition, namely something like 'love is faithfulness'. As Troilus attempts to reassert this the truth forces him to convert instance into its scholastic meaning and Cressida is seen as 'a case . . . in . . . disproof of a universal assertion', thus 'The bonds of heaven are slipp'd'.

Argument as physical evidence is plainly there before Troilus, and this brings us to the crucial concept for Shakespeare's drama, argument as manifestation in the sense of that which is made manifest by a situation or person or appearance or a thing. That is, action itself, independent of words, can constitute an argument. Examples where Shakespeare makes this plain are not difficult to find. After the defeat at Actium Antony sends his lowly ambassador to Octavius. As he appears Octavius asks, 'Know you him?', to which Dolabella replies:

> Caesar, 'tis his schoolmaster,
> An argument that he is pluck'd, when hither
> He sends so poor a pinion of his wing,
> Which had superfluous kings for messengers
> Not many moons gone by.

> (3.12.2–6)

On his entrance the status of Antony's emissary furnishes visual evidence of Antony's situation, which is subjected to Dolabella's dismissive irony. However, Hardin Craig comments on precisely this example as follows:

> In the case of *argument* or *proof* we have not only the common Elizabethan senses in Shakespeare but a number of instances where the word carries its logical application to the middle term in the syllogism, the proof or evidence; as, for example, in *Antony and Cleopatra* . . .[3]

Craig does not expand on this, but put crudely the syllogism would be something like the following:

Major	Inappropriate use of lesser servants indicates collapse of status.
Minor	This is Antony's servant.
Conclusion	Antony's position has collapsed.

A crucial factor in the development of English drama was the movement from the Senecan tragedy of declamation to a theatre which incorporated onstage action.[4] Though we take for granted action on stage, from small domestic incident to large-scale spectacle, in the classical tradition action is reported, not seen. Neoclassical emulation and imitation led to productions of the Senecan sensationalist tragedies of blood and revenge in the learned milieux of the universities and the Inns of Court. The earliest translations of Seneca into English were by Jasper Heywood between 1558 and 1561, of the *Troas*, *Thyestes* and *Hercules Furens*. In 1581 Thomas Newton made available the translations by various hands of *Seneca his Tenne Tragedies*. Rhetoric, eloquence and declamation in part characterise

Seneca. Action is discussed, not carried out on stage. Happenings are described or accounted for, usually with the distance of retrospect, often by a *nuncio* or other character who has witnessed or learnt of the event. Shakespeare retained the highly charged poetry of Seneca – not just in the early *Titus Andronicus* but in the great tragedies – but dramatised action on stage before an audience. For example, in chapter 8 below on *Antony and Cleopatra*, Shakespeare's staging of Antony being hoist aloft to the Monument by Cleopatra is an important dramatic argument of action in contrast to the comparison made in, for example, the Countess of Pembroke's translation of Robert Garnier's *The Tragedy of Antonie* (1595) where, in Senecan fashion, the same event is simply reported. As spectators of action audiences became witnesses not just auditors, witnesses of two kinds of evidence, not just of the verbal arguments between characters, and not just of the arguments of action, but witnesses of the relation between the two. This situation, for example, is presented to the stage audience, and the audience proper, by Brutus and Mark Antony in their famous speeches on the central action, the assassination of Julius Caesar.

To open up the possibilities of the argument of action some instances may be given here as a prelude to the more extensive studies, particularly of *Julius Caesar* and *Troilus and Cressida*. One of Shakespeare's most famous speeches occurs in *As You Like It*, namely Jacques' 'All the world's a stage' (2.7.139–66) on the ages of man, culminating in senility, 'second childishness and mere oblivion, / Sans teeth, sans eyes, sans taste, sans everything' (ll.165–6). It is not uncommon to find this quoted out of context, which rather misses the ironic point of what follows. The immediately succeeding stage direction reads '*Enter* ORLANDO *with* ADAM', and Duke Senior's response provides a cue for the director and actors, 'Welcome. Set down your venerable burden, / And let him feed' (ll.167–8). The entry is evidence which confutes Jacques' argument. We clearly see that age is not 'sans everything', but finds support in youth. In the terms of the play, 'service' is reciprocated by love within the larger affirmations of hospitality and courtesy. This is a very clear-cut unequivocal argument of action. Elsewhere, Shakespeare can be more ramified or ambivalent as when, for example, the Marshall commands, 'Stay, the king hath thrown his warder down' (*Richard II*, 1.3.118), which will be discussed in some detail.

Sometimes the action Shakespeare is concerned with is yet to come about or is hypothetical, as in the case of Caesar's triumph in *Antony and Cleopatra*. Here, consider the example of *King John*. The play, as E.A.J. Honigmann has shown, is largely structured around political confrontation which engages in 'nicely-argued disquisitions on moral concepts, often illustrating the conflict of two value-systems in a finely-pointed dualism'.[5] Honigmann enumerates these dualisms and finds at the heart of them right and might. On stage action is largely stiff and formal, befitting the subject of ambassadorial encounter and debate. However, in the midst of this emerges the image of the assassination of Arthur. For King John to keep his position assured Hubert is suborned as executioner (3.2.65–6). From this point we have the juxtaposition of two things: abstract argument about such matters as legitimacy, right and inheritance; and the concrete fact of an impending atrocity – the murder of an innocent young boy. Act 3 closes with the legate Pandulph explaining to the Dauphin that Arthur's murder would give rise to such a reaction against John that the French would be well supported. Therefore, Pandulph argues that he, Lewis, should precipitate Arthur's death by mounting an invasion. Lewis's reply closes the act: 'Strong reasons makes strange actions. Let us go; / If you say ay, the king will not say no' (3.4.182–3).

The action referred to here is the invasion, but it provides an ironic cue for what immediately follows with the opening of act 4. Hubert and the executioners enter ready to prepare for the death of Arthur: 'Heat me these irons hot' (4.1.1) Hubert commands, and young Arthur is eventually shown Hubert's written order, 'Must you with hot irons burn out both mine eyes?' he asks (l.39). A 'strange', in the sense of shocking, action indeed, the atrocity of which, measured in Arthur's pathos, outweighs any possible 'strong reason'. Thus the argument of action controverts any argument of 'policy', the key Machiavellian word in the play. Dramatic emphasis secures audience (and the executioners') recognition of a moral criterion which judges political action. Arthur's situation, his looks, gestures and speech combined create a pathos greater than his words alone. There is a 'speech' beyond words, as Volumnia says, in *Coriolanus*, 'Action is eloquence' (3.2.76).

To end this section let us turn to possibly the most notorious unperformed action in all of Shakespeare – Shylock's cutting off of his pound of flesh. Portia grants the sentence, the forfeit bond of a pound of flesh is awarded to Shylock, but then she qualifies it:

> This bond doth give thee here no jot of blood;
> The words expressly are 'pound of flesh'.

> (4.1.306–7)

Furthermore, Shylock is warned that one spilt drop of blood and his property will be confiscated. Commentators usually approach this from a legal point of view, quite rightly because the setting is indeed a court, finding a verbal quibble in the distinction between flesh and blood following the judge's acceptance of the legality of awarding the pound of flesh. Law of contract and the like might well be an issue here, but what is even more fundamental is the affront to logic. Definition was an elementary topic of logical invention, and Petrus Ramus, of whom more later, made it the beginning of his revisionary 'method'. There is no way in which living flesh could be defined without blood. From a modern point of view this recognition introduces a deconstructive turn. When we consider Portia's values and judgment, wholly shared by a Christian audience, in contemporary terms, New Testament mercy valorises a sophistry. Shylock is defeated not by justice but by a captious argument, regardless of any overall question of equity. But for the audience for which anti-Semitism was an unquestioned, normative fact of life, such a blatant ploy would have actually added to the comedy. The improbability of such illogicality succeeding in the real world makes its triumph in the play all the more farcical and Shylock all the more a greater comic butt.[6] Mention of topics of invention brings us to a major area of discussion; logic, rhetoric and argument in the education and culture of Shakespeare's period.

The following chapters in this study do not provide a systematic analysis of logic and rhetoric in Shakespeare's plays. Sister Miriam Joseph's erudite, painstaking and extensive study does that, albeit in a taxonomic rather than interpretative fashion.[7] What is intended here is to recreate the logical cast of mind of those of Shakespeare's audience who had undergone the standard grammar school education of the day. An argument on stage would have immediately engaged an audience trained to spot fallacies or captious arguments, an audience trained in various methods of logical construction and rhetorical amplification, in a sharper way than today's audience which, to some extent, is inclined to respond with somewhat uncritical absorption of 'poetry' or delight in visual 'spectacle' without realising the relationship between the two which came about on Shakespeare's stage. In order to re-evoke this major cultural factor of Renaissance England it is necessary to provide a brief sketch of some basic details. All critics who turn to the subject of Shakespeare and education owe a great debt to T.W. Baldwin's researches, as Miriam Joseph acknowledges. For the details which follow these authors are thanked, as well as the specialist study of Sister Joan Marie Lechner.[8]

In the course of the sixteenth century Tudor rhetoricians and logicians had absorbed, synthesised and revised their medieval and classical predecessors, providing textbooks which fostered humanism in the matrix of the Renaissance, the teaching of the trivium (grammar, logic and rhetoric) in the upper forms of the grammar school. The Renaissance enthronement of eloquence has long been something of a cliché: 'In the Renaissance medieval dialectic was rejected for the sake of rhetoric.' This is the kind of generalisation which can be found. Unfortunately, it simplifies and distorts a more complex truth. The Latin works of scholars such as Erasmus, Agricola, Melanchthon, Ramus and Susenbrotus draw on Quintilian, who was rediscovered in the fifteenth century. In some respects Quintilian rests on Cicero and the (pseudo-Cicero) *Rhetorica ad Herennium*, which in turn derives from Aristotle's works on logic which had become available since the twelfth century.

In the Renaissance eloquence was indeed an ideal to which students aspired, but the rhetorics they used for this purpose either shared features in common with logic or were designed to complement textbooks on logic. Traditional classical rhetoric, like that found in the influential *Rhetorica ad Herennium*, was divided into five parts: invention, disposition, elocution, memory and delivery. The last two, needed for public oratory, need not concern us here. Invention was the finding of arguments, disposition (judgement or *judicium*) was the due ordering of those arguments, and elocution, or style, was the figurative amplification in tropes and schemes of the discourse. The invention section overlapped with logic, since both were concerned with topics. Part of Petrus Ramus' reform of logic was to reclaim invention and disposition and to leave elocution for the rhetorician. In turn there was debate amongst logicians, some claiming that disposition should precede, not follow, invention. In sixteenth-century teaching are found these three kinds then: the neoclassical traditionalists, the Ramists and what Miriam Joseph calls the Figurists. In fact, the Ramists designed their logics to be studied alongside the textbooks of the Figurists. It is Miriam Joseph's contention that the Figurists were so thoroughgoing that they incorporated matter from invention and disposition anyway. In the chapters which follow, generally the technical language of rhetoric and logic will not be used, except when necessary.

Two areas of discussion in this subject are often found confusing by students of the period. They are, first, the topics and all the alternative words and phrases, often in Latin and Greek, they give rise to (categories, predicaments, predicables, *topica*, arguments, *loci*, commonplaces, and so on) and, second, the divisions of elocution between tropes and schemes of thought and schemes of language. Topic is from the Greek for place, i.e. *topos* in transliteration, plural *topoi*, in Latin *locus* and *loci*. The topic was a place a person went to, to be prompted into developing an argument. In fact Francis Bacon called the topics 'promptuaries'.[9] Sometimes they are called 'seats of argument' (*sedes argumentorum*), or 'storehouses', or 'fonts'. A popular figurative approach looked to field sports of the day; one hunted for arguments like following the hiding place of a fox, and so on. What were the topics? In his *Rhetoric* and *Topics* Aristotle had itemised twenty-eight. Some found these too extended and confusing; consequently Cicero in response specified sixteen basic topics, namely: definition, division, name, conjugates, genus, species, similarity, difference, contraries, adjuncts, consequents, antecedents, incompatibility, causes, affects, comparison. Logicians and rhetoricians often varied the number, sometimes drawing on Aristotle's basic categories or predicaments of any thing (substance, quantity, quality, relation, place, date, etc.), while Cicero in effect had already taken on board the predicables, i.e. that which can be predicated of any thing (genus, species, difference, property, accident).

In an important chapter, Lisa Jardine offers a very helpful summary of what took place in the development of medieval and Renaissance logic and rhetoric. There was a shift from the scholastic insistence on the demonstration of the formal validity of the syllogism to the freer practice of drawing on the topics as the basis for compelling arguments. The movement was from scholastic treatise to humanist dialogue, from the technical to the pragmatic. This humanist dialectic, in which Rudolf Agricola's *De Inventione Dialectica* is one of the most important texts, is commonly called 'topics logic' or 'place logic'.[10]

It was considered that, whatever the subject, you could apply it to the topics to find what was relevant, and develop it from there. As we have seen, both logicians and rhetoricians claimed the topics. However, there was some agreement that the dialectical topic was concerned with thesis and general truth, while the rhetorical topic was concerned with hypothesis and particular matter. Some topics would be more suitable than others, depending on the discourse in hand, whether a deliberative oration (proposed action as honest, possible, necessary, difficult, easy, etc.), or the demonstrative oration (a panegyric turning to topics of the person; mind, body, fortune, etc.). Materials for these were known as 'artistic' proofs. That is, drawing on the arts of logic and rhetoric. 'Inartistic' proofs are closer to what today we would regard as evidence and were used in judicial orations (testimony of witnesses, contracts, law, etc.). In fact, Cicero added testimony to his list of sixteen topics. Topics even in the Renaissance were often confused with commonplaces, to which we shall return, but not before losing sight of those tropes and schemes of thought and schemes of language. Indeed, as will be shown, there is an overlap of identity and use between some topics of the logician and some tropes of the rhetorician.

Elocution was concerned with figures, or figures of speech, which were divided by almost all Renaissance rhetoricians into tropes and schemes.[11] Tropes turned the literal meaning of a word or sentence into something else, and included such figures as metaphor, metonymy and periphrasis. Schemes of language were largely taken up with patterns of repetition and balanced arrangement, for example anaphora and parison. Schemes of thought used devices which rethought an idea, so to speak, like the dilemma, the antithesis and personification. These divisions are hardly watertight. Antithesis, parenthesis, periphrasis and sententia are all to be found under various headings in Renaissance rhetorics. Furthermore, since, as has been indicated above, Figurists incorporated much of invention and disposition into their discussion of elocution, it is not surprising to find that the logician's or rhetorician's topic has become the Figurist's trope. The dilemma, for instance, was regarded as a trope and as a topic of reasoning. Clearly tropes such as metonymy and synecdoche could be related to topics of, respectively, the adjunct (crown as adjunct of king), and genus and species (sword for swords – of an army).

There is a further area concerning commonplaces which has to be touched on. The topics discussed above are categories against which matter is placed to analyse it for division and development. Consequently these are sometimes referred to as 'analytic' topics. Alternatively, Aristotle suggested that there was another class of 'special' topics. As the analytic topics were abstract, so these were concrete and consisted of subject headings – war, marriage, government, vice and the like – with quotations gathered beneath. In the process of education boys were encouraged to make their personal commonplace books (Milton's survives)[12] drawing on particular authors or various kinds of compendia (like Erasmus's *Adagia*)[13] which came before them. One of the most famous in the sixteenth century was William Baldwin's *A Treatise of Morall Philosophie* (1547), the subtitle of which more accurately indicates the contents: *Wherein Is Contained the Worthy Sayings of Philosophers, Emperors, Kings, and Orators: Their Lives and Answers*...[14] Dipping into this the reader had at his fingertips a compendium of Greek and Roman 'sentence'. If a young scholar was asked to write on 'governance' for example, he could turn to this for subject topics and speedily find in the third book the thoughts of Aristotle, Plato, Marcus Aurelius, Plutarch, Cicero and many others. Choosing his matter – say, Cicero on favouritism and flattery – he could take them through the analytic topics to develop arguments, i.e. to define flattery, to look at its causes, its effects, things closely associated with it, comparisons and contrasts with, etc. Having then enriched his invention, the scholar must decide on the disposition of his matter which will depend on whether it is to be disposed dialectically or rhetorically.

Again, there was much debate concerning the appropriate division of the two. Some agreement was found in acknowledging that abstract and general questions were best left to the logician, while the particular issues concerning persons and actions were more properly the sphere of the rhetorician. But of course, it only takes the merest glance at this – assessing the rights and wrongs of one country declaring war on another, for instance – to see that it is difficult to uphold. However, the broad distinction between science and opinion, necessary propositions and probable propositions, characterise differentiation between logic and rhetoric. In short, logical disposition resorted to the varieties of syllogism, while rhetorical disposition took as its model variations on the classical oration. Petrus Ramus' *Dialecticae institutiones* (1543) was translated into English by Roland M'Kilwein ('M. Roll. Makylmenaeum Scotum') as *The Logike* (1574), followed by six more translations by 1632. Disposition following invention 'is parted into the proposition ... or syllogism and methode' (71). Disposition looks at the variety of propositions, simple and compound and 'method'. The latter was Ramus' recommendation to begin most generally with the topic of definition, thereafter dividing and subdividing matter.

Rhetorical disposition depended on what kind of oration was to be used since this would determine the appropriate topics. Conventionally, the oration consisted of exordium, narration, confirmation, confutation, peroration. At an early stage, the Renaissance schoolboy encountered one of the most well-used textbooks in early western education, Aphthonius's *Progymnasmata*.[15] The third and fourth of fourteen exercises contained therein, the *chreia* and the proverb, taught students both invention and disposition in the practice of amplification using a conventional procedure – praise, paraphrase or exposition, cause, contrast, comparison, example, confirmatory testimony, epilogue.[16]

Drawing on Aristotle's discussion of fallacies used for eristic purposes by the Sophists (notoriously Gorgias) in his *De Sophisticis Elenchis*, most logic textbooks included a section on sophistries. Fallacies arise from either a formally incorrect syllogism or a materially questionable proposition within a syllogism. Ambiguity of language and false assumptions together amount to the thirteen basic kinds of fallacy. The fallacy of accident and the *secundem quid* argument are probably the most common. Fallacy of accident occurs when the assumption that that which belongs only to a substance may be attributed to an accident or adjunct of that substance, and vice versa. *Secundem quid* assumes that what is partially true is wholly true, or vice versa. Another extremely common fallacy is that of the false cause, most blatantly found at the opening of *Richard III*, which is discussed below (p. 44).

Ramist logics and rhetorics actually used contemporary literature as illustration. Abraham Fraunce uses Spenser's *The Shepheardes Calendar* in his *Arcadian Rhetoric* (1588), for example. Schoolchildren were often asked to analyse their own work. In John Brinsley's *Ludus Literarius...* (1612) the scholars are asked to indicate stages of disposition and topics used, in the left hand margin, while the variety of tropes was to be pointed up in the right hand margin. A.H. Gilbert has shown how the logician teacher-pedant was exploited for comic purposes in Elizabethan drama, while Hardin Craig has briefly surveyed Shakespeare's plays to show the conscious use of terminology from formal logic. Logic and rhetoric were used in the formalised processes of analysis and oratory and, though it would be surprising to find a character who actually spoke in syllogisms, nevertheless forms of argument in the sense of persuading, dissuading, defending, debating, disputing, justifying etc., are found throughout Shakespeare's drama.

Characters do not speak in syllogisms but a particular way of thinking had come down from antiquity by which every educated person was accustomed to think, argue or debate *in utramque partem*, on both sides of the question. Sophistic rhetoric, like that of Gorgias, had encouraged this *dissoi logoi* ('double accounts'), and a lost work of Protagoras was entitled *Antilogies or Contradictory Arguments*. In Latin culture the rhetorical exercises known as the *controversiae* consisted of judicial declamations for and against. The exercise at the heart of Aphthonius' *Progymnasmata*, the thesis, was another form of this. Observing this element in the declamatory drama of figures such as Euripedes and Seneca, scholars have examined medieval and Renaissance drama for its continuing structural presence.[17]

In the chapters which follow the purpose is two-fold. First, to recognise the use of argument as a source of drama. That is to say, taking this chapter as a primer we can begin to take a particular Renaissance awareness to the plays. Second, in examining the given argument, often in relation to stage action, we will find that it directs us to the heart of the play's concerns – political, psychological, moral or social, as the case may be.

2
1 & 2 Henry VI

1 Henry VI

Shakespeare's English history plays largely depict fifteenth-century feudal society at war – with the foreign enemy or with itself, in rebellion. This consequence of European dynasticism, with all the problems of marriage, inheritance, law and diplomacy, created the aristocratic ideology of chivalry.[1] Chivalry needed war as its *raison d'être* since only with fame achieved by valorous deeds in battle could the knight fully realise honour. Valorous deeds enacted the bond of fealty between the knight and the feudal monarch, just as the act of homage enacted the receipt of inheritance and status. Both contracted the reciprocal obligation to fight and to defend.[2] The nexus between word and deed was the oath, the vow, the pledge, by which the knight's honour became the guarantee of meaningfulness in the correlation between utterance and action. This was the ideal conception, considered realised by such figures as Richard the Lionheart, Edward the Black Prince, Lord Talbot (as depicted in *1 Henry VI*) and Henry V. As founder of the most noble Order of the Garter, Edward III, the chivalric victor of Poitiers, had a special place in this roll-call. The obverse of the ideal was the looting, fire and massacre visited on town and countryside by those second and third sons who would not inherit; bastards from noble houses, lesser aristocrats and mercenary adventurers. For war brought not just honour but great wealth from loot and ransom, albeit legally attained according to medieval laws of war.[3] It must be emphasised, however, that there was no simple dichotomy of the ideal and the real. The historical record of knightly valour and the literature of chivalric romance provided models of aspiration and emulation for such celebrated figures as Guillaume Le Maréchal and the Chevalier Bayard whose actual deeds, almost within living memory by

Shakespeare's time, were idealised by subsequent chroniclers and poets.[4] The careers of the greatest of chivalric figures, like the Black Prince and John Talbot, included actions which by twentieth-century standards would be called war crimes, but according to medieval law of war were not so.[5]

For all the so-called decline of fifteenth-century chivalry the advent of print supplied a whole readership for chivalric romance and the institution of knighthood. Caxton printed not only such works as Malory's *Morte D'Arthur* and *The Recuyell of the Historyes of Troye* but also Ramon Lull's *The Book of the Ordre of Chyvalry* and Christine de Pisan's *The Book of the Fayttes of Armes and of Chyualrye*. The early Tudors fostered a revival of chivalric pageantry modelled on that of the famed Burgundian court. In the course of the sixteenth century the tournament became the site of knightly self-presentation. Elizabeth made the Accession Day tilts, the revival of the St George's Day festival and the Order of the Garter, central to the chivalric ideology of her court, which found its culmination in Spenser's *The Faerie Queene*.[6] Shakespeare's English history plays, which appeared in the course of the 1590s, can be seen as a complex response to the celebratory pageantry of contemporary idealisation. The complexity derives from the reluctance to adopt a one-sided approach of either shared adulation or committed scepticism. A simple definition of drama is 'conflict'. The argument of the histories derives from the conflict between these two conceptions. In dramatising overtly nationalist chronicles the deconstructive ambivalence in the word and deed of the printed page is brought to life in speech and action on the stage. In the very attempt to join in the glorification of such a hero as Henry V, for example, Shakespeare equally revealed the dubious grounds of such celebration.

In Shakespeare's addition of what is referred to as the Temple Garden scene (2.4) to the sources for *1 Henry VI* argument and action are immediately intertwined, like the rose briars on stage: the argument between the adherents of York and Lancaster and the action of plucking the red and white roses. Richard Plantagenet's opening words, 'Dare no man answer in a case of truth?' (2.4.2) and the following reference to the Temple heighten the legal meaning here. The 'truth' of Richard's legal 'case' – the state of facts juridically considered (*OED sb.*[1] 6) – is the 'argument' (2.4.57, 59) under dispute. Since it is not specified, the argument becomes the issue of legality itself (implicitly in relation to the hereditary title of the Duke of York, and as the following scene shows, the claim to the crown).

Given Shakespeare's withholding of the content, or evidence, of the argument, the opposed claims to 'truth' (2.4.20, 23) of Richard and

Somerset become assertions of verbal force. Richard, moreover, has pre-empted any debate from the outset since he presents only seemingly choice of judgement when no alternative is logically possible: 'Then say at once if I maintain'd the truth; / Or else was wrangling Somerset in th'error?' (2.4.5–6). Either way Richard wins. The action of plucking the red and white roses ironically supports this since the greater number choosing the white rose of York intimate that might is right. Right, however, is seen to support might since the lawyer tells Somerset, 'The argument you held was wrong in you' (2.4.57), whereupon his only supporter, Suffolk, reverts to the argument of might, to his sword 'Here in my scabbard' (2.4.60).

Is it Somerset's 'argument' that might will determine right, that armed force will ensure justice? Or, crudely, is it that might will *become* right, force will impose one factional 'right' over another? The latter is strongly suggested given Somerset's ally, Suffolk, earlier in the scene, who jocu-larly claims that as he never could quite bring himself to act according to the law, therefore he will 'frame the law unto my will' (2.4.9).

Another who appears to frame the law unto his will is Richard himself. In the arguments of the Temple Garden Somerset throws at Richard his father, the Earl of Cambridge's execution for treason under Henry V in 1415. Shakespeare subsequently dramatised this – the 'Cambridge con-spiracy' – in *Henry V* 2.2 (see the discussion below, pp. 91) where he follows Holinshed in confining the politics to treasonous subornation by a foreign enemy. In *1 Henry VI* the political argument is much more involved, as we hear in the next scene when Mortimer indicates the Yorkist claim on the crown. Richard defends himself against Somerset, 'My father was attached, not attainted, / Condemned to die for treason, but no traitor' (2.4.96–7). Richard's argument is ambiguous, question-begging and possibly treasonous in itself.

To be 'attached' is to be arrested, as the Earl of Cambridge and the other two conspirators certainly were, though he was 'not attainted' only in the sense that there was no specific parliamentary Act of Attainder *before* his arrest. Acts of Attainder were sometimes issued following appeal of treason by one person of another to get the accused to court to defend himself against the charge. Richard's father was apprehended in the 'open fact' as it was called, of committing treason. He was imme-diately executed and parliamentary attainder was confirmed later, in November 1415. But if the view is taken that Henry V, the son of a usurper, was therefore not a legal monarch, then, indeed, the Earl of Cambridge was 'condemned to die for treason' but could not be 'a traitor', especially since his own claim to the crown, as Mortimer argues, is stronger than Henry's. This may seem dangerous equivocation, but looking back from the sixteenth century with its 'horror of treason' there were the ironic reversals of history by which, for example, an act of attainder of 1461 found Henry VI guilty of waging war against Edward IV, and similarly an act of 1485 found Richard III a traitor against his sovereign lord, Henry Tudor.[7]

In this scene are found some of the major arguments of the histories: on the one hand the need for law to sanction action, on the other the abandonment of right for might; the inheritance of the Angevin dynastic divisions which would create war at home and abroad: the further divisions in feudal loyalties between the sovereign and rival families with all the ramified dynastic adherents. In short, the central paradox of the claims of honour which could be both unequivocal and absolute, as it is with Talbot's chivalry, or equivocal and relative as it is with Richard Plantagenet who appeals to the nobles in the Temple Garden: 'Let him that is a true-born gentleman / And stands upon the honor of his birth' (2.4.27–8) choose a rose. In the scene after Mortimer's dying speech Richard Plantagenet takes his feudal chivalric vow to his lord, the king, 'Thy humble servant vows obedience / And humble service till the point of death' (3.1.166–7), and then kneels before Henry who invests him with a sword and bids him rise as Duke of York.

Towards the close of the play Joan la Pucelle summons fiends to her aid who promptly appear: 'This speedy and quick appearance argues proof / Of your accustom'd diligence to me' (5.3.8–9), she comments. What 'proof', we might ask, does Richard Plantagenet's action in relation to his words 'argue'? We have to recognise a double standard. What from one point of view is complete betrayal of honour in the betrayal of word, from another is Richard's long-term plan to further the honour of the House of York by achieving what he believes to be the true title and inheritance by usurping the usurping line of the Lancasters. The design of *1 Henry VI* as a whole contrasts this and other divisive factions at home with the heroic fulfilment of the chivalric ideal in the sacrifice of Talbot and his son on the field of battle fighting for the honour of his liege lord, Henry VI. Shakespeare thereby dramatises a cultural argument of his day, the relationship between honour inherited through lineage and honour gained by valorous deeds.[8]

In dramatising the deeds of Talbot chronicle is brought to life and past renown finds present re-enactment on stage. This self-conscious metadrama and intertextuality is emphasised within the play. Recalling the great chronicler of the fifteenth-century feudal world, 'Froissart, a countryman of ours', Alençon remembers that he 'records / England all Olivers and Rolands bred' (1.2.29–30) in the time of Edward III. The epic dimension evoked by past chivalry, heroism and romance in both history and literature (*La Chanson de Roland* dates from the twelfth century[9]), anticipates the English hero who is to reincarnate martial glory as the oft-quoted lines of Nashe celebrate:

> How would it have joyed brave Talbot (the terror of the French) to think that after he had lain two hundred years in his tomb, he should triumph again on the stage, and have his bones new embalmed with the tears of ten thousand spectators at least (at several times), who, in the tragedian that represents his person, imagine they behold him fresh bleeding.[10]

Before we, the audience, actually 'behold' Lord Talbot, Shakespeare seems to prepare us with the Messenger's extensive narrative account of the battle of Orleans where 'valiant Talbot ... / Enacted wonders with his sword and lance'(1.1.108–40; 121–2), before being wounded and taken prisoner for a ransom. I say 'seems' because details of the Countess of Auvergne scene (2.3), another of Shakespeare's additions to the chronicle, must give us pause for thought. In reading the text we first encounter Talbot in 1.4.22ff, but the Countess of Auvergne scene suggests that how we *see* Talbot might somewhat compromise the heroic representations suggested earlier which themselves follow the play's opening elegy for the victories of Henry V.

The countess intends to capture Talbot on his visit to her castle. When he is admitted to her presence she seems bemused, 'What? is this the man? ... Is this the scourge of France?' (2.3.14–15) because what she sees before her is 'a child, a silly dwarf!', a 'weak and writhled shrimp' (2.3.22–3). Even allowing for some derogatory exaggeration there must be some correlation between her description and Talbot's stature, otherwise her remarks would have no point. Michael Hattaway notes that although the chronicler Hall describes Talbot's person as 'fearful, and terrible to his adversaries present', a sixteenth-century French account by André Thévet describes the soldier as of rather middling stature ('d'assez moyenne stature'). Andrew S. Cairncross conjectures that the same actor later played Richard of Gloucester, eventually Richard III, the crookback king.[11]

Before Talbot's actual appearance the Countess of Auvergne anticipates that sight of the fearful warrior will confirm reputation, 'Fain would mine eyes be witness with mine ears / To give their censure [opinion] of these rare reports' (2.3.9–10). Her expectation thwarted, she expostulates on the falsity of fame, for she had been led to expect another Hercules or a physically imposing Hector. In this brief incident, seemingly a farcical interlude, we can see what is to become a foundation of Shakespeare's dramatic art and vision which finds its most thoroughgoing expression throughout the whole of *Troilus and Cressida*. To recapitulate, what we first hear of Talbot repeats the idealisation of romance and chronicle and his first appearance confirms this with his lucky escape under attack beside the mortally wounded Salisbury. That is, the heroic role determines how we see the physical actor. The countess's reaction forces the audience to reverse this process and for a moment Shakespeare allows us to review the superhuman of the imagination as a less than impressive presence, cut down to size. This dualism of Shakespeare's vision determines much of the *Henry IV* plays and *Henry V*. In *1 Henry VI* the dualistic contrasts are found largely between groups or individuals, not within the individual character. Thus the first heroic account of Talbot at Patay also includes the contrastive story of the cowardly Sir John Falstaff fleeing from the field, betraying his general (1.1.131–4). Later, the Countess of Auvergne scene is reversed in act 3 scene 4 when, just before the coronation in Paris, Talbot meets the king for the first time, since 'Because till now we never saw your face' (3.4.24), Henry says as he confers the title of Earl of Salisbury, following Talbot's catalogue of victories obtained in pursuing 'duty' and 'loyalty' (3.4.4,10): a telling structural contrast with Richard Plantagenet's reinstatement of act 3, scene 1, discussed above. The chivalric emphasis develops in the next scene after Henry's coronation, when the hero confronts the coward.

Talbot tears the Garter from Sir John Falstaff's leg, thereby initiating ritualistic debasement. Then with an argument to persuade the king to complete the formal degradation, which is complied with, Talbot celebrates 'the sacred name of knight' (4.1.40) and the foundation of the Order of the Garter. These scenes (3.4, 4.1) are just two of the many ceremonial scenes in Shakespeare's histories, but they are not merely ceremonial in the modern somewhat reductive sense of colourful aristocratic pageantry. Medieval ceremony re-enacts the principles of feudal society. In the assembly against which the actions of ennoblement and coronation, and Talbot's argument, take place is not just the simple cowardice of Falstaff, but the enmity between church and state in the figures of the Bishop of Winchester and Protector Gloucester, the factional hatred of York and Somerset and, above all, the incipient ambition of the House of York to displace the reigning House of Lancaster. Not only is England bloodily immersed in the hundred years war with France, but it is also about to succumb to the carnage of the most protracted civil war that England was ever to experience, the Wars of the Roses. More immediately, with the resumption of war following the truce called for the coronation, it is the failure of the political in-fighting of York and Somerset to supply reinforcements that leads to Talbot's death, as much as French victory. Thus any response to the extensive pathos of the deaths of Talbot and his young son as the heroic fulfilment of true chivalric sacrifice has to be severely compromised by our awareness of the larger context of treachery and betrayal.

Three scenes are given to the Talbots' deaths (4.5, 6, 7) totalling 144 lines which are mostly taken up with arguments between father and son. In the highly formalised stichomythic exchanges the antitheses of youth and age, life or death, flight or fight, honour and shame are resolved in the logical synthesis of Talbot's 'Come, side by side, together live and die, / And soul with soul from France to heaven fly' (4.5.54–5). Scenes 5 and 6 have a certain amount of duplication. J.P. Brockbank conjectures that at some point Shakespeare went back to what we have as scene 6 and revised it in closer relationship to Hall's account of the deaths. Inadvertently, the revised scene as well as the old remained in the manuscript and both were printed in the Folio: act 4 scene 5 the new, and scene 6 the old.[12] Hall avails himself of the rhetorical licence of the humanist chronicler and invents Talbot's impassioned persuasions to his son to flee the battlefield. To heighten the pathos Shakespeare transfers the arguments to John, the self-sacrifice of youth working more emotionally on the audience:

> Then let me stay, and, father, do you fly.
> Your loss is great, so your regard should be;
> My worth unknown, no loss is known in me.
> Upon my death the French can little boast;
> In yours they will, in you all hopes are lost.
> Flight cannot stain the honor you have won,
> But mine it will, that no exploit have done.
> You fled for vantage, every one will swear;
> But if I bow, they'll say it was for fear.
> There is no hope that ever I will stay,
> If the first hour I shrink and run away.
> Here on my knee I beg mortality,
> Rather than life preserv'd with infamy.
>
>   (4.5.21–33)

Here we have the general indefinite thesis, 'Should a man flee from the battlefield?' converted to the hypothesis of the particular and definite of place, time and persons. The *in utramque partem* mode, arguing on both sides of the question, is not difficult to see. Applying the same topics of death and honour to each, young John is able to argue contrary positions in relation to the English army, the French enemy, reputation and cowardice. The rhetoric and logic are formalised even further by the rhyming couplets of the verse. Whatever the immediate audience response, Shakespeare's poetry is ultimately ironic, given the political manoeuvring which precedes and follows. The vindication of glory, name and fame is then enacted on stage before both perish, giving us a seemingly perfect correlation of argument and action. For an Elizabethan audience such artifice did not detract from the expression of emotion; it heightened it. This, Nashe tells us, brought those tears to the eyes of 'ten thousand spectators at least'. But Joan La Pucelle's reaction is rather different. On the field of battle Sir William Lucy recites the extensive catalogue of Talbot's titles (4.7.60–71): those of family, those awarded for valour, those of noble chivalric orders and finally Talbot's office as Marshal of France.

Joan's response is terse indeed, 'Him that thou magnifi'st with all these titles / Stinking and fly-blown lies here at our feet' (4.7.75–6). (There is a fascinating relationship between this sequence and Falstaff's better-known 'catechism' on honour and his subsequent stumbling on the corpse of Sir William Blunt [*1 Henry IV* 5.1. 3]). Talbot's titles are a comprehensive catalogue of honour; that of lineage, that of battle, that of nation, and the international honours of the chivalric orders of England, France and the Holy Roman Empire. We have two extremes: Lucy offers the enduring meaning of fame inherent in name, while Joan sneers at the proleptic putrefaction of a corpse. (Again we are reminded of an action in a later drama, when Hector discovers the 'putrefied core' [*Troilus and Cressida*, 5.8.1] beneath the suit of sumptuous armour he has seized as booty.) Joan's extreme reductiveness annuls the cynical response it calls for, but on the other hand it is not easy to share in the seemingly untrammelled emotion of Nashe's audiences. There is something in the deaths of Talbot and his son which compromises such an uncomplicated response since we see that what they believe they die for, spelt out for us in their arguments and actions, is not borne out by the larger dramatic situation.

The honour which underpins the chivalric code is transactional. An act of valour may be an autonomous enactment of a prescriptive ideal, but for its meaning to be fully realised it must be recognised by the collective community of honour which reciprocally confirms its validity.[13] With the pointed exceptions of Lucy, Essex and Salisbury, we see that the nobles are generally incapable of sharing authentic chivalric motivation since they are consumed by the power-hungry dignities of rival honour and status within the feudal hierarchy. In such circumstances the deaths of Talbot and his son become painfully futile. And behind this lies Shakespeare's essential insight into the deconstructive irony of feudalism itself. The very structure that relies on a centralised monarchical system of contractual defence ensured by homage actually fostered subinfeudation – the competing allegiances of the lesser nobility and gentry to their immediate lord. Dynastic rivalry was not an aberrance, but a natural outcome. The very person who celebrates Talbot's chivalry, 'Burgundy / Enshrines thee in his heart, and there erects / Thy noble deeds as valor's monuments' (3.2.118–20) is the noble whose divided feudal loyalties will lead him to betray his allies.

2 Henry VI

'God's will be done!' (3.1.86) is King Henry's response on hearing of the loss of his territories in France. The words provide a summary argument in relation to the action of the enemy, an argument that directs us to the larger argument of action in this and all the English histories – the issue of God's providence in relation to human deeds. Henry's utterance testifies to his unremitting piety when confronted with affairs of state. His Christian faith accepts that what has taken place must be part of God's just providential ordering of the world, however inscrutable that might appear to mere human understanding. From a secular point of view the king's response is a disastrous replacement of political action by words. Leadership, military tactics and retaliation are called for, not renunciation. An expression of faith is seen as one more failure of responsibility and as a provocation for York, standing close by.

In the scenes of conjuration, miracle, trial by combat and rebellion in *2 Henry VI*, Shakespeare mounts stage actions which directly contravene arguments of justice, both divine and human. Each contributes to the cumulative historical, political and religious significance of the *Henry VI* plays as a whole: the chaos which ensues when the monarch puts his complete faith and trust in the efficacy of God in human affairs. The elements of comedy and burlesque, travesty and carnival ultimately subvert the commonplaces of Tudor Christian ideology.[14]

First, let us examine the scene of Eleanor's conjuration (1.4) and its consequences. Eleanor's offence actually took place in 1441, four years earlier. For dramatic effect Shakespeare invented the enmity of the duchess and the queen, and added to the technique of commenting on the main action by means of several subplots as well as developing, following Margaret as symbolic successor to Joan La Pucelle, the demonic association of femininity and witchcraft.[15]

Out of ambition for her husband the Protector, and hatred for the queen, Eleanor wishes to learn of future events by witchcraft. Unknown to her, the agent she has used, Hume, is in the service of Suffolk and the Cardinal, who wish to see her and her husband brought down. In the conjuration the demonic burlesques the divine. As H.A. Kelly puts it, 'it was universally accepted by Christians in Shakespeare's day that only God had certain knowledge of the future, and that evil spirits could only conjecture future events from already existing causes. But we must no doubt admit that this doctrine was often contradicted in practice, and that men ascribed more knowledge to spirits than theologians could justify.'[16] There is a complex interplay in the action here. The conjuration derives from historical record, a reality. Yet in dramatising it a duplicity emerges. Past historical reality is now acted and, further, the characters have been suborned by Hume (to 'buzz these conjurations in her brain', 1.2.99). That is, the actors act characters who are putting on an act until the spirit 'Asnath' (an anagram for Sathan, obviously) arises. Is this a superlative actor or the devil himself? He trembles at the name of God and his prophecies are eventually fulfilled. Yet the stage tradition of the counterfeit devil was an established one.[17] However, the disappearance of the spirit and the arrest of the malfactors return us to the encompassing plot of the imposture on behalf of Suffolk and the Cardinal.

What is of great significance is King Henry's judgment, in the light of this, at Eleanor's trial. Execution for the witch and her associates and exile for the duchess is the sentence, for 'In sight of God and us, your guilt is great' (2.3.2), says the king. But when these words are put against Henry's reaction on first hearing of the witchcraft, 'O God, what mischiefs work the wicked ones' (2.1.181) a compromising irony emerges. In sight of the audience the 'mischiefs' of the 'wicked ones' are not so much the sins of Eleanor but the controlling machinations of Suffolk and the Cardinal, who have used justice for political ends. The crime was revealed not by God's providential ordering but by the actions of men. Something comparable takes place with the miracle of St Alban.

A miracle defies causation in the natural order as an intervention of God in response to faith. Man's faith is able to surmount the ordonnance of reason in cause and effect. One Saunder Simpcox, supposedly born completely blind, claims that in response to the supernatural voice of St Alban he had travelled to his shrine, where God had rewarded his faith by the miracle of restored sight. As Henry immediately declares, 'Now, God be prais'd, that to believing souls / Gives light in darkness, comfort in despair!' (2.1.65–6). Gloucester is less credulous and gets the imposter to identify some colours. Having trapped Simpcox he spells out the logic of his argument:

> If thou hadst been born blind,
> Thou might'st as well have known all our names, as thus
> To name the several colors we do wear.
> Sight may distinguish colors; but suddenly
> To nominate them all, it is impossible.

> (2.1.124–8)

As in miracle faith challenges reason, so now Gloucester's reason challenges Henry's faith. The logic of empirical experience defeats precepts of belief. Gloucester's judgement of an event is grounded in observation, an *a posteriori* endgame which traps Simpcox, with its pragmatic understanding of cognition, sight and language. His logical procedure derives from a sceptic's aetiology that abrogates the *a priori* assumption of God's miraculous revelation in human history – King Henry's belief. Here are focused the dramatised arguments of late medieval and early modern historiography. This constrast is particularly pointed since in Shakespeare's source, almost certainly Foxe, it is initially Gloucester who is credulous: 'having great joy to see such a miracle [Gloucester] called the poor man unto him, and first showing himself joyous of God's glory so showed in the getting of his sight.'[18] Shakespeare also added Simpcox's lameness to his source, thereby duplicating the farce as another 'miracle' is acclaimed when Simpcox flees from further punishment. Henry's faith never wavers, 'O God, seest Thou this, and bearest so long?' (2.1.151). An audience is surely left aghast at such single-minded piety which has rendered the king politically blind and lame.

The comic element is taken further in the trial by combat scene which some have taken to be a travesty of chivalric encounter.[19] However, Ralph Berry saw the more challenging implications. Of the apprentice's victory, celebrated by the king for the revelation of 'God in Justice' (2.3.102) Berry concludes, 'I put it that the play does not invite us to share the view of Divine Providence advanced by Peter and King

Henry'.[20] The chronicles provide very little detail of the circumstances of the combat, but, to judge from his manner of introducing the action – 'the appellant and defendant...to enter the lists' (2.3.49–50) – it is evident that Shakespeare knew that the combat was under the auspices of the courts of chivalry. Historical details of this background will bring out the fully burlesque nature of the argument of action in the combat.

Incurring the criticism of Parliament, which feared encroachment on the courts of common law, Richard II had fostered the power and scope of the civil court of chivalry to the extent that the articles of deposition against him included specific details of this abuse. It eventually became possible for any treason appeal to come before this court, although there were conditions which had to be fulfilled. In cases of treason trial by combat was used when there were no witnesses and no evidence, so that one man's word simply stood against another's, provided that both parties were of good repute and not felons.[21] The practice reached its height under Henry VI. Thus Cater and Davy, the originals of Shakespeare's Horner and Peter, appeared in historical fact in the chivalric setting of the lists at Smithfield.

They may seem an odd pair to have done so, but there were other cases concerning parties of less than knightly standing. A few years earlier, in 1441, for example, two thieves fought in combat 'at Totehill' according to Stow,[22] on what appeal he does not say, and in 1426 'a gentleman, Henry Knokkis' defended himself against an appeal of treason made by 'a certain plebian tailor' beneath the walls of Edinburgh castle.[23] Even more strangely, an elderly friar was ordered under Henry IV to fight a woman, who had accused him of treason, with one arm tied behind his back. (The charge was then withdrawn.) The *Brut* chronicle, also, records a fight to the death between a 'Welsh clerk' and a knight.[24]

By the Tudor period, such combat was considered against the law of arms. Spenser makes this clear by showing Calidore at first dismayed to see Tristram, who is 'no knight', slay a knight, 'which armes impugneth plaine'.[25] In Shakespeare's day, in a work which the playwright may have consulted for the combat scene of *Richard II*, Sir William Segar spelled out 'What sorts of men ought not bee admitted to triall of Armes'. Generally, 'the triall of Armes apperteineth onelie to Gentlemen, and that Gentilitie is a degree honourable, it were not fit that anie persons of meaner condition, should thereunto be admitted'.[26] In this judgement, amongst the ineligible, beside 'Theeves, Beggers, Bawdes, Victuallers, persons excommunicate, Usurers, persons banished the Armie', is ranked 'everie other man exercising an occupation or trade, unfit and unworthie a Gentleman or Soldier'. To sum up, then, Richard II

had promoted a situation in which history itself would furnish burlesques of chivalric practice, whilst Tudor aristocratic exclusivity had
heightened awareness of decorum. Thus when Horner and Peter appeared
on stage in the 1590s, one drunk, the other terrified, and both carrying
less than knightly weapons, the resulting burlesque confirmed the comic
tenor of Peter's petition:

Peter   Against my master, Thomas Horner, for saying that the
         Duke of York was rightful heir to the crown.
Queen   What say'st thou? Did the Duke of York say he was rightful
         heir to the Crown?
Peter   That my master was? No, forsooth; my master said that he
         was, and that the king was an usurer.[27]

(I.3.25–30)

Yet that exaggeration of the comic will prove to have its serious point.

Details of the combat deserve investigation. It is removed from the
traditional Smithfield venue to a 'Hall of Justice'. *Gregory's Chronicle*
mentions that Cater (like Davy, it is assumed) was in 'harnys' (harness)
that is, a suit of armour.[28] Shakespeare mentions a curious weapon, a
'staff with a sand-bag fastened to it', but no armour. The treason-duel of
chivalry, usually on horseback, was never fought without a sword and
spear. Shakespeare's weapon, in fact, is closer to the weapon of the duel-
of-law, the baton.[29] Sir Samuel Rush Meyrick, the Victorian antiquarian,
was somewhat baffled by the weapons of Horner and Peter: 'Shakespeare
arms his combatants with batons and sand-bags at the end of them, yet
this is the only authority I have met with for the use of this latter
appendage.' He then proceeded to speculate that 'probably such were
the weapons of the lower class of people, and were therefore considered
by him as appropriate to the parties'.[30] He quotes Samuel Butler's *Hudibras*
in support – 'Engaged with money-bags, as bold / As men with sand-bags
did of old' – and suggests a comparison with the fool's baton and bladder.
As early as Warburton's edition of the play, in fact, Butler had been
used as a gloss, as H.C. Hart recounts in his edition of 1909, where,
however, he shows no certainty as to what the weapon actually was.[31]
The weapons are in fact combat flails, as distinct from the metal military
flail or the agricultural wooden variety. Reference to them seems to be
rare, but an excellent illustration survives in one of the most detailed
examples of a Renaissance festival book, *The Triumph of Maximilian I*
(1526), with woodcuts by Hans Burgkmair and others. Plate 33 shows
'Five men with (leather) flails' preceding similar numbers of men with

quarterstaves, lances, halberds, battleaxes, and various swords and shields, all collectively representing *gefecht*, explained by the editor as 'combats on foot, considered beneath the notice of nobility or royalty until they were fostered by Maximilian, who took part in them himself'.[32]

By choosing flails with sand-filled leather bags Shakespeare placed a weapon associated with the lower orders in the high-born milieu of chivalric combat, bringing on his combatants without the expected arms and armour. He also made other significant alterations to the chronicle material. As has always been recognised, Shakespeare links the armourer's treason with York, although it was not so linked in the chronicles. In the sources the armourer is the innocent party and his servant the guilty. Holinshed, for example, following Fabyan, found Davy a 'false servant' and Cater 'without guilt', while Grafton, following Hall, saw Davy as 'a coward and a wretche'.[33] That wretchedness could follow from the cowardice, or it might be that Davy is called wretch for falsely accusing his master – presumably the latter, since the chroniclers see ultimate justice in his execution at Tyburn.

Hall introduced the notion of Horner's height and strength: 'he beying a tall and hardye personage'. Shakespeare changes this subtly to Horner's superior technique: Peter knows that 'I am never able to deal with my master, he hath learnt so much fence already' (2.3.77–8). Advantage is all on the side of the master, except for his over-confidence encouraged by drink. It could therefore seem that when the Armourer is struck and confesses treason before dying, Peter has 'prevail'd in right' (2.3.99); right seems to have defeated might, so that the combat could be seen as divinely ordered. As Segar puts it:

> all Nations . . . have (among many other trials) permitted that such question as could not be civilie prooved by confession, witnesse, or other circumstances, should receive judgement by fight and combat, supposing that GOD (who onelie knoweth the secret thought of all men) would give victorie to him that justlie adventured his life, for truth, Honor, and Justice. (sig. A^{2v-r})

At the beginning of the combat King Henry's invocation had been 'God defend the right!' (2.3.55), and his predictable response at the close is 'And God in justice hath reveal'd to us / The truth and innocence of this poor fellow' (2.3.102–3). York's comment is a little more worldly, 'Fellow, thank God and the good wine in thy master's way' (2.3.95–6). The staging of the combat has to take into account drunkenness, cowardice, inexperience and terror. Shakespeare's argument of action is transparent. Drunkenness becomes a warranty of providence. The king sees the hand of God, but the audience sees the folly of man, both Horner's fortified over-confidence and Henry's credulous faith in another kind of spirit, leading to complete lack of judgement in each case.

In the rebellion of Jack Cade, which dominates virtually the whole of act 4, Shakespeare shifted the argument from the question of divine justice to law in society that kept in place the hierarchic structure of rigid status division and exploitation. Cade's presentation has an affinity with the topsy-turveydom of the Lord of Misrule and the World Upside Down and in theatrical terms he is related to the Vice and the clown. Yet, ultimately, Cade is an inverted image of authority, both its distorted representative and its grotesque critic. To get into the subject I will isolate one argument from the very complex, dense and allusive opening of scene 2, when two rebels enter:

> *Hol*　　The nobility think scorn to go in leather aprons.
> *Bev*　　Nay, more; the King's Council are no good workmen.
> *Hol*　　True; and yet it is said, 'Labor in thy vocation': which is as
> 　　　　much to say as, let the magistrate be labouring men; and
> 　　　　therefore should we be magistrates.
>
> 　　　　　　　　　　　　　　　　　　　　　　(4.2.11–18)

Holland travesties the ideological foundations of the Tudor state, the *Book of Homilies*, specifically 'An Homily Against Idleness'. The 'Homily' repeats biblical and proverbial wisdom, 'everyone ought, in his lawful vocation and calling, to give himself to labour'. Holland's chop logic begins by misreading this as 'thy vocation is labouring'. Thus magistrates (rulers) should labour in this sense. He then reverses his own syntax into 'let labouring men be magistrates'. Further, Holland particularly discountenances the careful distinctions of the homily which we can assume were well known as they were regularly read in churches, as directed by authority. The homily considers:

> But when it is said, all men should labour, it is not so straightly meant, that all men should use handy labour . . . there be divers sorts of labours, some of the mind, and some of the body, and some of both . . . whosoever doth good to the commonweal . . . with his industry and labour . . . by governing the commonweal publicly . . . the same person is not to be accounted idle . . . though he work no bodily labour.[34]

The world is turned upside down first by turning language upside down: the king's magistrates are considered poor 'workmen', who should therefore carry out manual labour in a revised vocation, thereby taking the place of the regular workmen, like Bevis and Holland, who would assume their office. Deriving from classical *adunata* (or *impossibilia*) and the medieval *drolerie*, the pictorial tradition of the World Upside Down found on sixteenth-century broadsheets depicted a range of social and natural inversion. The social aspect concerns us here – such images as the peasant rides, the king walks; the servant arrests his master; 'the peasant judges the judge and teaches or refuses the advice of the learned' and 'the thief (or poor man) takes the judge or policeman to jail'.[35] It is this inversion which is enacted before us in Jack Cade's confrontation with Lord Say when the judge is judged.

Cade is many things – historical personage, clown, jester, Lord of Misrule and mock-king – all deriving from carnivalesque modes of inversion. This is seen at its most pointed when Cade presents an argument concerning society, law and justice:

> Thou hast appointed justices of the peace, to call poor men before them about matters they were not able to answer. Moreover, thou hast put them in prison; and because they could not read, thou hast hang'd them.
>
> (4.7.41–4)

Cade refers to the law of benefit of clergy. As in the matter of treason combat, history itself furnished grotesque materials, seeming travesties. In the Middle Ages benefit of clergy was the privilege, available to ordained clerks, monks and nuns accused of felony, of being tried and punished by an ecclesiastical court. As a consequence of the statute of *Pro Clero* (1350), which extended the privilege to secular clerks who helped the clergy in church services, it was later extended to all who could demonstrate the ability to read in Latin their 'neck verse', Psalm 51.1. By the sixteenth century royal courts had taken control, as benefit of clergy had become an involved law which could exempt those found guilty of certain felonies from the severity of the heavily used death penalty.[36] But what of those unable to read, who confronted the death penalty? Consider the case of one John Trotter, who claimed benefit of clergy when accused of murder during the reign of Edward III. Though illiterate he seemed able to 'read' the Psalter. He could still 'read' the verse even when a suspicious judge turned the book upside down. It transpired that a kind-hearted gaoler had allowed two boys to coach him. He was found guilty as a laymen, but if the boys had succeeded in teaching him to read more convincingly, his claim to clergy would have been upheld, though the gaoler would have been punished.[37] Such was the travesty of law in history.

At the conclusion of his argument Cade suddenly adds, 'Thou dost ride in a foot-cloth, dost thou not?' Lord Say is bemused and his inquisitor continues, 'Marry, thou oughtst not to let thy horse wear a cloak, when honester men than thou go in their hose and doublets' (4.7.46–51). Foot-cloths were the conspicuously sumptuous coverings that distinguished the privileged aristocratic mount. Cade's charge turns the logic of hierarchy against itself again. The implicit proposition is that though God created some men of higher degree than others, all men are created superior to animals: yet we see that the aristocrat treats his horse as superior to men of lower station. Furthermore, Say's criminal betrayal of office thereby renders him inferior to those 'honester men' who fulfil the role they were born into. Cade's logical implication plays on the discriminations of sumptuary laws still enforced in sixteenth-century England until King James's repeal in 1604.[38] In brief, an annual income of five pounds entitled the gentleman to wear silk, thereafter the further up the gradated social scale the more luxurious the legally worn cloth of gold, silver, sables, etc., whereas below the dividing line the peasant scratched a living in fustian, canvas, leather or wool cloth.[39] Clothing and class distinction are repeatedly referred to throughout the rebellion, perhaps most pointedly in Holland's 'The nobility think scorn to go in leather aprons' (4.2.12–13) and Cade's 'As for these silken-coated slaves, I pass not' (4.2.128).

The logic of Cade's charge to Lord Say applies an argument of inversion and reversal. Instead of being sentenced to death in effect for not being able to speak Latin, Lord Say is condemned for his words on Kent, 'bona terra, mala gens'. 'Away with him! Away with him! He speaks Latin' (4.7.57–8). Because of Cade's logic, in reciprocating authoritarian self-justification in kind, it is impossible to reject his judgement without recognising the preposterousness of such law in the actual world: this manifest injustice in the play serves to reveal the injustice of all so-called justice based on class.

The action which follows Cade's denunciation, the off-stage execution of Say and the public display of his head to the audience, is not merely Shakespeare's expression of anti-egaliterianism, his horror at the anarchic many-headed monster run wild, but the recognition that such rebellions become a grotesque mimicry of the barbarism of feudal hierarchy. The stage actions and arguments revealing the inscrutability and paradox of providential and human justice expose a world of humanity reduced to bestiality, as we see in *3 Henry VI*. The Cade rebellion is the most complex and provoking presentation of lower class insurrection in early modern drama. Its ambivalent dramatic power derives in large part from Shakespeare's dialectical invention which, *in utramque partem*, explores both sides of the rights and wrongs of degree, justice and society.

3

3 Henry VI and *Richard III*

3 Henry VI

In the course of the Wars of the Roses, before the gates of York, the Lancastrian party gaze up at the decapitated head of the Duke of York, ghoulishly aloft. The king feels pity and implores, 'Withhold revenge, dear God!' (2.2.7). In response, Clifford presents a lengthy argument against such lenity (2.2.9), to which the king's immediate reply is, 'Full well hath Clifford play'd the orator, / Inferring arguments of mighty force' (2.2.43–4). Clifford draws on natural history to illustrate how animals defend their young to the point of self-sacrifice and even the weakest will retaliate against attack. Whereas, on the contrary, Henry's action in disinheriting his son 'argued...a most unloving father' (2.2.25). The king continues his response to Clifford by asking, 'But, Clifford, didst thou never hear / That things ill got had ever bad success?' (2.2.45–6). There is, however, another supporting response, in view of the audience's experience of the play thus far.

The inference of Clifford's argument is that if 'unreasonable creatures' (2.2.26) act instinctively in such a way, then conversely even more so should man by virtue of superior reason. Ironically, staying with this passage, we may recognise that an animal will also act in precisely the reverse fashion, out of that same instinct. Clifford instances the parental lion: 'To whom do lions cast their gentle looks? / Not to the beast that would usurp their den' (2.2.11–12). Yet the same animal had been evoked in one of the most infamous and cruel acts of the play, the death of Rutland.

The Duke of York's youngest son is stressed throughout to augment the pathos and horror in the onstage slaughter of a child[1] – by no other than Clifford, in revenge for his father's death at the hands of the duke.

It is ironic enough to hear Clifford arguing for tenderness, solicitude and care before the head of the man he had helped to kill in one of the most poignant of execution scenes in all early modern drama, but when we hear such an argument from the man who had just slaughtered a boy in the most merciless fashion, before our eyes, it is quite grotesque and numbing. Before his killer, Rutland says:

> So looks the pent-up lion o'er the wretch
> That trembles under his devouring paws;
> And so he walks, insulting o'er his prey,
> And so he comes, to rend his limbs asunder.

> (1.3.12–15)

Rutland refers to a starved animal released to savage a condemned man, but that word 'prey' reminds us of the instinctive predator, nature red in tooth and claw, not the progenitor. Rutland evokes this parallel in his final desperate plea, 'Thou hast one son, for his sake pity me' (1.3.40). Clifford's one-line answer incorporates the fatal thrust of verbal argument and stage action. The argument of action carries out the inexorable logic of revenge, *lex talionis*, an eye for an eye – 'Thy father slew my father; therefore die' (1.3.47). The logic of argument and action rebounds on Clifford himself when at his death he is reviled by the Yorkists, as he reviled the Duke of York, and his head will replace that of the Duke on York gates (2.6.52–86), 'Measure for measure must be answered' (2.6.55). Returning to Clifford's argument before the gates of York, we can find yet a further deconstructive dimension: the lion acts according to the instincts of its animal nature because it cannot do otherwise, whereas man degrades his nature by abusing his humanity and debasing his reason in acting like a vicious animal. This is all enacted in yet another murder, the most notorious of all, the slaughter of Rutland's father in the following scene.

Queen Margaret's cruelty extends to mental torture as she delays the death of York by tormenting him with the news of his son's murder and wiping his face with a napkin dipped in Rutland's blood. In a much debated line York's response combines the animal and the human, 'O tiger's heart wrapp'd in a woman's hide!'[2] Margaret's action with the napkin and York's protracted answer even draws tears from the harsh Northumberland. York repeats, 'But you are more inhuman, more inexorable, / O, ten times more, than tigers of Hyrcania' (1.4.154–5). Part of York's argument is that Margaret's bestiality has turned her completely from her nature as woman and mother. A suspended irony comes full circle, as Rutland predicted, when Margaret witnesses the murder of her son Edward, another child, slaughtered by 'Butchers and Villains! Bloody cannibals!' (5.5.61). Her lament (see 5.5.50–67) echoes York's at the horror of men killing a boy, completely reversing positions. Action, situation and arguments are all preposterous, the word used at the opening of the next scene.

Richard Crookback, impelled by bloodlust and ambition, makes his way to the Tower and conventionally greets the imprisoned king, 'Good day, my lord' (5.6.1). Henry registers the sardonic implication of someone who is there to kill him, and replies:

> Ay, my good lord – my lord, I should say rather.
> 'Tis sin to flatter, 'good' was little better:
> 'Good Gloucester' and 'good devil' were alike,
> And both preposterous; therefore, not 'good lord'.
>
> (5.6.2–5)

Henry revokes the attribute automatically attached to the dignity of degree and title, the hallmark of honour deriving from lineage and/or valour. But then he takes it further. To grant Gloucester the epithet 'good' amounts to calling the devil the same and both are 'preposterous'. Preposterous is from the Latin *praeposterus* (*prae* – before; *posterus* – coming after) which meant, in the sixteenth century, inverted, reversed (having placed last that which should come first) and/or contrary to nature, monstrous and perverse. We know from the evidence of Tudor historians that Richard is to surpass even Clifford and Margaret by reversing inhumanity for humanity, evil for good. It is the monstrous inversion not so much of the likes of Jack Cade and his followers, but from the heart of the feudal system, the House of Plantagenet itself – and by extension the whole knightly caste – in the complete reversion of honour for infamy.

Consider Clifford. Eager to fight York, he has to be restrained by Northumberland, 'Hold, Clifford' (1.4.54), who declares, as they capture the duke, 'It is war's prize to take all vantages, / And ten to one is no impeach of valor' (1.4.59–60). As Margaret torments York she points out 'That valiant Clifford with his rapier's point' (1.4.80) killed Rutland. Given the unchivalric odds and such atrocity, what meaning could 'valor' and 'valiant' possibly have here, especially when we recall that 'valiant' was the key epithet for Talbot? (See *1 Henry VI*, 1.2.21, 4.7.61.) Honour and renown gained by valorous deeds are rewarded by the record of your name in the annals of fame. For all the preposterousness of that 'valor' and 'valiant', justice was done since, as Sir William Dugdale records, Clifford's 'name' in history was recorded as 'the butcher'.[3]

Nobility, chivalry and valour may be summed up in that single word 'honour'. The essence of the word was put with almost touching simplicity in a famous fourteenth-century treatise on warfare, *The Tree of Battles* by Honoré Bonet. 'I tell you,' he writes,

> that the first and principal thing is that [good knights] should keep the oath which they have made to their lord to whom they belong, and to whom they have sworn and promised to do all that he shall command for the defence of the land, according to what is laid down by the laws. He is no true knight who, for fear of death, or of what might befall, fails to defend the land of his lord, but in truth he is a traitor and forsworn.[4]

In contrast, in chapter 18 of *The Prince*, 'How princes should honour their word', Machiavelli gave his recommendations, 'He should appear to be compassionate, faithful to his word, guileless, and devout', 'But one must know how to colour one's actions and to be a great liar and deceiver.'[5] As we have seen, Lord Talbot acts according to Bonet's principles, whereas practically everyone else follows the *realpolitik* of the Florentine. Shakespeare not only stages oath-breaking in the arguments of action, but he also has Richard of Gloucester provide a verbal argument of Machiavellian rationalisation. The staging, action and words are all 'preposterous'.

Act 1 scene 1 is opened by telescoping the events of 1455 and 1460 as if the Yorkists had rushed from the battle of St Albans to ascend the throne in the parliament house. Following the Folio's stage direction *They go up*, Capell's direction indicates York's installing himself on the raised throne or chair of state. 'My lords, look where the sturdy rebel sits, / Even in the chair of state' (1.1.50–1), Henry cries. The outcome of the confrontation is that Henry agrees to 'unnaturally...disinherit' (1.1.193) his son and entails the crown to the House of York, after his death, on condition of the duke's oath of acceptance, which is given, 'This oath I willingly take and will perform' (1.1.201). At this point Capell added the stage direction *Coming from the throne*. The preposterous inversions are overwhelming: Henry reverses his son's inheritance; the king addresses a subject sitting on the throne; the subject descends in order to accept his future enthronement. Furthermore, what value can York's oath have when we have already witnessed his complete perjury in *1 Henry VI* on taking his oath of homage when reinstated as duke

(3.1.166–7)? Yet, from another point of view, King Henry's decision derives more from immediate coercion than from choice. Staged before us in the course of the scene is no less than a *coup d'état*. Warwick orders the king, 'Do right unto this princely Duke of York, / Or I will fill the house with armed men' (1.1.166–7), which he does without waiting for a reply, *He stamps with his foot, and the Soldiers show themselves* (Folio stage direction). Even though the armed men are withdrawn to Tuthill Fields (1.1.179),[6] Henry is surrounded. In the circumstances it is Henry's weakness and compliance which save him (temporarily); anyone more belligerent would almost certainly have met his end, there and then. Once again, might enforces an equivocal right, for division between those who support the third generation of Lancastrian kings, the son of the victor at Agincourt, and those who support the technical right of lineal descent of the Yorkist claim, seems irresolvable. As the Prince of Wales later says, 'if that be right which Warwick says is right, / There is no wrong, but every thing is right' (2.2.131–2). Thus the preposterousness of Henry's resolution only ensures further civil war, which immediately breaks out when York's son persuades him to seize the crown: 'for a kingdom any oath may be broken' (1.2.16), says Edward.

Proverbial *reapolitik* is blunt enough, but Richard offers to resolve his father's qualms with an argument to prove that for his father to break his oath is not perjury:

> An oath is of no moment, being not took
> Before a true and lawful magistrate
> That hath authority over him that swears.
> Henry had none, but did usurp the place.
> Then seeing 'twas he that made you to depose,
> Your oath, my lord, is vain and frivolous.
>
> (1.2.22–7)

Editors point out the legal meaning of 'frivolous' – 'manifestly insufficient or futile' (*OED sb.* 1b). Richard restricts the meaning of taking an oath to the externals of circumstance. Legalism of procedure rather than the ethics of honour is all that matters as a pretext for public expediency. It is hardly a salve for conscience since no genuine conscience could possibly accept such chicanery. Thus the doubly ironic force of that 'frivolous' from the master of sophistry and staging whose arguments are as crooked as his back. York, easily persuaded by this, then learns that Margaret is massing troops against him, thereby rendering Richard's argument redundant and giving him the moral high ground with a line that anticipates his son's ethical inversions: 'trust not simple Henry nor his oaths' (1.2.59). Perhaps the lowest point of such moral distortion, and far from comic, is when Margaret, having wiped the captive York's face with the bloody napkin and crowned him with a paper diadem, reminds him of his oath as part of her argument to justify her action: 'But how is it that great Plantagenet / Is crown'd so soon, and broke his solemn oath?' (1.4.99–100).

Words such as 'solemn' measure the debasement of such savage mockery. Yet Margaret had been quick to see the fallacy of Salisbury's argument in *2 Henry VI* when he links oath-taking and barbarism: 'It is a great sin to swear unto a sin, / But greater sin to keep a sinful oath' (5.1.181–2). He goes on to ask, 'Who can be bound by any solemn vow' to murder, rob, rape and cheat?' Margaret's response is 'A subtle traitor needs no sophister' (5.1.191). She does not expand on this as she takes the sophistry to be self-evident – Salisbury identifies his oath of allegiance to the king (5.1.179) with an oath to commit crime, etc. The full irony of Margaret's sharpness is realised when, at the end of York's torment, she joins Clifford in his oath to revenge his father's death – 'Here's for my oath' (1.4.175) – as they both stab York to death. Salisbury's fallacious argument is thus literally realised in an argument of action, an action infamous even amongst the atrocities of the Wars of the Roses.

In a scene of Shakespeare's invention he introduces a concept of oath-taking which, since the early fourteenth century, was to have far-reaching consequences in English constitutional history. Two keepers come across the disguised Henry musing on kingship and other matters such as Warwick as a 'subtle orator' who 'Inferreth arguments of mighty strength' (3.1.33, 49) as ambassador for Edward IV in the French court. As sworn subjects of the new king the keepers seek to arrest Henry, who reminds them of their oath to him: 'we were subjects but while you were king' (3.1.181), the first keeper replies. That is, their oath is to the office of kingship and whoever its occupant might be.[7] However serious as a political issue, the travesty here derives from such matters being argued by those entirely different in degree: a monarch of the realm, albeit deposed, and two lowly gamekeepers. Henry graciously enables them to keep their oath by voluntarily surrendering to them, but not without pointing out the irony of the logic of their proposition, 'We are true subjects to the king, King Edward' – 'So would you be again to Henry, / If he were seated as King Edward is' (3.1.94–5).

We see how King Edward is 'seated' in the following scene (3.2) in which the keepers' idea of sovereignty is contrasted with the sovereign's lascivious insinuations which capitulate to the counter-argument of Lady Grey's resolute virtue, 'Her looks doth argue her replete with modesty' (3.2.84). Not so much the mystique of the king's two bodies, politic and natural, but an autocratic carnality which wrecks the diplomatic marriage negotiations with France in the next scene. When the king enters with his new queen (4.1) another contrast between the ideal of the sovereign state and the reality of the sovereign's actions occurs in the arguments of the assembled nobles. The loss of a French diplomatic alliance is lamented by Montague, but Hastings argues the sixteenth-century commonplace of independent nationalism, 'England is safe, if true within itself' (4.1.40).[8] Then an extraordinary argument breaks out (4.1.47–66) between the king and his brothers, Clarence and Richard, concerning the use of the royal prerogative of the Courts of Wards in marrying off well-endowed aristocratic heiresses to reward his loyal supporters. Accession is consolidated by the power base of devolved property in the feudal marriage market in which royalty becomes a 'broker' (4.1.63).

In the great world of the French court news of Edward IV's marriage while Warwick was in the midst of negotiating an advantageous French liaison for him leads the earl to reverse allegiance and side with Queen Margaret and Henry. Far from adducing 'arguments of mighty strength' here Warwick's present shame suddenly makes him recall a whole sequence of dishonourable actions (3.3.186–91) which allegiance to the House of York had brought him to. The extremes of honour and shame appear to depend entirely on the expedience of opportunist memory. Warwick goes on to argue that Edward put his lust before honour and the 'strength and safety of our country' (3.3.211) which he will now redress, he hopes, by invading England with a French army! His reasoning would seem quite preposterous were it not for the fact that it has now become virtually the acceptable norm, as *Richard III* makes very clear.

Richard III

Richard of Gloucester was born preposterous, feet first,[9] and his role thereafter – compounded of Vice, devil, Machiavel, Tudor bugbear and Senecan villain-hero-tyrant – is to pursue the logic of ambition by way of sophistry, guile and murder. Yet the deeper logic his casuistry serves is the logic of providence. Having challenged the nature of divine and human justice in the *Henry VI* plays, now chronologically approaching the foundation of the Tudor nation-state, Shakespeare prudently shifts his own dramatic argument by emphatically following Tudor historical mythology in making Henry of Richmond the divinely appointed restorer of peace by unification of the red and white roses in a new dynasty.[10] Conversely, Richard of Gloucester has an additional role to those outlined above: he is the scourge of God. God may intervene as first cause in human history, as in miracles, or he may work through a second cause, man, to carry out his providential purposes. Sometimes an evil person was chosen as a scourge of God (*flagellum dei*) for the sins of man. This accomplished, the scourge of God is then scourged by God.[11]

In terms of genre, Shakespeare stresses the pattern of revenge tragedy, the logic of reprisal and slaughter voiced by Clifford, discussed above, and echoed by Warwick, 'Measure for measure must be answered' (*3 Henry VI*, 2.6.55). Richard argues for revenge on life for his misshapen body, whereas God's vengence for Richard's villainy is repeatedly invoked by the suffering characters. The fallacy of Richard's arguments is exposed by his own careful deliberation, the comedy of outrageous logical self-justification seemingly flying in the face of metaphysical justice, yet Richard is an instrument of the divine. The final dialectical irony is that in spite of the concession to Tudor historiography the rationality of providence is equally exposed by the inner contradiction of its own doctrines.

In his opening soliloquy Richard claims that, given his deformity, 'therefore, since I cannot prove a lover . . . I am determined to prove a villain' (1.1.28, 30). This is the common fallacy of the false cause. If we allow that deformity precludes the conventional conduct of amatory courtship, it doesn't necessarily proscribe love completely and it certainly doesn't mean that the only alternative is to be a villain. In his essay 'Of Deformity' Francis Bacon points out that the scorn aroused by such an affliction is usually overcome by virtue or by malice. Richard chooses malice.[12] Over and above this, for all his self-consciousness and quips, laughing at others' religiosity, Richard does not realise that he is the agent of 'God's just ordinance' (4.4.184), as the play shows.

The Old Testament ordinance is first heard in Deuteronomy 32.35, but its most quoted wording is that of Romans 12.19, 'Vengeance is mine; I will repay, saith the Lord'. Revenge ('revenged', 'venge', 'vengeance', 'avenged') is mentioned slightly more often in *3 Henry VI* than in *Richard III*, but there is an all-important, highly conscious shift in meaning. Nearly every instance in *3 Henry VI* refers to the personal vendetta of blood feud between individuals and between families, whereas in *Richard III* almost all occurrences refer to the revenge of God. As William Tyndale put it, in *The Obedience of a Christian Man* (1528), 'God hath taken all vengeance into his own hands, and will avenge all unright himself; either by the powers or officers which are appointed thereto, or else, if they be negligent, he will send his curses upon the transgressors, and destroy them with his secret judgements.'[13]

In *3 Henry VI*, before the gates of York, King Henry, once again responding to everything from the depths of his faith, recognises the force of scripture: 'Withhold revenge, dear God!' (2.2.7). In contrast, throughout *Richard III* God's vengeance is urged by character after character beginning powerfully with Lady Anne, widow of the slaughtered Prince Edward. When confronted with the 'lump of foul deformity' Richard of Gloucester before the coffin of Henry VI; she cries 'O God! . . . revenge his death!' (1.2.57, 62). Consequently, from this point of view, the argument of the plot becomes a particular kind of argument of action, namely the argument of providence, the proof or manifestation of divine justice. Clarence raises this as part of his desperate argument before his murderers:

> the great King of kings
> Hath in the table of his law commanded
> That thou shalt do no murther. Will you then
> Spurn at his edict, and fulfil a man's?
> Take heed; for he holds vengeance in his hand,
> To hurl upon their heads that break his law.

> (1.4.195–200)

To unravel the convolutions of irony here calls for a casuistic temperament. As the second murderer immediately replies, 'And that same vengeance doth he hurl on thee / For false forswearing and for murther too' (1.4.201–2). The second murderer rationalises the murder he is about to commit, but since he unknowingly acts on behalf of the scourge of God he is carrying out divine providence. Yet it is the first murderer who actually stabs Clarence and drowns him in the malmsey butt, while the second murderer shows compunction and hands over his share of the blood money, but he cannot hand over his share of guilt as accessory after the fact.

In the confrontation with Henry's murderer, Lady Anne throws just this pity at Richard, 'Villain, thou know'st nor law of God nor man: / No beast so fierce but knows some touch of pity' (1.2.70–1). With the chop logic characteristic of the morality Vice Richard deflects this to his witty advantage. Anne's charge is that not only is Richard beyond the laws of God or man, he is even worse than the fiercest beast which shows some 'pity' (i.e. towards its young). Richard's answer is 'But I know none, and therefore am no beast' (1.2.72). Richard's fallacy derives from the false syllogism: 'Beasts feel pity. I do not feel pity. Therefore . . . ' Thus Richard turns Anne's argument around, since if 'no beast' he must be man (i.e. 'human' rather than 'inhuman').

Richard goes on 'To leave this keen encounter of our wits' and turn to something of 'a slower method' (1.2.115–16). As ever, he chooses his words carefully and 'method' indicates the fundamental practice of Renaissance rhetoric and logic, the choice of topics for invention and disposition, here 'cause' of the deaths of King Henry and Prince Edward.[14] 'Thou wast the cause, and most accurs'd effect' is Anne's rejoinder. Alerted by Richard's rhetorical signal she tries to crush his argument by the pun on 'effect' as 'executioner', but as ever the Crookback is one step ahead as he turns both meanings of effect back on her and separates cause: 'Your beauty was the cause of that effect' (1.2.120–1) is his reply. In his grotesque courtship Richard is then able to imply that his jealousy derived from her beauty, the internal is externalised and the cause of Edward's death placed in her. But though the complete imposture of this deadly courtship has already been admitted to the audience, however vicariously mesmeric Richard's spell, we also know that the prior cause is God's will, which Richard carries out. This oscillating irony is made blatant in the next scene when Richard retorts to Queen Margaret, 'God, not we, hath plagu'd thy bloody deed' (1.3.180) of murdering Rutland and tormenting York. Partly to emphasise this self-reflexive irony, in addition to God's law, justice and revenge invoked by Anne (1.2.62–70), Shakespeare includes the prolepsis within the sequence of stichomythia:

> *Glou*   By such despair I should accuse myself.
> *Anne*   And by despairing shalt thou stand excused
>   For doing worthy vengeance on thyself,
>   That didst unworthy slaughter upon others.

> (1.2.85–8)

The words 'revenge' and 'despair' appear in Richard's final soliloquy, before Bosworth, along with the very things he had denied, 'I, that have neither pity, love, nor fear' (*3 Henry VI*, 5.6.68), when killing Henry, which he can no longer argue against.

Before examining Richard's final soliloquy, we may turn to the extensive reprise to the wooing of Lady Anne, the wooing of Princess

Elizabeth by way of her mother, Queen Elizabeth (4.4). The wooing occupies lines 204–33, while most of the preceding dialogue is taken up with the choral lamentation of Elizabeth, Queen Margaret and the Duchess of York. In the performance history this whole scene has been subjected to lengthy cuts, not least because of the heavily rhetorical nature of its stichomythia.[15] The speech I wish to draw attention to is Richard's series of arguments to persuade Queen Elizabeth, lines 291–336, only found in the Folio. The speech is a rhetorician's *tour de force* since it derives from a seemingly impossible position. What conceivable arguments could the murderer of the princes in the Tower – the sons of the queen, the brothers of the princess – find to persuade? Richard has to turn such heinous action into some sort of advantageous topic. Richard appears to resort to the outrageous antitheses of sophistic rhetoric, the inheritance of Gorgias, most notoriously. Richard outdoes even the Sophists in the specialty of the *dissoi logoi*, the double arguments, of making 'the weaker cause the stronger'.[16] But in fact what we have here is the language of the devil, which Queen Elizabeth recognises, 'Shall I be tempted of the devil thus?' (4.4.418), as Christ was by Satan.

It has always been recognised that a considerable part of Richard's characterisation derives from the dramatic provenance of the Vice and the devil.[17] 'Devil' is thrown at Richard many times in the play, and by Anne particularly in the first wooing scene where, like Queen Elizabeth, she recognises the arguments as demonic, following a passage analysed above: 'O wonderful, when devils tell the truth' (1.2.73). Richard admits to seeming 'a saint, when most I play the devil' (1.3.337) as we see when Richard plays the Christian at the opening of his speech to Elizabeth by linking the notion of amendment with that of repentance (4.4.291, 293), echoing the Geneva Bible, Matthew 3.8, 'Bring forth therefore fruit worthy of amendment of life', which is glossed, 'True repentance is an inward thing which hath his seat in the minde and heart.'

The devil is the source of all duality, polarity and contrariety in the fallen world. Irony is the trope of contrariety and its favoured demonic expression is antithesis, the rhetoricians' *contentio*.[18] Richard works through the antithesis of take / give (4.4.294–5), killed / beget (4.4.296–7), vexation / comfort (4.4.305–6), son-king / daughter-queen (4.4.307–8), foreign / home (4.4.312–13), ruin / repair (4.4.318–19): the kingdom taken from Edward V will be given to his sister; Elizabeth's blood, killed in the issue of her womb, will be renewed in that of her daughter's, and so on. In a satanic parody of godhead, 'good' will come from evil. For those educated in rhetoric and logic, the devilish audacity of this would have been mesmerising. Yet Richard's control of his audience breaks down when in his last soliloquy he becomes, in effect, onstage auditor of the 'frantic play' (4.4.68) of his evil actions.

One of the most remarkable aspects of Richard's last speech, within a tetralogy particularly characterised by the general formalism of its verse, is the way it develops through the perceptible structure of *in utramque partem* debate, on both sides of the question, to something approaching relative naturalism. Richard controls the world by words. As king his word is law in peace and war. In his progress to the throne his witty arguments had displayed his performance to the audience – with the comic daring of sophistry by which he controlled audience, victim, situation and his own exuberance. But now he discovers the one thing he cannot control, his dreams, or put another way, the expression his conscience finds through dreams.[19] As he had addressed the captive audience, now he is the sole auditor, captive in sleep, before the tableaux of staged recrimination. The juristic aspect in Shakespeare's drama of argument as evidence, discussed in the concluding chapter, is apparent here. As Clarence had anticipated, 'these things . . . now give evidence against my soul' (1.4.66–7) and Richard's accusers 'throng to the bar' to give voice to what we the audience have witnessed – 'Guilty! Guilty!' (5.3.199).

The nightmare of the morrow's battle brings out his first utterance, otherwise entirely characteristic of Henry, 'Have mercy, Jesu!' (5.3.178). Then Richard tries to exercise his characteristic control by arguing against conscience. Madeleine Doran has touched on the debate structure here.[20] Richard presents himself with a question, 'What do I fear?' (5.3.182), which is answered by the methodical division into self or others. Others are to be feared in the form of a murderer but the self-loving king is alone and thus self-protective. Yet that same person is indeed a murderer. Murderers must be fled from, an impossibility for the self. To resolve the anomaly Richard systematically develops the argument. A murderer would take revenge. How could the self-loving ego take revenge on itself? Then the topic of definition implicitly undermines Richard's whole argument since any definition of love must entail the idea of the good and he knows that he is solely evil in thought and deed, therefore the protective self-love he claims is really self-hatred, as he acknowledges – 'I rather hate myself' (5.3.190).

Richard's cold rationalism is subverted by the 'fear' he earlier claimed he never felt, 'Cold fearful drops stand on my trembling flesh' (5.3.181). Selfhood divides between the present accusing conscience and the past conscienceless acts of evil, revealing the soul in despair, unpitied and unloved, guilty before the court of last judgment. Richard's pitilessness and hatred had snuffed out one life after another, but he cannot extinguish meaning: 'pity, love and fear' return to haunt him like the ghosts.

The onset of some degree of *anagnorisis*, or self-knowledge, here, as an aspect of Shakespeare's tragic development going well beyond his sources, is controverted by reversion to Machiavellian type. Armed for battle, in the light of day, Richard urges:

> Let not our babbling dreams affright our souls;
> Conscience is but a word which cowards use.
> Devis'd at first to keep the strong in awe:
> Our strong arms be our conscience, swords our law!
>
> (5.3.308–11)

And he goes on to fulfil his role as the scourger scourged, the unwitting agent of Tudor unification celebrated in the closing speech by victorious Richmond, encapsulating the 'Tudor myth' of Hall's chronicle.

> We will unite the White Rose and the Red.
> . . .
> O now let Richmond and Elizabeth,
> The true succeeders of each royal house,
> By God's fair ordinance conjoin together!
>
> (5.5.19, 29–31)

The concluding emphasis here is plain enough and it is not difficult to envisage the endorsement of the contemporary audience response. There was, however, as William R. Elton has shown, a section of the late sixteenth-century audience which anticipates that of the twentieth century, for whom the argument of providence would have presented a difficulty in the issue of suffering, evil and justice. For example, Elton discusses John Carpenter's *A Preparative to Contentation* (1597), in which

> Doubters of providence emphasise 'this heavy consideration . . . that the . . . wicked be preferred, and live in long prospertie: that the unrighteous do unrighteously, & God (as *Job* saith) doth not charge them with follie, or plague them: that injustice and oppression is seene in the place of judgement' (p. 278). Such discontent regarding providence is spread among 'The common sort of men' who 'do argue of the want of power and force in God', implying government by fortune. Even 'manie of the godlie themsleves . . . are by . . . such like

spectacles, mooved to expostulate agaynst the Lorde...*should not the Judge of all the world do justice?'* There are 'not a fewe' who are 'desperate of GOD, and of the divine providence...' (pp. 279–80)[21]

In short, given the emphasis on the innocence of such figures as Rutland, Prince Edward and the princes in the Tower, quite how do their deaths fit in with the providential scheme of things? Further, some characters such as Edward IV and Queen Margaret, seem to remain relatively unpunished.[22] Justice seems quite arbitrary. Some, such as Buckingham and Clarence, are punished for their crimes, others seem to be punished for their blamelessness. Retributive and distributive justice seem irreconcilable. The customary answer to this draws on St Augustine's formulations: if all were duly punished on earth, nothing would seem to be reserved for the Last Judgement. Conversely, if nobody were punished on earth, it would appear that there were no divine providence at all. Where the good and bad seem equally to receive punishment in the form of calamity and misfortune, suffering purges the righteous but damns the sinner.[23]

Unfortunately, when Tyrrel relates the murderers' account of the death of the princes – full of 'tenderness', 'compassion', 'tears', and the beauty and innocence of the 'most...sweet work of nature' (4.3.7–18) – it is difficult to reconcile such atrocity with any scheme of justice. If we reconsider the issue in theological terms of particular and general providence, then the use of particular evil means to justify a general end seems more the work of a Machiavel than a loving God. If we take up the common position that all are born sinful, we still have the problem that the princes received punishment for acts they could not have possibly had any part in. Alternatively, a reverse view would be that after death they share blessedness with God in heaven sooner than they otherwise would. Such beliefs in a state of sin which inherits suffering and suffering which merits a state of blessedness would seem to defy the credulity of any faith. The second position would lead us to endorse Richard's sardonic suggestion to Anne concerning the dead king: the grotesque Vice-devil suggests, 'Let him thank me that help to send him hither; / or he was fitter for that place than earth' (1.2.107–8). In summarising God's distribution of 'suffering' on earth St Augustine writes:

whatever affliction good men and bad men suffer together in this life, it doth not prove the persons undistinct, because so they do jointly endure like pains. For the sufferers remain distinct even while enduring the same suffering, and virtue and vice remain distinct between the burden of the same affliction.[24]

Thus it appears that God, like the formal vice, Iniquity, moralises two meanings of 'suffering' in one word. While Shakespeare seems to comply, at the end of the tetralogy, with the political ideology of the Tudor myth, his representation of theodicy is disturbingly radical. The question of the origin of evil in relation to the Godhead repeatedly arose in Reformation controversy nearly always focusing on the divine 'permission' of evil as part of God's absolute will. As a consequence, the difference between authority and agency could seem merely a question of argument.[25] Richard's 'God, not we, hath plagu'd thy bloody deed' (1.3.180) in relation to this context takes on a dangerous ambivalence. Only on Judgment Day, St Augustine tells us, 'we shall learn, and know also, why God's judgements are generally incomprehensible to us'.[26] In a play that seemingly endorses a providential view of history Shakespeare calls into question the possibility of any justice, natural or metaphysical.

4
Richard II

Richard II opens with the 'argument' (1.1.12) which Richard rather edgily questions John of Gaunt about: the nature of the accusation his son Henry Bolingbroke has made against Thomas Mowbray. Bolingbroke's charge of treason leads to the trial by combat at Coventry which is stopped, as it was in the historical record, by Richard's action, 'Stay, the King hath thrown his warder down' (1.3.118). After these ceremonially long-drawn-out scenes, the action moves quickly: Bolingbroke is banished; he returns; Richard is deposed; Bolingbroke ascends the throne, Richard is murdered.

To begin by examining the opening arguments and Richard's action, I wish to put forward a case that is not usually found in critical discussion of this play: Bolingbroke's argument and intended action, the combat, are the first move of a hoped-for *coup*. The plan seems to go wrong since Richard does not allow the combat, but Bolingbroke succeeds anyway when he takes another risk and breaks the terms of his banishment. One of the crucial details for this interpretation is Bolingbroke's inclusion in the charge against Mowbray: 'That he did plot the Duke of Gloucester's death' (1.1.100). This Duke of Gloucester is Thomas of Woodstock, Bolingbroke and Richard's uncle. Because of the plethora of repeated titles in the English histories, I shall refer to him as Woodstock. There are two things to note at the outset here. In Holinshed Bolingbroke's charge against Mowbray is rather general, 'a traitor, false and disloiall to the king, and enimie vnto the realme' (II, 844).

It is an anonymous knight supporting Bolingbroke who brings up the specific crime of Mowbray: 'he hath caused to die and to be murthered your right déere uncle, the duke of Glocester, sonne to King Edward' (II, 845). Second, well in advance of the actual combat, the king knows what the stakes are, so he obviously has time to plan. The approach

52

taken here, seeing Shakespeare's grasp of *realpolitik* beneath the protocols of ceremony and courtliness, is in fact found in Holinshed where, at Bolingbroke's accession, he looks back and summarises: 'The duke of Glocester chéefe instrument of this mischiefe...his nephue [Bolingbroke] tooke vpon him to reuenge his death' (II, 869). At this point it would be appropriate to look back to that period of Richard's reign immediately preceding the two years dramatised in the play, to estimate the state of knowledge in the chronicles and thus available to Shakespeare's audience.[1]

Richard either banished or executed any noble opposition. He converted parliament into an instrument of his will with his favourites wielding power.[2] Holinshed provides a general paragraph which says so much:

> Manie other things were doone in this parliament [at Shrewsbury, 1398]...namelie, for that diuerse rightfull heires were disherited of their lands and liuings...the King and those that were about him...came into great infamie and slander...the King...forgot himselfe, and began to rule by will more than by reason, threatening death to each one that obeied not his inordinate desires...the lords of the realme began to fear their owne estates, being in danger of his furious outrage, whome they tooke for a man destitute of sobrietie and wisdome. (II, 844)

A later account in Holinshed shows how Richard hit upon a legal method of killing off the disaffected baronage. Using the procedures of the court of chivalry he had fit young supporters accuse his older opponents of treason, subsequently killing them in trial by combat (Holinshed, II, 850), unless they submitted to the accusation. Parliament had expressed misgivings about the court of chivalry, fearing its encroachment on common law. Thus Richard combined a chivalric occasion of imposing ritual with a deadly political weapon. (Ironically, the official who drew up the rules for the order of combats was Thomas of Woodstock.)[3] When we turn to Froissart we find in one place virtually the popular basis for Bolingbroke's *coup*. Froissart is always fascinated by the political power of the Londoners and he provides them with a speech in support of Bolingbroke at the time of the confrontation with Mowbray:

> howesoevere the matter tourne, ye shall scape with honour...we knowe well this mater is made and conveyed by envy, to the entente

to drive you out of the realme, bycause ye be well beloved with many men. And if so be that ye departe in trouble, ye shall entre agayne with joye, for ye ought rather to rule than Rycharde of Burdeaulx ... ye be more nerer to the crowne of Englande than Rycharde ... [4]

Shakespeare, however, chose to stress Richard's recognition of Boling-broke's popularity after the sentence of banishment, as made manifest in his departure (1.4.1–36), yet Richard's speech ends on a note which seems to reflect the second half of the above Froissart passage:

> A brace of draymen bid God speed him well,
> And had the tribute of his supple knee,
> With 'Thanks, my countrymen, my loving friends',
> As were our England in reversion his,
> And he our subjects' next degree of hope
>
> (1.4.32–6)

As we have seen, Shakespeare emphasises the most damning fact which symbolised the gross misrule of Richard's last years, the murder of Woodstock. In Shakespeare's invention of a scene not found in any of the sources, act 1, scene 2, Woodstock's death is the sole concern in the dialogue between John of Gaunt and the Duchess of Gloucester, beginning with the opening line, 'Alas, the part I had in Woodstock's blood'.[5] The duchess pleads for Gaunt to take vengeance against Wood-stock's murderers, and in doing so her argument gives voice to the unanimous historical record: Mowbray killed Woodstock on Richard's orders. These brutal facts were common knowledge (see Holinshed, II, 837) and the duchess reminds the audience in a private scene set between the chivalric and ceremonial scenes of challenge and trial by combat.

Before continuing with this contrast we need to look at Gaunt's argu-ment in reply for not taking revenge for his brother's assassination:

> God's is the quarrel, for God's substitute,
> His deputy anointed in His sight,
> Hath caus'd his death, the which if wrongfully,
> Let heaven revenge, for I may never lift
> An angry arm against His minister.
>
> (1.2.37–41)

These lines amount to an epitome of what is usually referred to as the absolutist theory of divine right and its corollary of passive obedience. The most famous expression of these ideas is by the Bishop of Carlisle in his later protest at Richard's deposition and Bolingbroke's imminent installation (4.1.114–31). For newcomers to the play, Carlisle's speech, particularly, has often been the source of one-sided confusion concerning late medieval and early modern political thought and it will be re-examined here shortly as part of the dramatic structure of arguments of law in relation to political action. What often passes without comment in Gaunt's argument is its trenchant irony: a divinely appointed king is also a murderer, yet that murder may be an aspect of divine justice, and equally it may not – 'the which if wrongfully'. On theological, political and moral grounds this is provocative, indeed, and arguably undermines the very thing it protests, divine justice, which also seems to be forgotten in the combat at Coventry.

By 1398, Holinshed tells us, Richard's tyranny seemed so powerful that 'whatsoeuer he then did, none durst speake a word contrarie therevnto' (II, 843). Bolingbroke's accusation against Mowbray in the same year (Holinshed, II, 844) is an explicit defiance of this fear, giving voice in Shakespeare's emphasis to what everyone saw as Richard's greatest crime, the death of Woodstock. Bolingbroke's accusation insists on the right to 'the rites of knighthood' which Mowbray's answer confirms, embracing the 'chivalrous design of knightly trial' (1.1.75, 81). With the accusation of treason, trial by combat was followed when there were no witnesses and no evidence, one man's word simply standing against another's.[6]

Mowbray protests his 'spotless reputation' and his 'honor' (1.1.178, 182), which is paradoxical since his earlier argument specifically answering Bolingbroke's charge concerning Woodstock seems both to prevaricate and yet to admit guilt: 'For Gloucester's death,' he says, 'I slew him not, but to my own disgrace / Neglected my sworn duty in that case' (1.1.132–4). Mowbray delayed carrying out Richard's orders for Woodstock's immediate execution, which was eventually done under his supervision after a few weeks (Holinshed, II, 837). Mowbray's words are confusing. He seems to be casuistically disclaiming direct agency as a murderer, yet at the same time apologising to the king for not speedily fulfilling his obligation as Richard's Earl Marshall. How this is compatible with 'spotless reputation' and 'honor' is difficult to see unless we recognise a double standard. Mowbray may claim 'spotless reputation' since he did carry out the king's orders regardless of questions of legality or political morality. Honour, as has been discussed above

(p. 22), may be understood as the honour attached to the name and status automatically deriving from noble birth, anterior to the chivalric honour deriving from valorous deeds or the civic honour deriving from virtue.[7] For aristocrats like Mowbray the honour of cumulative lineage is greater than the honour assumed by any individual bearer of the name whose personal acts could thus not impugn the greater glory of inheritance unless, as here, the consequences of proven treason could jeopardise a noble line.[8]

The most important fact to grasp about the chief action of the combat is that Richard's pre-empting any battle by throwing his official warder down (1.3.118) was entirely within the rules of trial by combat and was often done.[9] Although a modern-day director may wish to emphasise a high-camp arbitrariness to bring out Richard's character, the historical situation was an invidiously political one. Richard had two main political options, either to allow the combat or to prevent it with his judgment. The outcome of any battle would have divided into three possibilities: Bolingbroke kills Mowbray; Mowbray kills Bolingbroke; they kill each other. The last would have been perfect for Richard and, though it occasionally happened, the odds were against it. If Mowbray killed Bolingbroke this might trigger a rebellion and it would leave alive the person who had become Richard's chief political liability. If Bolingbroke killed Mowbray this might be taken as divine endorsement, by proxy, for removing the king himself and rebellion might well ensue, Bolingbroke's *coup* taking shape.

This political reading is borne out by the words of Westmoreland in *2 Henry IV*, answering Mowbray's son:

> The Earl of Herford was reputed then
> In England the most valiant gentleman.
> Who knows on whom fortune would then have smil'd?
> But if your father had been victor there,
> He ne'er had borne it out of Coventry;
> For all the country in a general voice
> Cried hate upon him; and all their prayers and love
> Were set on Herford, whom they doted on
> And bless'd and grac'd and did, more than the King –

(4.1.129–37)

Bolingbroke took a major gamble that the king would allow the combat since he must have known of the alternative procedure. Once again

Richard resorted to one of his main political ploys, banishment, thought out well before he halts the combat and withdraws to take counsel (1.3.121–4).[10] Richard's judgment is less inflammatory than any other outcome and, ironically, it is perfectly even-handed since he shortly hints privately that Bolingbroke, like Mowbray, will never be allowed to return (1.4.20–2).

In *2 Henry IV* Mowbray's son suggests:

> O, when the King did throw his warder down
> (His own life hung upon the staff he threw),
> Then threw he down himself and all their lives
> That by indictment and by dint of sword
> Have since miscarried under Bolingbroke.
>
> (4.1.123–7)

Most modern commentators, however, would take the view that Richard's action of seizing on the dead John of Gaunt's estate and disallowing Bolingbroke's feudal right to homage and inheritance was the crucial factor, as indeed within the play the Duke of York tries to explain to the king (2.1.186–208). This view would accord with Holinshed, where Bolingbroke's banishment begins on St Lambert's day, 17 September 1398; Gaunt dies early in 1399; Richard began his Irish wars in April 1399 and then, following representation from the English nobility and magistracy, Bolingbroke landed at Ravenspurgh at the beginning of July 1399. That is, in Holinshed (II, 844–53) there are approximately ten months between Bolingbroke's banishment and return, ten months for the exile to learn of Richard's action against his inheritance and all the various political and economic outrages of the king (many indicated in Gaunt's dying speeches, 2.1.57–66, 110–14). Yet this does not accord with Shakespeare's play, where a crucial difference occurs with the greatest deliberation since it is in such marked contrast to the historical record.

Nearly two-thirds of act 2, scene 1 are taken up with Richard's acrimonious confrontation with the dying Gaunt, who gives voice to some of the most celebrated and anthologised lines of all the English histories ('This royal throne of kings . . .' etc., 2.1.40ff). The last third of the scene is as neglected as the first two-thirds are celebrated – perhaps unsurprisingly, following the passionate drama of what precedes, since the scene is largely taken up (l.225ff) with the grievances of disaffected nobles. Yet there is great subtlety in the way

Northumberland sedulously sounds out the degree of political revolt before he plays his trump card and to unite them all in the complicity of rebellion announces that Bolingbroke with an armed fleet is already sailing for England[11] – before, that is, he could possibly have heard of Richard's dealings with his father. Bolingbroke's prospective *coup* following the combat was pre-empted. Now with a small army and eager support in England, he comes to claim no less than the crown, since the political situation his return creates is unilateral: there can be no compromise, whatever the pretext, it must be success and the throne, or failure and execution. This is the argument of Bolingbroke's action in sailing from Brittany. On landing at Ravenspurgh and learning of Richard's depredations against the House of Lancaster he has a perfect pretext – he has returned to claim his inheritance as Northumberland insists (2.3.148–9) and Bolingbroke repeats before the king (3.3.196).

Initially, however, the Duke of York sees things quite differently, for to him the argument of Bolingbroke's action is 'gross rebellion and detested treason' (2.3.109). Bolingbroke's response to this is a sophistry: 'As I was banish'd, I was banish'd Herford, / But as I come, I come for Lancaster' (2.3.113–14). To York, Herford-Lancaster is a rebel and a traitor. Bolingbroke's ambiguous argument suggests several things: that banishment is somehow nullified by failure of inheritance, i.e. that the failure of a general law, feudal succession, annuls the king's particular sentence. Nowhere in his speech does Bolingbroke mention the grounds of Richard's judgment (however much a pretext, it was nevertheless accurate): the danger of civil dissension (1.3.128). Further, his initial reasoning fallaciously suggests that the sentence of banishment was only on Herford which he no longer is, but now the Duke of Lancaster come to claim that title, as if change in status actually changed the individual's culpability. (Put in terms of scholastic logic, Bolingbroke treats an accident (title) as if it were substance (person).) Herford-Lancaster pursues the legal argument in words which specifically recall York's earlier outburst to the king, namely:

> If you do wrongfully seize Herford's rights,
> Call in the letters-patent that he hath
> By his attorneys-general to sue
> His livery, and deny his off'red homage,
> You pluck a thousand dangers on your head

> (2.1.201–5)

York spells out for Richard the political analogy.

> Take Herford's rights away, and take from Time
> His charters and his customary rights . . .
>   . . . for how art thou a King
> But by fair sequence and succession?

(2.1.195–6, 198–9)

But Richard is quite deaf to his argument. With Bolingbroke's return the logic of the political situation has changed, crucially: 'If that my cousin king be King of England, / It must be granted that I am Duke of Lancaster', he says (2.3.123–4). It is precisely because Richard is king that he is not the Duke of Lancaster. The implicit logic of thought and action now is that to ensure becoming the Duke of Lancaster he must also become King of England.

The cornerstone of Bolingbroke's argument is for his 'rights' (2.3.119), 'I am subject, / And I challenge law' (2.3.133–4) ('challenge' in the sense of 'lay claim to' legal rights [*OED v.* 5]). This is the foundation of his oath at Ravenspurgh. In one of the symmetrically patterned correspondences emphasising diametrical contrasts in the play, on Richard's return from Ireland he reasserts another kind of 'right':

> Not all the water in the rough rude sea
> Can wash the balm from an anointed king;
> The breath of worldly men cannot depose
> The deputy elected by the Lord;

(3.2.54–7)

and 'heaven still guards the right' (3.2.62) (as it was supposed to do at the combat where it was conveniently put aside). Bolingbroke's implicit and Richard's explicit view of kingship are completely opposed and both are found in medieval and early modern political thought. Perhaps surprisingly, both are also found together in the English coronation ritual.

The Roman civil law inheritance from the formulations of Justinian had included a warrantee for absolutism which was encapsulated in three pronouncements: *quod principi placuit leges habet vigorem* (what pleases the prince has the force of the law); *rex legibus solutus est* (the king is above the law); *omnia iura habet princeps in pectore suo* (the prince has all law in his breast).[12] The last was specifically included in the articles of deposition against Richard, item fourteen: 'he said, that the lawes of the realme were in his head, and sometimes in his brest, by reason of which fantasticall opinion, he destroied noble men, and impouerished the poore commons' (Holinshed, II, 860).[13] This was particularly obnoxious to the common law tradition in England and to its spokesmen, such as Sir John Fortescue, the fifteenth-century jurist.

On the other hand, in the course of the Middle Ages, there had always been resistance to the claims of hieratic absolutism in both the church and the state. From this standpoint, neither pope, emperor nor king was above the laws of God from which derived the laws of reason, nature and society that are reflected in the laws of man. Therefore none could act against the law without ultimately infringing divine ordinance. Put another way, by way of Latin jurisprudence Christian culture had inherited Greek ideas of natural law and equity in spite of Hebraic concepts of the Fall. Such law existed for the sake of the people as a corporate body, and kingship was seen as the office of a guardian-protector of such laws. The oft-quoted clarion call of such thought was Cicero's *salus populi suprema est lex* (the health – or safety – of the people is the highest law).[14]

The law of the kingdom, the *lex regia*, enshrined the idea of the sovereignty of the people. Also found in Justinian was the formulation *lex digna vox*, interpreted as 'it is a word worthy of the majesty of the ruler that the prince professes himself bound by the law'. In England, by the fifteenth century, this aspect of Roman law had combined with the tradition of positive, custom or common law, by which the king could not make law without the assent of the people, since, in Fortescue's phrase, England was a *dominium politicum et regale*. One point of view sees such political ideas as taking shape to forestall the danger of tyranny, another stresses such a movement as incipiently contributing to the formation of constitutionalism.[15] Be that as it may, the notion of the king's obligation to uphold the law was built into the coronation oath.

Richard II's coronation ritual included the four questions of the oath, beginning with his vow to 'keep, and . . . confirm, to the people of England, the laws and customs granted to them by the ancient Kings of England'.[16] These laws and customs are those granted to the church and those of the realm generally. In fact the three other questions repeat these in different ways, but the fourth contained a vital shift in emphasis: 'Sir, do you grant to hold and keep the laws and righteous customs which the community of your realm shall have chosen, and will you defend and strengthen them to the honour of God to the utmost of your power?'[17] (*Concedis iustas leges et consuetudines esse tenen-*

das, et promittis eas per te esse protegendas, et ad honorem dei roborandas quas uulgus elegerit secundum uires tuas.[18])

The fourth question was forced on Edward II as part of his coronation order, thereby binding the king to whatever future laws might be chosen, determined or enacted (*elegerit*). Just before, the assembled nobles, '*the people*', are asked to grant '*their will and consent about the consecration of the said king*'.[19] The elective element was made stronger for the coronation of Edward III and thereafter by the additions of the *Liber Regalis* by Abbot Lytlington in the fifteenth century which was followed for the coronation of Richard II.[20] Items eleven and nineteen of the articles of deposition against Richard specified the breaking of his coronation oath. Item fourteen has been quoted above and this, along with item twenty-three, encapsulates Richard's absolutism: 'he most tyrannouslie and vnprincelie said, that the liues and goods of all his subiects were in his hands, and at his disposition' (Holinshed, II, 861). However, following the will and consent of the people and the oath, the consecration and ritual signify that the king has also been chosen by God.

Here is the foundation of the arguments we have seen in *Richard II* by Gaunt, the Bishop of Carlisle and the king. The coronation ritual dramatised the sacred nature of biblical priest-kingship. The *Liber Regalis* compares the English king with Melchisedek, high priest and king (Genesis 14.18) and its description of the coronation robes resembles those of priestly vestments.[21] Before the twelfth century some had considered the king's consecration by anointing to be a sacrament. Thereafter the number of sacraments was limited to seven, but nevertheless it is common to find the hieratic aspect of the ritual, harking back to Samuel's anointing of King David, as a sacrament.[22] Following tradition, Richard was elaborately anointed on the hands and breast, between the shoulders, on the elbows, and with the sign of the cross on the head, as God's deputy, vice-regent, or vicar on earth: thus fulfilling the biblical pronouncement of such texts as Proverbs 8.15, 'By me Kings reign', and the ubiquitous sanction of Romans 13.1, 'Let every soul be subject unto the higher powers. For there is no power but of God: the powers that be are ordained of God.'[23]

The Bishop of Carlisle's language – 'And shall the figure of God's majesty, / His captain, steward, deputy, elect, / Anointed, crowned, planted many years' (4.1.125–7) – is much more hieratic than his speech in Holinshed (III, 6). Such language, however, had a contemporary resonance for Elizabethans, since the Tudor monarchy in the world of the Reformation had reasserted the absolutist language of biblical priest-kingship. This is perhaps nowhere more evident than in the *Homilies*, above all in 'An Exhortation concerning good order and obedience to rulers and magistrates', at the heart of which is the example of David refusing to harm the sleeping Saul (1 Samuel 18–26): 'Here is evidently proved, that we may not withstand nor in any wise hurt an anointed King, which is God's lieutenant, vicegerent, and highest minister in that country where he is king.'[24] Such a view, supported by the concomitant ideas of non-resistance and passive obedience before a malign ruler, could lead to the absolutist extreme of the following:

> He that judgeth the king judgeth God; and he that resisteth the king resisted God and damneth God's laws and ordinance.... The king is, in this world, without law, and may at his lust do right or wrong and shall give accounts but to God only.

This is quoted from William Tyndale's *The Obedience of a Christian Man* (1582 edition).[25]

On returning from Ireland Richard reverts to this language (first introduced into the play by Gaunt, as we have seen).

> Not all the water in the rough rude sea
> Can wash the balm off from an anointed king;
> The breath of worldly men cannot depose
> The deputy elected by the Lord;
>
> (3.2.54–7)

This is not merely rhetoric, neither is it adequate to account for its claim solely in terms of Richard's histrionic character. First, the argument is completely at odds with the argument of Richard's preceding actions, which culminate in the expropriation of Gaunt's estate. Notions of divine kingship are seen to be completely incompatible with extortion and fraud, theft and murder. But from a religious point of view the anointed sanctity of a king was considered an indefeasible fact right up to Shakespeare's time. To shift the ground from the ritualistic to the legalistic, Richard has a point. Though the king may not be above the law he was outside the law in the sense that there was no legal basis or procedure to try a criminal monarch, since it was the monarch who sanctioned and inaugurated such procedure for major state trials. The estates of the realm, expressing consensus through parliamentary representatives, made political authority the enabling instrument of legalism.[26] Further, deposition ran into trouble if the king were not willing to resign

his office, title and kingdom: the breath of worldly men could not legally depose God's deputy without his uncoerced cooperation. Hence the
importance of that word 'willing' in York's speech before Carlisle's
outburst, Richard 'with willing soul / Adopts thee heir' (4.1.108–9).

Lancastrian chroniclers stressed Richard's renunciation at Conway
and subsequently his official resignation in the Tower of London 'with
cheerful countenance' ('*vultu hilari*'), an account which is inscribed in
the Rolls of Parliament.[27] Shakespeare's king is resigned to the role York
presents but he is fully aware of the political reality beneath Bolingbroke's pretexts. Richard knows it is 'the crown [Bolingbroke] looks for'
(3.3.95) and 'the strong'st and surest way to get' (3.3.201), just as he
knows, in facing Bolingbroke, that he is his prisoner and must adopt
the appropriate demeanour for deposition, but not without a wry protest:
'What you will have, I'll give, and willing too, / For do we must what
force will have us do' (3.3.206–7). It is deeply ironic that Richard has
this clear-sighted view of the reality of the Lancastrian's political
actions when he is quite blind to how his actions, as a 'tyrant by
oppression', have been seen by others.[28] When Northumberland insists
that the king read the list of his 'grievous crimes', Richard refers to them
as merely 'follies' (4.1.223, 229).

Bolingbroke stages the deposition to pre-empt any charge of conquest
or usurpation, 'that in common view / He may surrender; so we shall
proceed / Without suspicion' (4.1.155–7). This anxiety nevertheless recurs
in York's directive 'To do that office of thine own good will' (4.1.177)
and with Bolingbroke's 'I thought you had been willing to resign'
(4.1.190), 'Are you contented to resign the crown?' (4.1.200). In fact, at
one point Bolingbroke had to be dissuaded from claiming the grounds
of conquest.[29] After recording the articles of deposition, Holinshed records
that the king's servants spelt out the situation:

> they aduised him willinglie to suffer himselfe to be deposed, and to
> resign his right of his owne accord, so that the duke of Lancaster
> might without murther or battell obteine the scepter and diademe,
> after which (they well perceiued) he gaped: by meane whereof they
> thought he might be in perfect assurance of his life long to continue.
> (II, 861)

'Gaped' is dramatic, indeed, but Shakespeare explores an altogether different approach. The counsellors' argument here is explicit, whereas
Shakespeare leaves it implicit in the argument of action, unspoken
except for that word 'willing'. Shakespeare thereby derives great tension

from the drama of Richard's theatrical character – will he comply with the expected role or will he throw defiance in their face? The drama is heightened to its uttermost as Richard does both.

The king's posturing culminates in the request for a mirror, the prop and cue by which he upstages everybody, but only because he is allowed to do so. It is Bolingbroke, not the antic Death, who allows 'a little scene' (3.2.164). In this there is a daring political analogy between Tudor state politics and theatre censorship, between political reality and the kind of official 'reality' the Elizabethan theatre was allowed to stage. Staging the chronicle of Richard's last years, however, was dangerous as it brought together the official doctrine of the sanctity of kingship and the circumstances by which a king might be deposed and another elected, the very situation by the 1590s as a result of decades of developing resistance theory from every direction at home and abroad.

By the 1590s varieties of resistance theory developing arguments for deposition and election were everywhere. With the resistance theory of medieval political thought in the background[30] we find the Marian exiles, Presbyterians, radical Puritans and the Huguenots all concerned with persecution under an oppressive monarch. Further, with the French King Henry III sympathetic to the Huguenots and then the accession of a Huguenot monarch, Henry IV, the Catholic Holy League of the Guise, and the Jesuits, took up theories of deposition with a vengeance.[31] Finally, it was believed that these pernicious doctrines had spread to English Catholics.[32] Pope Sixtus V set about renewing his predecessor Pius's 1570 bull against Elizabeth, a redaction of which appeared in England as *A Declaration of the Sentence and deposition of Elizabeth, the usurper and pretensed Quene of England* (1588), to sanction the Armada.[33]

In a sermon of 1593, *Dangerous Positions and Proceedings*, Richard Bancroft (later Bishop of London), lumped together Marian exiles such as John Ponet and the French Huguenot theorists Hubert Languet and Phillipe du Plessis Mornay, castigating the principles of election, deposition and tyrannicide, quoting in horror '*Evil Princes ought (by the Law of God) to be deposed*...Examples allowed of Kings deposed. Edw. II Rich. II'.[34] No wonder the staging of the deposition scene of *Richard II* was not printed until 1608 in the fourth quarto.

To recapitulate – circumstances had played into Bolingbroke's hands, he finds overwhelming support from the nobility, whereas on his return from Ireland Richard found that all his forces had deserted him. Therefore there was no battle, no bloodshed, and Bolingbroke did not have to seize the crown by force, a factor which ever afterwards would have gravely undermined whatever claims he might make to the throne. Consequently, the way is open for legal accession by proto-constitutional means, if Richard can be persuaded to resign the crown and abdicate without coercion.[35] Illegal rebellion will be replaced by judicially sanctioned deposition. Shakespeare chose not to use the hereditary claim made by Bolingbroke in his speech at Westminster, through descent from Henry III and the blessing of God who 'hath sent me, with the helpe of my kin, and of my friends, to recouer' the realm of England (Holinshed, II, 865).[36] Both in Shakespeare and Holinshed, Bolingbroke's dilemma is that he must be seen not as a usurper but as responding to the consensus of the body politic, the 'commons' (see 4.3.134, 4.1.272), and yet for his own future position he must ensure a right independent of election by parliament.

Richard is allowed his 'little scene' of poetic self-deposition. As it is all he has left, he seizes the theatrical moment, which culminates in the word-play of the 'shadow' and 'substance' of grief. But the shadow and substance of political reality are something altogether different. The shadow is the emptiness of metaphysical kingship and the substance is that of Machiavellian *realpolitik* negotiating legitimacy by proto-consti-tutional means. All of Bolingbroke's actions add up to this argument, whereas all of Richard's arguments add up to this mere 'breath' and 'a little scene, / To monarchize' (3.2.164–5).

The new king, however, was well aware that a little scene to monar-chise could, in appropriate circumstances, carry great political weight. In his coronation ritual Bolingbroke ordered the use of a specially sanc-tified chrism for the anointing from a miraculous phial said to have been given by the Virgin Mary to Thomas Becket and recently discovered in the Tower of London after two centuries of hiding in Poitiers.[37] An opportune occasion of the prudential and providential with which to begin the reign.

5
1 & 2 Henry IV

Falstaff's celebrated 'catechism' begins with an avowal to delay a debt – death owed to God – and the 'honour' speech follows:[1]

> ...honor pricks me on. Yea, but how if honor pricks me off when I come on? how then? Can honor set to a leg? No. Or an arm? No. Or take away the grief of a wound? No. Honor hath no skill in surgery then? No. What is honor? A word. What is in that word honor? What is that honor? Air. A trim reckoning! Who hath it? He that died a' Wednesday. Doth he feel it? No. Doth he hear it? No. 'Tis insensible, then? Yea, to the dead. But will ['t] not live with the living? No. Why? Detraction will not suffer it. Therefore I'll none of it, honor is a mere scutcheon. And so ends my catechism.
>
> (*1 Henry IV*, 5.1.129–41)

S.L. Bethell's briefly incisive remarks point up the identifiable fallacy of such an argument:

> This is one of the oldest sophistries, to confuse the notion signified with the signifying word. 'What is in that word honor? What is that honor? Air'. *Flatus Vocis*, the extreme Nominalists said ... It is the evacuation of all spiritual significance from life.[2]

Though we might disagree with Bethell's conclusion, nevertheless this observation directs us towards the significance of Falstaff's logic and rhetoric. The sceptical basis of nominalism distrusted syllogistic logic as a means to truth. Universals were considered mental constructs only, for reality lay in things not words. Falstaff uses a sophistry for a provocative rhetorical end. Cause (honour) and effect (injuries and death) are conflated, so juxtaposing the abstract and the concrete. By excluding intermediary explanatory propositions, Falstaff confronts us with the brutal facts of war, which force us to face the question raised by all warfare. Does the invocation of a cause (patriotism, honour, etc.) ever justify the reality of human suffering, or does the shock of the effect call into question the validity of the cause, possibly forcing us to see it as an ideological simplication for something more complex and less ennobling: in this case power struggles arising from dynastic rivalries.

Of course, the speech can be taken in a more naturalistic way, in terms of Falstaff's character, as a witty rationalisation of his own self-preservation ('Give me life', *1 Henry IV*, 5.3.59). A longstanding formulaic view is that Hotspur and Falstaff represent the excess and deficiency of honour while Hal realises the Aristotelian golden mean. There is a point here, but if Falstaff's argument is taken beyond that of character, it obviously makes a critical point about the context of honour, name and fame – the anonymous carnage of those who are 'food for powder' (*1 Henry IV*, 4.2.65–6). Even this has proved controversial. Is it a gross instance of Falstaff's exploitation and corruption, or is it Shakespeare's use of Falstaff to represent a common military abuse of the time?[3]

Falstaff's argument forces home a disjunction between words and things, the irreconcilability of certain facts, like dead bodies, with ideas as cause, motive or ideal. Coming across one of the dead shortly afterwards Falstaff exclaims, 'Sir Walter Blunt. There's honor for you' (*1 Henry 1V*, 5.3.32–3), presumably in ironic contrast to his own troops: 'I have led my ragamuffins where they are pepper'd' (*1 Henry IV*, 5.3.35–6). The illogicality forces us to reappraise words and actions and to recognise that Falstaff's argument brings to the fore a process that is taking place throughout the *Henry IV*s. Yet, as we shall see, Shakespeare is not simply dramatising a nominalist scepticism, but actually balancing his own dramatic argument with a thoroughgoing dualism, until, that is, the rejection by the successor to the throne.

On his deathbed King Henry claims that rebellion, usurpation and deposition were 'an honor snatch'd with boist'rous hand' (*2 Henry IV*, 5.5.191) as if political reality were nothing but a playful game. In similarly euphemistic vein, we have heard:

> God knows, my son,
> By what by-paths and indirect crook'd ways
> I met this crown ...

> (*2 Henry IV*, 4.5.183–5)

That disingenuous 'met' invites the Falstaffian rejoinder of an earlier context, when Henry challenges Worcester's disclaimer at Shrewsbury:

> *Worc*   I have not sought the day of this dislike.
> *King*   You have not sought it? How comes it, then?

Falstaff replies, 'Rebellion lay in his way, and he found it' (*1 Henry IV*, 5.1.26–8). It would appear that kingship lay in Henry Bolingbroke's way and he found it. If, in the shadow of death, Henry's words gloss over the argument of his actions, nevertheless he retains a sense of the reality of the political problem of Prince Henry's succession. Succession itself would constitute a kind of legitimacy, but the political use of a foreign war would give it greater strength. Henry himself had intended a crusade, now forestalled by death, thereby proposing the same political manoeuvre which was pre-empted at the outset of *1 Henry IV*.

Shakespeare does several things with the chroniclers' record that Henry intended a crusade at the end, not at the beginning of his reign. Holinshed and Samuel Daniel record that Henry planned a crusade to unite the opposed Christian princes of France and England against the common pagan enemy. Here in *2 Henry IV* Shakespeare narrows the political ploy to England and the circumstances of Henry's accession – his dependence on accessories: 'Lest rest and lying still might make them look / Too near unto [his] state', Henry 'had a purpose now / To lead out many to the Holy Land' (4.5.209–12).

Further, the symbol of the Holy Land is introduced at the end of *Richard II*, immediately after the report of Richard's death, and at the beginning of *1 Henry IV*. Reacting to the death of Richard, the new King Henry's words close *Richard II*. In apparent remorse, he proposes to 'make a voyage to the Holy Land, / To wash this blood off from my guilty hand' (5.6.49–50). This sounds more like a pilgrimage than a crusade, and Henry speaks both personally and collectively, inviting all those present, and thus parties to his accession, to unite behind him and the coffin, in what becomes a symbolic admission, ritualistically subsuming the political embarrassment of Exton's entry. But the political significance of this is suffused by the tragic coda and emotional quietism.

Again, at the opening of *1 Henry IV* Shakespeare chose to use the argument for a crusade in a specifically political and dramatic way. Henry's declared intention of a crusade 'As far as to the sepulchre of Christ' is to prevent continuance or renewal of civil war:

> Those opposed eyes . . .
> Shall now, in mutual well-beseeming ranks,
> March all one way and be no more opposed
> Against acquaintance, kindred, and allies.

> (1.1.9, 14–16)

And of course against himself. Thus in terms of the plays as a whole Shakespeare provides an ironic frame of Christian reference for the ideas of debt and redemption, as well as obligation, in the crusade, but Henry's motives are as far removed from authentic piety as the Jerusalem chamber in which he dies is from Jerusalem itself.

Henry's act in leading a crusade would be a public argument of self-legitimation by allowing unquestioned religious sanction to subsume questionable political credentials. To be seen as a Christian monarch fulfilling the noblest end of chivalry by rescuing the holy places from the heathen would draw the consensus of Christendom, thereby immeasurably strengthening his claims at home. 'What is in that word crusade?' as Falstaff might well ask.[4] However, Henry's political strategy is aborted by the very thing it sought to overcome, insurrection in Wales and the North. Yet behind this is yet another strategy, as the king well knows.

By dwelling on the crusade a political dimension, otherwise absent in the sources, is particularly stressed. In building upon the allusions to the Holy Land at the end of *Richard II* Shakespeare dramatises a para-dox. Even if an English audience might baulk at the Bishop of Carlisle's absolutist insistence on Richard's divine right (*Richard II*, 4.1.114–49), nevertheless the office of late medieval kingship was imbued with a sense of the sacred by way of the symbolic chrism in the consecration of the coronation ritual of an anointed king.[5] That is to say, having broken Christian sanction in one form, Henry seemingly pursues it in another. 'Seemingly', because prior to the announcements concerning the crusade at the beginning of *1 Henry IV*, Henry has already begun an argument of action which will contravene the declared intention of his words. Why else did Henry send such a foppish courtier north (not found in the sources) to demand of the irascible Hotspur the prisoners of war unless he wished to provoke Henry Percy and thus the whole of that powerful family? Just as Henry is celebrating Hotspur as 'the theme of honor's tongue' (1.1.81) he is weighing the probability of a Percy rebellion provoked by himself.

The argument concerning Hotspur's prisoners is a complex one, and in response to the emphasis it receives in Hall and Holinshed Shakespeare adjusted the narrative to explore its dramatic possibilities as part of Henry's political strategy. Holinshed gives this account:

> [Northumberland, Worcester and Hotspur were] especiallie . . . gréeved, bicause the king demanded of the earle and his sonne such Scotish prisoners as were taken at Homeldon and Nesbit: for of all the captiues which were taken in the conflicts foughten in those two places, there was deliuered to the kings possession onlie Moredake earle of Fife, the duke of Albanies sonne, though the king did divers and sundrie times require deliuerance of the residue, and that with great threatenings: wherewith the Persies being sore offended, for that they claimed them as their owne proper prisoners, and their peculiar preies . . . (III, 22)

But for the addition of the colourful 'and that with great threatnings', this agrees substantially with Hall, who continues the above: 'and to deliuer theym vtterly denaied, in so muche that the Kyng openly saied that if they wolde not deliuer them, he wolde take them without deliuerance'.[6] Shakespeare's insistence on denial (*1 Henry IV*, 1.3.25, 29, 77) seems to indicate his memory of Hall here, though he has the Percies deny the denial. In both Hall and Holinshed Worcester then approaches Henry with the question of paying the ransom for Edmund Mortimer who, by marrying his captor Glendower's daughter, had committed a treasonous act. Shakespeare links the denial of prisoners with this, making Hotspur's condition that he will release the prisoners if the king pays Mortimer's ransom. Henry knows that Mortimer has a claim to the crown, so his argument with the Percies over the prisoners is cleverly used to insist on one right (to prisoners) to reinforce another (not 'to redeem a traitor home, *1 Henry IV*, 1.3.86), thereby putting Hotspur in the position of insisting on one wrong to bring about another.

The Percies claim to 'their owne proper prisoners, and their peculiar preies' is expressly against the laws of war, even apart from the specific instructions Henry is known to have made following the battle of Holmdon: orders were sent from the Council of Westminster (dated 22 September, 1402) forbidding the ransom or freeing of any prisoners for any reason and giving reassurance that the captors would eventually receive what was their due.[7] Holinshed at one point simply states that

Northumberland and Hotspur were 'to keepe them [the prisoners] to the kings vse' (III, p. 21). An authority of the Middle Ages, Honoré Bonet, closely following John of Legnano's *De Bello, de Represuliis et de Duello*, confirms that a prisoner belongs not to his captor but to his captor's lord.[8] Northumberland and Hotspur were, respectively, the Wardens of the West and East March and thus legally indentured to fight on behalf of their sovereign lord, the king. There is considerable documentary evidence on the status of prisoners, not least the 'Ordinances of War' issued in 1385 for the English forces advancing on Scotland.[9]

King Henry's problem is that *de facto* possession of the crown without peace must find some acceptable sanction to ensure rule and succession. This can be conferred by the use of religion or law in proto-constitutional politics, unless of course he chooses to rule without any sanction by force and personal dictat – as a tyrant. The argument for the crusade was a gesture only for ideological display, since to have left the kingdom for any length of time in the circumstances would have been almost certain to have encouraged a coup, as we soon learn when the fully articulated plot involving Douglas and the Scots, the Archbishop of York, Glendower and Mortimer, is revealed (*1 Henry IV*, 1.3.260–76).

Richard II transgressed feudal law by denying Henry Herford the right to sue for his succession, and Henry transgressed divine law, some would protest, to succeed in Richard's place. Shakespeare leaves out Holinshed's details of Henry being urged to return to England to expel Richard by nobles alarmed by his depredations. Instead, Shakespeare focuses on argument and action by repeatedly alluding to Henry's oath on landing at Ravenspurgh as the crucial motive for the action of the Percies: or at least an ostensible motive. Shakespeare exposes the *realpolitik*, the truth of actions in the reality of dynastic power struggle beneath the professed reality of argument – of words as cause, motive and rationalisation. Both sides, the king and the Percies, persist with a language of pretence and pretext which is exposed by their actions, as it is exposed by Falstaff's 'What is in that word honor?'

Henry's reason for returning to England from his banishment, he argues before the Duke of York, was to claim the right to his inheritance, and this was the substance of his oath at Ravenspurgh we are told several times in *1 Henry IV*, yet we are also told that he left France before news of his father's death reached him as we have seen above (p. 58).

With Richard's actions and Henry's reactions, given the evident impossibility of reconciliation, compromise or accommodation, everyone knew what the real political situation was: Henry, the Percies, and eventually even Richard, long before the necessary legalism of the deposition. As Richard acknowledged at Flint Castle: 'Your own is yours, and I am yours, and all' (*Richard II*, 3.3.197). We do not hear Henry's oath at Ravenspurgh, but what we do hear is his guarantee to the rebels of reward upon success. When introduced to Hotspur Henry declares, 'And as my fortune ripens with thy love, / It shall be still thy true love's recompense' (*Richard II*, 2.3.48–9). And to Ross and Willoughby:

> All my treasury
> Is yet but unfelt thanks, which, more enrich'd,
> Shall be your love and labor's recompense ...
> Evermore thank's the exchequer of the poor,
> Which, till my infant fortune comes to years,
> Stands for my bounty.
>
> (*Richard II*, 2.3.60–3, 65–7)

With success, the crown on his head, it is time to pay up. Henry knows it, the Percies know it and Richard anticipated it:

> Northumberland ...
>   Thou shalt think,
> Though he divide the realm and give thee half,
> It is too little, helping him to all;
> He shall think that thou, which knowest the way
> To plant unrightful kings, wilt know again,
> Being ne'er so little urg'd, another way
> To pluck him headlong from the usurped throne.
>
> (*Richard II*, 5.1.55, 59–65)

Characteristically, King Henry later recalls Richard's speech but stops short – 'so went on' (*2 Henry IV*, 3.1.77) – of the hard political reality described.

To follow through his early promises Henry would increase only the power of those dynastic rivals whose power largely put him on the throne. They have a candidate for the throne, Mortimer, whose claim is stronger than Henry's; they are disaffected towards him (we are told of Worcester's 'malevolence' [*1 Henry IV*, 1.1.97]); and they have a popular hero as a figurehead in Hotspur. As we have seen, Henry has begun his political strategy – to provoke Hotspur, not to ransom Mortimer, to confront and defeat the Percies, thereby ensuring the House of Lancaster and keeping his coffers and lands intact. The justification for Henry's decision is seen immediately with the Council assembled at Windsor (*1 Henry IV*, 1.3). Henry's use of a Council pre-empts the charge of tyranny and provides a dramatic forum that enlists support – we the audience are privy to this Council and recognise the manifest danger of Worcester. Henry knows that he must be seen to be rightly defending the country against anarchy and insurrection, not to be seen as just killing off those who put him where he is. In fact, this is the only 'sanction' left open to him: the political manoeuvre to engineer rebellion, then put it down, and thus 'save' the country from the perils of anarchy by inaugurating peace and prosperity. Given Shakespeare's selection and presentation of materials from the chronicles, the argument of his plot, in light of the above we see that Henry demonstrates an unrivalled daring and Machiavellian astuteness that is proved to be exactly right, not least in the first words of Worcester:

> Our house, my sovereign liege, little deserves
> The scourge of greatness to be us'd on it,
> And that same greatness too which our own hands
> Hath help to make so portly.
>
> (*1 Henry IV*, 1.3.10–13)

Henry did not really need the provocative fop he sent north; clearly Hotspur is not the only outspoken member of the family. Worcester is dismissed from the Council but returns at the end of the scene to reveal a plot well underway which we have noted above. Henry's strategy was completely justified. The much discussed 'travesty by parallel' between the main plot and Eastcheap–Gadshill subplot is made even stronger. The 'I know you all' beginning Hal's notorious speech announcing his calculated use of his cronies for political ends (*1 Henry IV*, 1.2.195–217), is precisely the reciprocal case with his father – Henry 'knows' the rebels well enough, indeed.

Talk of the 'crusade', like the arguments of 'honour', is the public language of collective chivalric idealism. At the outset, we are not given a full-scale soliloquy of Henry's private thoughts but we are left to deduce such from the argument of his action. Though Hotspur has an eye on fame, honour and posterity and wishes to erase the shame of Richard's death in future chronicles, for all his romanticism he recognises the final reality of Henry's political manoeuvring. In the privacy of conspiracy he spells it out in a language altogether different from that public vocabulary of feudal 'fealty', etc. Henry will 'answer all the debt he owes to you, / Even with the bloody payment of your deaths' (*1 Henry IV*, 1.3.185–6), Hotspur says. A view which Worcester argues shortly after:

> The King will always think him in our debt,
> And think we think ourselves unsatisfied,
> Till he hath found a time to pay us home.

> (1.3.286–8)

The language of 'owe', 'pay' and 'debt' will prove to be of the greatest significance along with 'that word honor' in understanding Falstaff's otherwise rather mystifying reaction to his rejection by the new king, Henry V, 'Master Shallow, I owe you a thousand pound' (*2 Henry VI*, 5.5.73). But here note how the arguments of the Percies justifying their rebellion is quite different from the materialism of the above *realpolitik*. Once again Shakespeare exploits a resource of drama in the disparity between what men say and what men do.

At Shrewsbury both Hotspur and Worcester appeal to Henry's perjury, the breaking of his oath at Doncaster after landing at Ravenspurgh. Before the battle Hotspur reminds Sir Walter Blunt, the king's emissary, of the role of the Percies in attracting others to Henry's cause after accepting his oath that he was returning to his own and nothing more. Later at Shrewsbury, when Worcester parleys in the king's camp, the same arguments are used:

> It was myself, my brother, and his son
> That brought you home . . .
> And you did swear that oath at Doncaster
> You . . .
> Forgot your oath to us at Doncaster.

> (*1 Henry IV*, 5.1.39ff)

But this argument is all a formalised pretext. If we look to the actions, not the words, of the Percies in this matter, then an entirely different argument emerges.

Northumberland and Hotspur were parties to Richard's capitulation at Flint Castle. Northumberland was present at Bristol when Henry sentenced Bushy and Greene, and it was he who supervised their execution. At Westminster, Northumberland, without prompting, summarily arrested the Bishop of Carlisle after his absolutist objection to Henry as he ascended the throne, while Hotspur stood by. Northumberland carried out a prominent executive position in Richard's self-deposition in his repeated insistence on the king reading out the articles. Northumberland conducted Richard to Pomfret Castle. Northumberland and Hotspur exited behind the coffin bearing Richard's body. Evidently, at every stage the Percies actively assisted Henry in his assumption of regal authority and his deposition of Richard. Hotspur and Worcester are at Shrewsbury not because of Henry's oath-breaking, but to make their bid for power in a dynastic struggle between feudal war lords.

In his portrayal of the politics of rebellion Shakespeare clearly points up a potential anarchy that proceeds not just from something like the proposed division of the kingdom or the disunity at Shrewsbury but in a potentially anarchic state of language itself. We see not only a division of territory but, like property, meaning is appropriated, because it is less readily divisible. With Hotspur's response to Mortimer's outline of the Archdeacon's division of the kingdom, Shakespeare makes a simple but telling point. In Holinshed there is no difference of opinion concerning the 'indentures tripartite' (*1 Henry IV*, 3.1.79). Here in the play Hotspur's disagreement, Glendower's objection and then capitulation, followed by Hotspur's retraction, signals an arbitrariness which promises civil war between themselves even should they defeat Henry.

Military disunity at Shrewsbury is largely Shakespeare's invention. In Holinshed Northumberland's 'sickness' occurred early in the rebellion, and in the case of the delay of Glendower's force Shakespeare chose to follow Samuel Daniel rather than Holinshed who records that they actually joined Hotspur. Thus before the eventual outcome of the battle Shakespeare not only creates circumstances as a foil for Hotspur's chivalric egoism, but signals the likelihood of political repercussions had the battle gone differently. As a kind of logical regression the outcome of division and disunity is followed by a form of anarchy.

Northumberland's invocation upon learning of the death of Hotspur, is often quoted:

> Let heaven kiss earth! now let not Nature's hand
> Keep the wild flood confin'd! let order die!
> And let this world no longer be a stage
> To feed contention in a ling'ring act;
> But let one spirit of the first-born Cain
> Reign in all bosoms, that each heart being set
> On bloody courses, the rude scene may end,
> And darkness be the burier of the dead!

(2 Henry IV, 1.1.153–60)

The macrocosmic chaos of nature itself succeeding upon large-scale microcosmic fratricide would seem to stamp Shakespeare's portrayal of the politics of rebellion here with Tudor orthodoxy. If these lines are taken wholly in a choric sense, then this is, indeed, the case. But the arguments of Lord Bardolph and Morton which immediately follow suggest that Northumberland's hyperbole represents a rhetorical compensation for guilt, a deflected self-recrimination. The image of anarchy remains powerful, but it is anarchy not as a reversion of hypostatised nature, but anarchy as proceeding from a specific chain of cause and effect. Morton argues that all that took place was foreseeable, given the circumstances of rebellion, and the character of Hotspur, concluding:

> What hath then befall'n?
> Or what hath this bold enterprise brought forth,
> More than that being which was like to be?
>
> (*2 Henry IV*, 1.1.177–90)

Morton's opening remonstration was, 'Sweet Earl, divorce not wisdom from your honor' (l.162). This is not said cynically though in its dramatic placement Shakespeare confronts the audience with an ironic collision of values. How could any real 'honor' be consistent with Northumberland's self-indicting language, let alone his obvious failure as head of the family to support Hotspur, Worcester and the others at Shrewsbury?

Morton's words, 'divorce not wisdom from your honor', echo Falstaff's catechistic confrontation with feudal society, no less. As an ideology feudal 'honor' provides a ramified, all-encompassing sanction for action, conduct and relationship. In the Christian, militarist, later Middle Ages of feudal England, as depicted in the chronicles, the chivalric code of honour supposedly provided the bonds of fealty. At least this was the ideal conception of something like Ramon Lull's *The Book of the Ordre of Chyvalry of Knyghthode* published by Caxton in 1484. Feudalism regulated private and public allegiances whereby an individual's relationship was determined by loyalty sustained by legitimacy. Relationship to kith, kin and king observed the feudal hierarchy, at the apex of which was the feudal monarch.[10] Ties or bonds were comparatively legal and institutional, rather than affective. 'England' was a composition of feudal tenures rather than a nation-state. Arguably John of Gaunt's 'This England' speech in *Richard II* is more monarchist than nationalist. But once the legitimate king was removed, his replacement was just another feudal lord put there by his peers.

Honour underpinned the militarist ethic of feudal society. In an hierarchic structure honour was what you were born into, according to your degree, from the knightly class upwards. Honour was title, status and identity, since selfhood and honour are inextricable. Honour was also glory and fame acquired in battle, particularly against the pagan. For honour to be meaningful it depended on a larger structure of meaning which in turn was dependent on the structure of society. Words like 'liege' and 'fealty' reflect the structure of feudalism itself. Fealty, the idealised conception of feudal loyalty, was the cement which held the fabric together. Once removed, as with the deposition and killing of the king, meaning collapses.[11] Thereafter, the struggle for the crown is the struggle to sustain a meaning in language no longer supported by reality. We see not reciprocal service and loyalty in exchange for feudal tenure, but power for power, favour for favour. This contradiction of feudalism turned against itself is brought out very forcefully in Lord Mortimer's urging Glendower to gather 'Your tenants, friends and neighboring gentlemen' (1 Henry IV, 3.1.89) *against* the feudal lord, not for him. Chivalric honour perpetuated in literature an ideal which men were not consistently capable of, and at their worst, acted entirely contrary to. The meaning of honour in the plays is tested by placing it within a scale of language ('redeem', 'due', 'reckoning', 'owe', 'payment') containing through metaphor polarised possibilities running from the sacred to the profane. That is to say, the language of material and reductive modes of transaction which has been touched on above is continually contrasted with arguments of honour.

Hotspur tells Worcester and Northumberland, 'time serves wherein you may redeem / Your banish'd honors' (1 Henry IV, 1.3.180–1). Romantic egoism, not to say homicidal mania, carries Hotspur away, and he would

> ... pluck bright honor from the pale-fac'd moon ...
> So that he that doth redeem her thence might wear
> Without corrival all her dignities;

> (1 Henry IV, 1.3.202, 206–7)

Hotspur's argument for exclusiveness reverses chivalric priorities and honour is at the service of an individual, not an individual serving honour. Prince Hal is also concerned with a form of redemption. In the soliloquy which has caused so much comment Hal sees his low-life associations and subsequent 'reformation' as a strategy, payment of a 'debt' he 'never promised', thereby 'redeeming time' seemingly wasted (*I Henry IV*,

1.2.209–17). It has been shown that Hal misrepresents the Pauline injunction of Ephesians (v.16) – past time cannot be redeemed, but one's life may be amended in the present.[12] When the king confronts him with the heroic image of Hotspur, Hal's defensive argument seems closer to accountancy than chivalry:

> I will redeem all this on Percy's head . . .
> For every honor sitting on his helm . . .
> Percy is but my factor, good my lord,
> To engross up glorious deeds on my behalf,
> And I will call him to so strict account
> That he shall render every glory up,
> Yea, even the slightest worship of his time,
> Or I will tear the reckoning from his heart

(1 Henry IV, 3.2.132–52)

While Hotspur and the rebels are corporate raiders on the body politic, the commercial metaphors here ambivalently suggest that Hal is a prospective asset-stripper. And even the greatest symbolic asset of all, the crown itself, is weighed and measured in the scales of transaction.

> Thy due from me
> Is tears and heavy sorrows of the blood,
> Which nature, love, and filial tenderness
> Shall, O dear father, pay thee plenteously.
> My due from thee is this imperial crown

(2 Henry IV, 37–41)

In both cases, with Hotspur's reputation and with the crown, the language is reductive, to a certain degree. However formalised and solemn the language leading up to the second quotation, and however ritualised the personal emotion of Hal, nevertheless irony is inescapable. The warmth of tears is chilled by the coldness of metal. The plentifulness of weeping comes not from depth of emotion but as the due price for gold. Two separate things, grief and succession, private feeling and public office, are levelled by the priorities of the latter in the public world of 'payment'.

For Henry gaining the crown is 'But as an honor snatch'd with boist'rous hand' (*2 Henry IV*, 4.5.191). This is indeed just what Hal has literally done when he took the crown from his father's bedside, believing the king was dead: 'this imperial crown . . . This lineal honor' (*2 Henry IV*, 4.5.41, 46) he calls it. Here the distinction between the signifier and the thing signified is collapsed – the meaning of the crown is immanent within the material object, thus honour becomes possession of the thing. The conceptual is materialised and legitimacy resides in possession. Possession is might and right. Similarly, with the honour of the person, in titles where it is taken to be absolute not contingent.[13] Thus, as we have seen above, Morton's plea to Northumberland 'Divorce not wisdom from your honor' (*2 Henry IV*, 1.1.162). Simply to be born into a certain feudal class is to inherit 'honour': meaning and value are assumed rather than fulfilled. Furthermore, in Shakespeare's dramatisation this honour becomes quantifiable, not merely hierarchic. Size of family and armed retainers determine the scale of honour. The materialism and verbal totemism becomes society's enabling and disabling sanction as both Falstaff and Prince John of Lancaster demonstrate.

As editors point out, in the chronicles it is Westmoreland who treaties with the rebels at Gaultree. Shakespeare made the youthful Prince John the chief negotiator, thus allying his coldly calculated betrayal of honour with the House of Lancaster he represents. In agreeing to redress the grievances of the rebels Prince John swears 'by the honor of my blood' (*2 Henry IV*, 4.2.55). By means of a sophistry – John separates the grievances from those who made them – the rebels are arrested and executed, and the disbanded army is pursued. On his arrest Mowbray protests, 'Is this proceeding just and honourable?', and the Archbishop of York seconds him with 'Will you thus break your faith?' Prince John's immediate answer is terse indeed: 'I pawn'd thee none' (*2 Henry IV*, 4.2.110–13). For John, words are objects whose value is not intrinsic but expedient. 'Faith' and 'honor' are not ideals or concepts but counters in the game of political pawnbroking which the rebels unwittingly lose. John pledged the truce with a drink as a ritualised visual symbol, for the onlooking soldiers, of 'our restored love and amity' (*2 Henry IV*, 4.2.65). No sophistry can get round that. And when he declares ' . . . by mine honor / I will perform with a most Christian care' 'redress of these grievances' (*2 Henry IV*, 4.2.114–15) the religious enlistment and rationalisation are chilling. Shakespeare makes an indirect dramatic comment on this in the following scene when Sir John Coleville surrenders passively to Falstaff, the reputed victor over Hotspur. Prince John's honour is as empty as Falstaff's valour.

As art intervening in history, comedy subverting chronicle, Falstaff ultimately both suggests and burlesques an ideal order of value which appraises the dramatised historical actuality of the feudal world.

Though reality falls short of the ideal and calls it into question, we are left to measure the relative claims of both in terms of the human, fallible and attainable. Shakespeare does not make homiletic recommendations. He does not moralise or suggest a simple black and white, either/or answer to the complexity of human experience. He leaves the audience with a question salvaged from barbarism and carnage, laughter and gaiety, power and weakness – what is it that we owe to one another?

At the moment of rejection Falstaff acknowledges a debt, 'Master Shallow, I owe you a thousand pound' (*2 Henry IV*, 5.5.73). This has proved resonantly baffling for editors, though it is crucial for an understanding of the two plays. At a simple dramatic level it partly checks our hostile feelings towards Hal with an element of comedy. A fat chance Shallow has of seeing any cash from Falstaff, and yet that posture of probity in such unpropitious circumstances! There are so many aspects to Falstaff: he has been seen, variously, as a Renaissance sceptic (Chauduri); humanist 'fool' (Kaiser); holy fool (Battenhouse); Elizabethan soldier (Draper); carnival (Rhodes); morality vice and devil (Dover Wilson); Lord of Misrule (Barber); clown (Wiles); anthropological scapegoat (Stewart); narcissistic libido (Alexander); declassed feudal retainer (Jackson); bourgeois ego (Holderness).[14]

The list could be extended considerably, but underlying all of these is Falstaff as a comic performance. That is to say, most of the above categories are critical and intellectual abstractions mostly derived from the text, rather than performance. As Calderwood reminds us, Falstaff is a creation of and for the stage.[15] He has a *relationship* to the Elizabethan world, to dramatic forebears, and to history, but his reality, his life, is the reality of comic stage performance. The role of Falstaff is multidimensional. Comedy establishes a mutual compact between actor and audience. Falstaff acts as much on behalf of the audience as on that of the plot. Downstage, playing to the audience, Falstaff stands midway between the 1590s and the fifteenth century. The whole point about the encounter in the Boar's Head after the Gadshill fiasco is that everyone is made party to the comic set-up – Hal, Poins, Falstaff and the audience. The Gadshill incident certainly has serious parodic undertones but from 'A plague of all cowards, I say' (*1 Henry IV*, 2.4.4.114ff) onwards, the scene builds upon the comic momentum of Falstaff's theatrical posture of self-righteousness undermined by incremental exaggeration. The progression is shaped by the design of protest, exposure and comic reversal – 'By the Lord, I knew ye as well as he that made ye' (*1 Henry IV*, 2.4.267–8) – not naturalism. Falstaff's 'cowardice' at Gadshill is a necessary circumstantial precondition to prime audience expectation, engineered by Hal, the 'interior' playwright as Calderwood calls him. Comic cowardice and cowardice normally considered are simply not the same thing, and should not be judged as such.

Superimposed on history Falstaff becomes the metadramatic figure of art itself free from the empirical constraints of chronicle, challenging the ideal ethos of chivalric honour. Falstaff's comedy is not just a matter of his verbal wit. Comedy creates a duality which checks simple moral judgment. As such the presentation of Falstaff is not unique in the plays. Shakespeare provides a dualistic perspective on almost every main character.

Over the dead Hotspur, Hal bids 'Adieu, and take they praise with thee to heaven! / Thy ignominy sleep with thee in the grave' (*I Henry IV*, 5.4.99–100). 'Praise' yet censure, 'ignominy' – the audience has relished Hotspur's own particular comic exuberance throughout, as well as recognising his dangerous egotism. Hotspur's wife provides a moving epitaph in *2 Henry IV* (2.3.18–32), but we have always been made aware of the political danger of such blind rashness. Hotspur is, in turn, the embodiment of knighthood and its abuser. Similarly, Douglas is jeered at by Hal (*1 Henry IV*, 2.4.342–6), yet pardoned after Shrewsbury for his chivalric valour. Hal is celebrated by Vernon's glowing evocation in a panegyric unrivalled in Shakespeare ('I saw young Harry with his beaver on' (*1 Henry IV*, 4.1.104ff)), yet he is commonly censured for his calculation and lack of warmth. However, the claims of birth and kingship have to be met, and however we react to the manner of Falstaff's rejection, Hal as Henry V could hardly do otherwise in the circumstances. Similarly with King Henry himself, either he allowed Richard to seize his inheritance or he returned to England to claim it, which of necessity entailed confrontation with the king and all that followed. Either way Henry's feudal peers could not let Richard get away with what was not a singular instance, but the culmination of irreversible political abuse. What he did once he could do again. Whatever we feel about the personal shortcomings of Henry we recognise that he has to act politically as he does, or go under. From one point of view he can be seen as a usurper, from another he is preserving the country from anarchy. Though Jorgensen has provided evidence that not only was the Gaultree treachery hardly unique as a political strategy, but that divine sanction was claimed for such acts, nevertheless no commentators exonerate Prince John.[16] Yet within the play he is congratulated by Hal and Henry for his valour at Shrewsbury (*I Henry IV*, 5.4.16–23): 'praise' and 'ignominy' again.

This duality occasionally structures whole scenes, if not both plays, when we consider the relationship of comedy, chronicle, and 'travesty-by-parallel'. Consider act 3, scene 1 of *1 Henry IV*. The rebels are assembled at Bangor to plan the carving-up of the country after the presumed success of their rebellion. A politically self-indicting scene of great seriousness, yet from the outset a comic circumstance – Hotspur has mislaid the map – is developed by Hotspur's hilarious mockery of the pompous Glendower. Then suddenly the mood is reversed as Lord Mortimer outlines the division of the kingdom and Hotspur queries his portion (ll.69–114). To effect a transition Shakespeare uses Hotspur's humour to modify the tone (ll.115–62), again at Glendower's expense. Lord Mortimer redresses the balance by presenting a brief encomium on Glendower (ll.163–70), and Worcester follows this with a crushing epitome of Hotspur's faults (ll.175–87) – both examples of the dualistic points of view taken on all the main characters by themselves, or others, throughout the plays, but of course pre-eminently in the play-acting scene (*1 Henry IV*, 2.4) with Falstaff-as-king on Falstaff, and Hal-as-king on Falstaff. The rest of act 3 scene 1, with the entry of the ladies, is like a scene from an early comedy with the contrasted pairs: the lovers, Lord Mortimer and Glendower's daughter, romantic, poetic and moving; the husband and wife, Hotspur and Lady Percy, ironic, gamesome and down-to-earth.

This dualism strongly echoes the tradition of the sophists' *dissoi logoi* (double accounts) as reflected in the *in utramque partem* mode (arguments for and against), particularly, as Joel B. Altman has shown, the inheritance of the *laus* and *vituperatio* (praise and denunciation) topics from Aphthonius's *Progymnasmata* by which the student 'learned how the same person may be described from opposing points of view'.[17] Such dualism makes us suspend judgment, the sceptical position advocated by Erasmus, 'I...want to analyze and not to judge, to inquire and not to dogmatize'.[18] Structural dualism explains Falstaff's stabbing of Hotspur.

In parodic functional terms the action offers the counterpart to Hal's chivalric gesture over the dead Hotspur, 'But let my favors hide thy mangled face', (*1 Henry IV*, 5.4.96), and signals Falstaff's succumbing to honour and reputation. As the comic performance in part surrenders to the imperative of history so it is corrupted by it – to some extent. The character Falstaff is now drawn into the consequences of history by the burden of his acquired reputation and he enters the contingent world of time. Shakespeare stresses time as successive events, the matter of the chronicles, but Falstaff has lived a daily life of cocooned indulgence. Now the body is subject to time as Falstaff is caught up in the linear progression of history. In contrast a seasonal recurrent time of a continuing world outside the rise and fall of great ones is suggested by the Gloucestershire scenes – the sowing of the hade land, the bringing of beasts to market. The king dies, but nevertheless 'praise God for the merry year' (*2 Henry IV*, 5.3.18). Hal may wish to redeem time, but the greater, all-encompassing truth, is that we owe God a death. The debt Falstaff recognises, 'do not bid me remember mine end' (*2 Henry IV*, 2.4.235), is towards the living; the debt, obligation and relationship he feels for Hal, as well as for Poins and Bardolph.

After the Gadshill robbery Hal and Poins, waiting for the return of their cohorts amuse themselves with Frances the drawer in the Boar's Head tavern. As indirect self-reproach Hal, the 'truant' from chivalry, attempts to make Francis a truant from his obligation and duty as apprentice, with the temptation of a thousand pounds, the seductive figure Mistress Quickly claims Falstaff says is owed to him by Hal, and the figure Falstaff acknowledges at the rejection, 'Master Shallow, I owe you a thousand pound' (*2 Henry IV*, 5.5.73). Roundly rebuked and rejected by Henry V, no longer Hal, Falstaff cannot say what he wants to say and so deflects it into the oblique utterance concerning the debt to Justice Shallow. His acknowledgement works on many levels, including a masterful insight into the psychology of shock. Until he succumbs to reputation, Falstaff has never recognised the validity of the claims of the public world. His order of value has always depended on the private and personal. The confrontation of the two men is a confrontation of these two worlds: Falstaff and company, sweaty and unkempt, and the king in coronation robes nobly attended from Westminster Abbey.

What Falstaff wants to say has been said before in Eastcheap in the scene we have touched on already:

Host   [Falstaff] said this other day you ought him a thousand pound.
Prince Sirrah, do I owe you a thousand pound?
Fal   A thousand pound, Hal? a million, thy love is worth a million; thou owest me thy love.

(*1 Henry IV*, 3.3.133–7)

At the rejection Falstaff, recognising the king's righteous posture, wants to say 'Hal, you owe me your love', but he knows he cannot. In Eastcheap Falstaff had been using his pious puritan posture in echoing the Bible to evade answering the question by amusing Hal, yet at the same time giving voice to his real feelings, the satirical pre-empting any direct affective appeal.

The passage echoed is from St Paul's epistle to the Romans 13, immediately following one of the most well-known sources of political comment for the Middle Ages and the Renaissance in the whole of the Bible: 'Let every soule be subject unto the higher powers: for there is no power but of God: and the powers that be, are ordeined of God' (Geneva Bible). Thus begins the chapter seized on by royalists, monarchists and absolutists with its following complementary doctrine of non-resistance to 'the minister of God' (v. 4).

Critics of tyrannical absolutism supporting the principle of resistance, such as John Ponet and Peter Martyr Vermigli, had to take St Paul's words into account.[19] J.W. Allen wrote of this passage, 'The thirteenth chapter of the Epistle to the Romans contains what are perhaps the most important words ever written for the history of political thought'.[20] As one would expect, it appears as a cornerstone in what may be regarded as the foundation of Tudor orthodoxy under Elizabeth, 'An Homily against Disobedience and wilful Rebellion' which quotes verses 1–7.[21] In terms of debt and obligation v. 7 reads:

> Give to all men therefore their duetie: tribute to whom yea owe tribute: custome to whom custome; feare, to whom feare: honour, to whom ye owe honour. (Geneva Bible)

Here is found that alignment of debt and honour which we have seen is central to an understanding of *1 & 2 Henry IV*. Hal stands before Falstaff as Henry V, the English Caesar, one of the higher powers, sternly rebuking his old associate in this identifiable fashion. Though shocked, Falstaff's mind registers the situation and seizes on St Paul's larger intuition of charity and his allusion picks up where the *Homily* leaves off. As the epistle proceeds, St Paul turns from the contemporary historical world of Caesar, with its local political obligations, to the larger universal Christian ordinance of charity to which all men, Caesar, citizens and slaves, are bound.

> Owe nothing to any man, but to love another: for he that loveth another, hath fulfilled the Lawe. (v. 8. Geneva Bible)

This is the verse Falstaff had mimicked earlier 'thou owest me thy love', which is now deflected into 'Master Shallow, I owe you a thousand pound'.

Shakespeare's irony has Falstaff both burlesque and yet act as vehicle for this 'love'. The burlesque derives from the obvious inconsistency in

Falstaff's overall behaviour when measured against St Paul. Falstaff's love is not the disinterested love of Christian charity, but it is closer to it than anything Hal says, which sounds inevitably Pharisaical. The very partiality of Falstaff's affections glows like Bardolph's nose in a world increasingly darkened by loveless relationships of power, possession and property, the exchange and mart of feudal honour. Fulfilment of either Christian charity or chivalric honour is fraught by egoism and hypocrisy, self-interest and necessity. But Falstaff's oblique avowal of love is the reverse of Prince John's blatant betrayal of honour, which is paralleled by the necessity of Hal's succession and the institutional betrayal of love.

'[S]weet wag...sweet wag...mad wag...the most comparative rascalliest sweet young prince' (*1 Henry IV*, 1.2.16, 23, 44, 80–1): this is difficult to construe as anything other than a manifestation of affection which betokens something deeper. Similarly, immediately before the rejection, it is hard to take Falstaff's excited anticipation at anything other than face value. It is true that Shakespeare shapes a crescendo for dramatic ends – it is the most long-awaited dramatic moment in the two plays – but we are not merely witnesses, the purely dramatic equally engages us as audience with Falstaff's emotions:

> *Fal*   God save thy Grace, King Hal! my royal Hal!...
> God save thee, my sweet boy!...
> My King, my Jove! I speak to thee, my heart!
> *King*   I know thee not, old man.
>
> (*2 Henry IV*, 5.5.41, 43, 46–7)

To call the build-up to this cynical is cynical in itself. It would have been cynical if Falstaff *had* 'bestow'd the thousand pound' on 'new liveries' (*2 Henry IV*, 5.5.11–12). The drama of the confrontation is shaped by the audience's emotional compact with both Falstaff and the new king: emotion, psychology and situation are heightened by precise dramatic antitheses – travel-stained clothing and coronation robes: impetuousness and formality; personal claims and impersonal duty; private 'love' and public conduct; disorder, order; comedy and innocence, seriousness and experience. Two laws collide, the inevitability of Falstaff's own nature and necessity of state. Relegating Falstaff's parasitic qualities, drama has always bestowed the carnivalesque endowment of comic generosity, and however we regard Hal's personal character, the leading imperatives of kingship must supervene, at least in the public actual world of both the chronicles and the 1590s. But in the dramatic world of *1 & 2 Henry IV*, Shakespeare suggests a humanist revision of the actual by enlisting the audience in a rejection of history for the sake of Falstaff. Emotional impetus is stronger than public sanction. Prince John's offstage valour never compensates for his onstage perfidy, so who could possibly agree with his closing remark endorsing the rejection, 'I like this fair proceeding of the King's' (*2 Henry IV*, 5.5.97)? Shakespeare knew the answer to this. The epilogue plays with the idea of the audience as creditor owed a successful play. On the contrary, by the end of *1 & 2 Henry IV* Shakespeare knows that we are in Falstaff's debt, and we owe him our love. By way of the text of St Paul which underpinned monarchism, in Shakespeare's confrontation with ethics and politics, art triumphs over history.

6
Henry V

In the concluding play of Shakespeare's second tetralogy a singular argument and action dominate the whole drama.[1] The action is war, which culminates in Agincourt, and the argument is its justification, which is challenged immediately before the battle. This singularity, however, is subjected to a highly consistent patterning which, in turn, has led to a polarised critical reception of the play. Commentators are divided between those who support Chorus's patriotic view of 'This star of England' (Epilogue, 1.6) and those who, looking more closely at the representation of Henry in relation to the design of the play, find an ambivalent critique of warmongering.[2]

I shall demonstrate that in *Henry V* Shakespeare reveals by travesty the betrayals of history and art to honour the claims to truth, particular or universal, associated with both.

> ...Poesie historicall is of all other next the diuine most honorable and worthy, as well for the common benefit as for the speciall comfort euery man receiueth by it. No one thing in the world with more delectation reuiuing our spirits then to behold as it were in a glasse the liuely image of our deare forefathers, their noble and vertuous maner of life, with other things autentike ...[3]

Medieval and Renaissance historiography and literature are, however, more complex than such a claim to 'things autentike'.[4] The combined influences of rhetoric and idealism, romance and nationalism, patronage and providentialism, subjected the partiality of historical evidence to the pressure of political ideology whereby the record of the past was adjusted to the needs of the present governed by authority and censorship. Thus, for example, the *Gesta Henrici Quinti* celebrates the English royal hero.[5] Shakespeare dramatises this official version but problematizes it with the representations of art.

Given the Prologue and Choruses to each act, Shakespeare appears to be capitulating to post-Armada nationalism, to be sharing in the ambience which created *The Famous Victories of Henry the Fifth* (1594). From this point of view, art like history is seemingly at the service of ideology. But Shakespeare's parodic elements point to a deconstructive radicalism that is overt in the contrasting scenes of epic and burlesque and covert in the complexity of the character of the king himself. The non-comic scenes seem to be showing how the representation of nationalist epic heroism in the warrior-king is not just the expression of a unifying need to idolise, but is a means of sanctioning the Tudor dynasty in the continuity of Englishness established by divinely appointed victory. Whereas the alternation of comic scenes provides an allusive travesty which develops as the two worlds of high and low begin to encroach on each other in the same scene, culminating in the confrontation of the disguised king with three ordinary soldiers before Agincourt.

The dualism we have observed in the *Henry IV* plays is formalised here in the whole structure of *Henry V* as well as in the character of the king. Put another way, Shakespeare takes the idealised argument of history, the *speculum principis* or mirror for princes, dividing it between the acts and scenes, but interpolating destabilising points of view in further scenes to provide an ironised perspective. Mirror and perspective are Shakespeare's terms: the opening Chorus of act 2 celebrates Henry as 'the mirror of all Christian Kings' (l.6), at the close the French king says of Henry's view of a French city and a French maid, 'you see them perspectively' (5.2.320–1). By act 5 this is exactly how the audience has learned to see the play as a whole. Or put less categorically, those members of the audience who resist direct jingoism and recognise comedy as functional, will develop a response to this perspectivism.[6]

In 'the mirror of all Christian kings' the mirror is usually glossed as pattern or exemplar. *Speculum* literature is an extensive and varied mode, the most famous title of which is undoubtedly William Baldwin's *The Mirror for Magistrates* (1555, 1559), one of Shakespeare's sources for the histories.[7] Within the didactic mirror the reader or spectator 'saw' exemplars of various kinds running all the way from the most heinous to the most admirable (from Richard III to Henry V, some might say). The perspective referred to by the French king almost certainly refers to something familiar to most members of the audience since an unsophisticated version was popular as a childhood toy.[8] This was the corrugated pictorial device which showed two, usually contrasted, images when viewed from opposite angles. Two pictures were cut into strips and then mounted alternatively, strip by strip. When folded at each strip to create a series of rightangles the 'perspective' was then displayed. In *Antony and Cleopatra*, Cleopatra refers to the 'perspective' nature of her lover in this way, 'Though he be painted one way like a Gorgon, / The other way's a Mars' (2.5.116–17).[9]

In *Henry V* the French king suggests two pictures, one of the maid and one of the city, which have been assembled in this way. Thus from one point of view in this final scene history is resolved into the banter of romantic comedy, from another we see the hard politics of diplomatic marriage – the two recalling the combined significance of rape in siege warfare, as threatened at Harfleur (3.3.1–43). Yet Shakespeare's perspectivism is more complex than the pictorial device. It is multidimensional: what we see *and hear* in immediate succession; what we see and hear in relation to what immediately precedes; what we see and hear in relation to the earlier plays of the tetralogy; what we see and hear in relation to other representations of history and art available at the time. Above all, we recognise that this perspectivism is the visual parallel to the antithetic practices within rhetoric and logic: arguing on both sides of the question, *in utramque partem*, arguments *pro* and *contra* of the thesis, the rhetorical topics of *laus* (praise) and *vituperatio* (denunciation). These issues will be focused on here following the methodology of the whole study, the nature of verbal argument in relation to the argument of action.

The first scene of the play is given to two senior divines, the Archbishop of Canterbury and the Bishop of Ely, discussing the financial affairs of the church in relation to state politics. Henry V's parliament has revived a bill of the preceding reign which, if carried through, would halve the church's wealth (1.1.7–8). The historical material is taken from Holinshed (III, 65). Canterbury reveals his strategy, to offer a greater sum towards the king's war with France than the church had ever contributed to the state before. Canterbury explains (1.1.83–9) that the offer was accepted, but because of the arrival of a French embassy there had not been time for the Archbishop to supply what Henry had asked for as part of the bargain – approval of his claimed inherited rights to some dukedoms in particular and to the realm of France in general. This is hard-nosed *quid pro quo* politics in which both sides get what they want, with the king as the outright gainer. For Henry to have supported the bill would have alienated the church whose agreement he must have. The king knows that he cannot proceed unless his action can be argued as a just war, an argument which will be returned to in detail later in this chapter. Canterbury knows that the huge sum he proposes gives the king the necessary finance as well as his judgment ensuring the church's theological endorsement of dynastic claims.

In the midst of the cleric's account, however, occurs something in contrast to Henry as the tough, astute, calculating son of Bolingbroke, that is the portrait of the former Hal as an ideal Renaissance prince. Having introduced the parliamentary politics (1.1.1–20), the prelates then rehearse the legendary story of Prince Hal's 'reformation' (1.1.33) upon his father's death, and his becoming 'a true lover of the holy Church' (1.1.22), a 'scholar' (1.1.32) who has mastered 'divinity' (1.1.38), state affairs (1.1.41) and international politics (1.1.43, 45), subjecting theory to 'the art and practic part of life' (1.1.51). Actors do not need to give these lines a satirical edge since the dramatic context itself creates the euphemism of the 'art and practic part of life', namely the political subtext of the prelates' recognition that Henry will see that his best political self-interests lie in expedient mutuality not autocratic confrontation. Here they rehearse the public perception of the king, with the kind of panegyrical *topoi* of official celebration with which they might embellish a sermon.

It was from these and other similar epideictic materials that John H. Walter constructed his model of the ideal epic hero and text-book king in his Arden introduction (pp. xvi–xvii). I say 'text-book' king because that is precisely what he does. Walter takes two of the most famous humanist handbooks on the ideal prince, Erasmus's *Institutio Principis* (1516) and Chelidonius's *Of the Institution and firste beginning of Christian Princes* (Chillester's translation, 1571), and selects various categories of virtuous behaviour and aligns them with passages from the play. But Shakespeare's text is a play, not a florilegium, and the prelates' praise occurs within an immediate dramatic context. Canterbury and Ely are in private, with us the audience eavesdropping on the stratagems of politics and such a revealing exchange as 'This would drink deep', "Twould drink the cup and all' (1.1.20). The language of worldly colloquial materialism is quite at odds with the reverence of the speakers' status made manifest by the appropriate ceremonial robes donned for their public presentation before the monarch and his council. Thus their portrait of the ideal ruler, the evident *laus* of panegyric, is somewhat compromised by the deconstructive perspective we are given before we actually meet the king in the next scene.

When Henry appears, surrounded by his nobles, and summons the primate of the English church to his presence we all know the political situation, the reality beneath the ceremony in which the king insists that Canterbury's argument must be guided by 'truth' (1.2.17) of the validity of the dynastic claim, one way or another ('Or should, or should not, bar us in our claim', 1.1.12). It is in this speech that the beginning of a certain pattern emerges, Henry's shifting of responsibility, for the king insists that it is Canterbury's judgment that will initiate invasion and war, 'Of what your reverence shall incite us to' (1.2.20).[10] But the exact opposite is the case. It is Henry who has incited the prelate by making ecclesiastical sanction a necessary stipulation in the prior agreement which the preceding scene has made us party to. Yet from another point of view if we shift our perspective and remember just the ideal portrait of scene 1, then it could be said that here we see the ruler publicly seeking and accepting council from the senior personages of the realm. Much of the play is structured by this alternation.

For example, let us look forward to the Cambridge conspiracy at Southampton (2.2). This commonly draws critical comment on the omission of any direct reference to the Earl of Cambridge's motive as having a legitimate claim to the throne of England. Here I wish to look at the question of responsibility, judgement, argument and action. Cambridge, Lord Scroop and Sir Thomas Grey are known to be conspiring against the king's life as we hear in the first words of the scene. Before their arrest, Shakespeare invents a little parable that is not found in the sources: Henry orders Exeter to release a prisoner who had been arrested the previous day for drunken insults against the king. In Henry's judgment it was mere drunkenness. Not so for Scroop, who argues that such mercy is naïve forebearance which might lead others to expect like leniency, therefore the prisoner should be punished. Henry replies that he wishes to show mercy but Cambridge supports Scroop by urging that punishment is consistent with mercy which Grey endorses by insisting that punishment falling short of the capital sentence is mercy enough. Henry's response is to point out that if, following their recommendation, such a small offence could not be overlooked but punished with such harshness, then major offences could only be regarded with the utmost severity. Upon their arrest the conspirators appeal to Henry's mercy. The king replies, 'The mercy that was quick in us but late / By your own counsel is suppress'd and kill'd' (2.2.79–80). In effect the conspirators' prior judgment has sentenced them to death and they are led off to execution. In his design Shakespeare juxtaposes the ideal king showing invented clemency with the historical actuality of high treason (subornation by a foreign enemy) in which no mercy could have been legally and politically possible, but the responsibility for the verdict is shifted by the king on to the conspirators themselves.

Returning to the Archbishop of Canterbury and his argument, we find that Shakespeare makes one crucial division in his source material which somewhat dents the political front. Canterbury's extensive account of the Salic law (1.2.33–95) is taken almost word for word from Holinshed (III, 65–6), but it is made ludicrous by separating it from its initial premise in the chronicle which is stated in the Canterbury–Ely exchanges of scene 1, summarised above, namely Henry's claims ' . . . to some certain dukedoms, / And generally to the crown and seat of France, / Deriv'd from Edward, his great-grandfather' (1.1.87–9). Before the king and council this is left out. (Perhaps unsurprisingly since the claim for descent through Isabella, the mother of Edward III and daughter of Philip IV of France, does not bear close examination.[11]) In the midst of all the digressive pomposity the core of Canterbury's argument is the evidence of two usurpers and one conscience-struck son of a usurper inheriting the French crown by way of a female line (respectively, Pepin, Hugh Capet and Lewis the Ninth, 1.2.65, 69, 77–9).[12] As if to rub home the sardonic point to the conscience-struck son of the usurper Henry IV ('O, not to-day, think not upon the fault / My father made in compassing the crown!', 4.1.293–4), the closing lines of Canterbury's argument claim that the titles of the contemporary French monarch are 'Usurp'd from you and your progenitors' (1.2.95). Then, almost as an afterthought, following Henry's question, 'May I with right and conscience make this claim?', the primate delivers the imprimatur, 'Look back into your mighty ancestors; / Go, my dread lord, to your great-grandfather's tomb, / From whom you claim' (1.2.96, 102–4). When we look back and go no further than to Shakespeare's representation of the death of Henry IV, we find an altogether different imperative of father to son:

> Be it thy course to busy giddy minds
> With foreign quarrels, that action, hence borne out,
> May waste the memory of the former days.
>
> (*2 Henry IV*, 4.5.213–15)

With the first major confrontation of war in France, the siege of Harfleur, we find a pattern similar to that we have examined with the divines and with the Cambridge conspiracy. The law of siege warfare allowed for a process of parley, as Henry's words remind us, 'This is the latest parle we will admit' (3.3.2).[13] If terms of surrender, 'composition' as it was called, were resisted, then destruction and the horrors of war would follow, since 'The gates of mercy shall be all shut up' (3.3.10). Holinshed and Hall make no mention of the word 'mercy'. To persuade the governor of the town, Henry's argument evokes the horrors of war; the rape and murder of virgins, the slaughter of the aged and infants, in all – 'heady murther, spoil, and villainy' (3.3.32). If this comes about, Henry tells the governor, 'you yourselves are cause' (3.3.19), just as he had, through his ambassador, explained to the French king that he would be responsible, 'on your head' (2.4.109), for all the ensuing bloodshed if he didn't hand over his crown. In transferring responsibility Henry's sophistry lies in making the governor's decision the efficient cause of slaughter rather than his own action as invading conqueror. Whatever decision the governor makes he is forced into it by an external cause, Henry's war. However, the governor surrenders and Henry commands, 'Use mercy to them all' (3.3.54).

So, the graphic threats of the mercilessness of vile atrocity produce mercy. The king's procedure was to follow 'the disciplines of war' as Fluellen constantly reminds us (see 3.2, *passim*) and by evoking horror prevent the very suffering he threatened. Once again, in Shakespeare's design Henry may be seen as the merciful mirror of princes, or as the most calculating tactician, like his brother prince John at Gaultree. Unfortunately, we recognise that here mercy and mercilessness are equal options to the same end, the defeat of the town. Mercy is not an inalienable principle of humanitarianism but a negotiable tactic for a general. Chivalry and barbarism were quite compatible in medieval warfare. Because Edward the Black Prince's adviser, the Bishop of Limoges, had handed over the city to the French in 1370, he ordered an assault without terms of surrender and no quarter to be given. Three thousand innocent men, women and children were slaughtered and the city plundered, burnt and destroyed, as Froissart recorded for posterity.[14] In reality the town of Harfleur, as Shakespeare found in Hall and Holinshed, was sacked by the English. Shakespeare delays confronting the actual atrocities of war until Agincourt, when heightened arguments of patriotism could be juxtaposed against the immediate evidence of butchery.

In the confrontation of the disguised king and the common soldiers, Williams, Bates and Court, the whole argument of *Henry V* – the design of Shakespeare's plot, Henry's cause and military action – is put to the test in a heavily pointed way, the debate on the king's responsibility. We are on the eve of the legendary action, the battle of Agincourt, the outcome of the English king's argument for his right to the crown of France. For the Middle Ages the absolutely essential criterion for any such argument and action of war is that the cause must be seen as just.

Henry raises this, 'his cause being just and his quarrel honorable' (4.1.27–8). Williams's response is immediately sceptical, 'That's more than we know', whereas Bates comments, 'If his cause be wrong, our obedience wipes the crime of it out of us'. Williams continues by developing the theological implications, 'But if the cause be not good, the King himself hath a heavy reckoning to make' (4.1.129–35).

The legal concept of the 'just war' is a very involved topic.[15] The Christian fighting the infidel in a crusade was straightforward enough and defence of national boundaries against a foreign invader seems 'just', but what if that very invader were also claiming a just war in restoring his own national boundaries? From one point of view Henry's war was just in so far as he could legally make it such simply by virtue of his declaration of war as a sovereign prince. A just war (sometimes referred to as a public war in contrast to private feuding), legitimised otherwise criminal acts (killing, destroying, etc.) and, most important of all, made legal the taking of unlimited spoils and prisoners for ransom. But the question of a just *cause* remained. In practical politics this meant that whatever the sovereign prince declared just, providing it was supported adequately, was so. As 'imperial' (4.1.261) within his own kingdom Henry doesn't really have to answer to anyone else and, as we have seen, he has secured the full support of the church. Yet we have also seen, particularly in relation to the Cambridge conspiracy and Canterbury's paradoxical justification, that Henry's 'cause' is far from unimpeachable.

As Williams's reply (4.1.135–8) makes plain, he is referring to the Day of Judgment at which Henry's soul will be weighed in the balance. If his cause is bad, then all those killed in battle on his behalf will bear witness in his judgment. When Williams says, 'Now if these men do not die well' (4.1.144), he is not referring to the spiritual estate of their souls at that moment, but to the manner of their death – violent, bloody and painful. Williams is not saying that Henry is responsible for the unconfessed past sins of his soldiers but he is suggesting that as killing ('blood is their argument', 4.1.143) is the business of battle and killing is a sin, then Henry is implicated since they fight on behalf of his cause. According to the theological implications of the laws of war, Honoré Bonet (following John of Legnano) considers:

> if a soldier die in battle in a just war and to maintain a just quarrel he ... will be saved in Paradise ... [but] if he die or be killed in unjust warfare he is in the way of damnation, for we hold according to our Faith that the souls of those who die in mortal sin go to hell.[16]

Such a view puts Henry's evasion of responsibility in sharp relief. The king ignores Williams's opening charge and seizes on the argument concerning the individual's responsibility for the spiritual estate of his soul.

Henry uses a series of analogies and concludes, 'The king is not bound to answer the particular endings of his soldiers, the father of his son, nor the master of his servant' (4.1.155–7). That is to say, if a person in a state of sin dies while going about his business, it has nothing to do with the person on whose behalf he was acting. The analogies are to a merchant sending his son to sea and a master likewise employing a servant on the road. But the analogies are false. Henry evades the parallel question of cause which would reveal the inadequacy of the analogies ('only when the business is criminal and the cause unjust is the case the same' for Jonathan Hart).[17] Death is a constant likelihood for a soldier fighting for his king, whereas in ordinary business it is unlikely. Henry's analogies attempt to neutralise and distance the issue in what can only be called a disingenuous fashion, 'for they purpose not their death when they purpose their services' (4.1.157–8). This is manifestly untrue for a solider for whom it is glaringly obvious that the reverse is the case. As if aware of this Henry tries to argue that God works on the king's behalf by punishing criminals in war who have escaped justice at home, seemingly a variant on the argument that war purges the body politic of the ill humours of criminality. But the implicit false proposition that all soldiers are criminals reveals the fallacy of *secumdem quid*, taking the part for the whole. Late medieval and early modern armies often consisted of many criminals, but many conscripts were volunteers.[18] The king flounders further, vainly grasping at various arguments, but all to no avail since the initial question of his own soul on Judgement Day is completely ignored.

Even when left alone, in soliloquy, Henry persists in misrepresenting Williams's fundamental case, 'let us...our sins lay on the King!' (4.1.230–2). The cares of kingship speech which this begins provides a conventional anthology piece but within the immediate context it is in part subverted by what has just taken place. This can be brought out by running two passages together:

> What infinite heart's ease
> Must kings neglect, that private men enjoy!
> ...
> Not all these...
> Can sleep so soundly as the wretched slave;

> Who, with a body fill'd and vacant mind,
> Gets him to rest...

$$(4.1.236–7, 267–70)$$

Yet we have just seen in the common soldiers that there is neither heart's ease, sound sleep, or vacant mind, as they anxiously pass a restless night, loyal certainly, but as Henry finds, full of the human dread of death in battle.

The hollowness of the conventional tropes of Henry's soliloquy on kingship is anticipated in a particular way by Shakespeare's undermining another convention in the Henry–Williams debate. In several English history plays between 1587 and 1600 Anne Barton has studied scenes in which the disguised king becomes involved with the lower orders, usually in some form of altercation or advice. The licence of fictional romance and comedy allows a breach of the status quo, but hierarchy is suspended to reinforce hierarchy since the resultant harmony reaffirms the concord of a natural social order, divinely ordained. In *Henry V*, with the encounter of king and soldiers, Barton sees a development of this motif, but 'to question, not to celebrate, a folk convention... [Shakespeare] used Henry's disguise to summon up the memory of a wistful, naïve attitude toward history and the relationship of subject and king which the play rejects as attractive but untrue: a nostalgic but false romanticism'.[19]

The scene of Henry, Williams, Bates and Court comes from Shakespeare's invention; it is not to be found in the sources. As, in effect, a prologue to the field of battle, the argument is breathtaking. In terms of dramatic emphasis, that is, the significance of Agincourt is bound up with this extensive encounter in which all action stops and we are forced to concentrate on argument. Furthermore, there is no comparable treatment of plebeian characters elsewhere in Shakespeare, or elsewhere in early modern drama for that matter, since Williams and Bates are given the dignity of plain English speech quite free from the customary comic idioms of country-clown mummetshire. Shakespeare actually takes a few of the 'ciphers to this great accompt' (Prologue, l.17) and gives them names, not that King Henry enquires this far. On the contrary, in the resonant Saint Crispin's day speech he anticipates the heroic memory of nobles such as Warwick and Talbot who were not there at all (4.3.54). Similarly, Henry repeatedly insists that victory at Agincourt came from the 'arm' of God, 'without stratagem' (4.8.106–8), when as everybody knows the stakes defending the deadly archers were responsible for success, and it was the developed arm of the bowman that had the strength to ensure the vital armour-piercing velocity of the arrows. The king allows patriotic enthusiasm to carry him away to the extent of falsifying the record, like Chorus who wishes us to see what is not there, alternatively 'minding true things by what their mock'ries be' (4.53). When it gets to the actual battle we certainly see that 'mockery' in Pistol's travesty of ransom in his taking prisoner Monsieur le Fer. (Or does the travesty reveal the social and economic 'truth' beneath all the chivalric and legal superstructure of medieval ordinances of war?)

The comic subplot of the Eastcheap low lives has long been accepted, like that of the *Henry IV* plays, as having a parodic relationship with the main plot.[20] In the battle of Agincourt Henry orders the death of the prisoners: earlier he had ordered the execution of Bardolph. I wish to examine here Pistol's vain argument in defence of Bardolph's crime of stealing the pax (a decorative tablet kissed during communion). As all editors point out, in the chronicles it was a pyx (an ornamental box for the host) and in his ordinances of war King Henry had forbidden any such spoliation.[21] Needless to say, critics have pointed out the ironic parallel of pax as peace, seized by Bardolph and broken by Henry. Pistol sees it differently:

> Bardolph, a soldier firm and sound of heart,
> And of buxom valor, hath by cruel fate,
> And giddy Fortune's furious fickle wheel,
> That goddess blind,
> That stands upon the rolling restless stone –
>
> (3.6.25–9)

Fluellen interrupts and offers a pedantic exposition of the iconology of fortune, but he eventually sides with authority against the miscreant, who is to be hanged. J.H. Walter glossed this by accepting T.W. Baldwin's elaboration of an eighteenth-century suggestion that the extensive passage on fortune might be taken from the *Rhetorica ad Herennium's* examination of some lines of poetry by Pacuvius.[22] The quotation in *Herennium*, which Shakespeare would have encountered in Stratford Grammar School, is cited as an example of faulty reasoning. In the view of the *Herennium*, Pacuvius' argument that events come about more by accident than by fortune is weak in itself since neither is compelling as an explanation of causality. In Shakespeare's adaptation of this allusion to Bardolph's situation we see a version of Henry's constant transference of responsibility. For a past criminal action of Bardolph, Pistol puts the responsibility onto fortune. Henry repeatedly shifts the responsibility for his actions on to others. Neither accepts the cause, and thus responsibility, for action as deriving from oneself. Henry, however, gets France, Bardolph gets hanged. Perhaps Chorus wryly comments on this at the close, for 'Fortune made [Henry's] sword', smiling on the king, it appears, but frowning on Bardolph.

Henry's command 'Then every soldier kill his prisoners' (4.6.37) is probably the most discussed line of the play. All the arguments concerning right and justice, war and responsibility, are tested by the evidence of this action.

Discussion of the line usually concentrates on the questions of sequence and causality, and the question of legality. Is Henry's command in revenge for the French slaughter of the camp boys, as Gower assumes (4.7.5–10)? If not, what is the legal, moral and theological significance of such an action? Before examining the questions we should note the structural placing of the king's order in relation to what precedes it. Henry's words close the brief scene which is otherwise wholly taken up with Exeter's account of the deaths of York and Suffolk (4.6.7–32), an account of Shakespeare's invention, again. The epic quality of Exeter's anticipation is sounded in the Homeric 'Thrice...thrice' (4.6.4–5). Exeter's portrayal evokes heroic sacrifice in battle as the dying York kisses his dead compatriot in honour of '"this glorious and well-foughten field"' in which '"we kept together in our chivalry"' (4.6.18–19), and his last words affirm the ideals of feudal and emergent, nationalist knighthood, '"Commend my service to my sovereign"' (4.6.23). Then we hear: '...every soldier kill his prisoners' (4.6.37). Here we have, brought together in sharp juxtaposition, the two extremes of the representation of historical warfare in literature: idealism transforms the actual into the rhetorical *ekphrasis* (recalling the death of Talbot in *1 Henry VI*, 4.7) and realism indicates the harsh barbarity of battlefield expedience.

In the Oxford edition, on Henry's command the prisoners who were brought on stage with him are killed there and then in front of the audience, and for good measure Oxford follows the Quarto at the end of the scene and has the otherwise silent Pistol throw in his catchphrase, '*Coup' la gorge*', cut their throats. In my view there is a compelling logic for this, besides that of textual principles and practice, the logic of Shakespeare's disjunction between the argument of action and verbal argument. Oxford's decision gives us, in addition to the perspectivism noted above, the ineffability of the act itself and the revealing collision of clowns and subplot superimposed on, not parallel to, the leaders in the theatre of war (throat-cutting as symbolic of atrocity is a motif that is sounded throughout: see 2.1.21–2; 2.1.69, 71, 92; 3.2.111–12; 4.1.193; 4.4.14, 32, 39; 4.7.9–10, 63). Consequently, we are forced to ask whether Chorus's imagined 'truth' of chivalry is a mockery, or whether so-called 'mockery' is closer to the reality we actually see?

In the sequence of events as dramatised by Shakespeare he makes one crucial change to the source. Holinshed's account (III, 81) is as follows: realising that the English camp was distant and unguarded, the French attacked and slaughtered the boys; the cries of those escaping were heard by Henry; fearing the regrouping of the French and the possibility of French prisoners rebelling in support, Henry ordered their slaughter. Hall's record (pp. 69–70) is substantially the same, with the addition of King Henry receiving a message as he hears the cries of those escaping. The authority on Shakespeare's sources, Geoffrey Bullough, points out that *The Famous Victories of Henry the Fifth* omits the killing of the prisoners whereas in Shakespeare's play 'the killing of the French prisoners [was] ordered after the illegal attack on the King's camp and baggage train'.[23] This is not how Shakespeare presents it: Henry's commiseration with Exeter is interrupted, 'But hark, what new alarum is this same?' An 'alarum' is the call to arms and Henry realises the danger, 'The French have reinforc'd their scatter'd men' and immediately gives the order, 'Then every soldier kill his prisoners, / Give the word through' (4.6.35–8). T.W. Craik believes that what Henry hears is the alarum sounded by Bourbon's rally of 4.5.11.[24] At the opening of 4.7 Fluellen laments the death of the boys and Gower mistakenly attributes the king's order to this:

'Tis certain there's not a boy left alive, and the cowardly rascals that ran from the battle ha' done this slaughter. Besides, they have burn'd and carried away all that was in the King's tent; wherefore the King, most worthily, hath caus'd every soldier to cut his prisoner's throat.

(4.7.5–10)

As Craik points out, the 'cowardly rascals' refers to another group of Frenchmen who are clearly identified by Holinshed (III, 81), though J.H. Walter claims they are Bourbon's rally, just as he disingenuously notes that the king's command is found in Hall and Holinshed. Ironically, Bullough goes on to quote a contemporary justification for his assumed sequence which, in fact, is closer to Shakespeare since it leaves out any mention of the killing of the camp boys and Andrew Gurr presents evidence to indicate that it might well have been Shakespeare's source: the following is from Richard Crompton's *The Mansion of Magnanimitie* (1599).

> ...the French, as they are men of great courage and valure, so they assembled themselves againe in battell array, meaning to have given a new battell to King Henry, which King Henry perceiving, gave speciall commaundment by proclamation, that every man should kill his prisoners...[25]

I agree with Craik and Gurr that when Henry enters with Bourbon as his prisoner his first words – 'I was not angry since I came to France / Until this instant' (4.7.55–6) – indicate that he has just learnt of the death of the boys. So Shakespeare gives one reason for the king's action whereas Hall and Holinshed give two. Or, put another way, Shakespeare withdraws the emotional slaughter of the boys as some kind of justification by *lex talionis* for Henry's atrocity. Even with this, Holinshed, repeating Hall, is very uneasy about the prisoners' deaths, 'this dolorous decree, and pitifull proclamation...this lamentable slaughter' (III, pp. 81, 82). Then and now the morality of Henry's action was questioned, apologised for and defended. Shakespeare's version deliberately aggravates the issue. In contrast, the *Gesta Henrici Quiniti*, written by an eye-witness, Henry's chaplain, records the killing of the prisoners as a spontaneous prudential act carried out by the captors without any orders from the king at all.

Unfortunately, Meron's assessment of Henry's order in relation to the laws of war is somewhat vitiated by his acceptance of Bullough's misrepresentation, but part of his discussion remains valuable. Meron shows that the baggage train was a lawful object of attack; however, the question of the immunity of the baggage train personnel where they do not resist, was the subject of legal debate.[26] So even if we follow the causal sequence in Holinshed the legality of Henry's order is called in question since he could not claim lawful reprisal, as the French action may not have breached any code. Thus the fundamental situation falls back on necessity as justification in itself, a situation which John of Legnano had granted.[27] Henry's troops were vastly outnumbered and extremely fatigued, and at that point he didn't know the outcome of the battle. The danger was too great so the prisoners had to be killed. Ironically, modern historians supply information which retrospectively supports Shakespeare's bifocal view of Henry's action – the king exempted the high-born French nobility whose status determined that their ransom went to him.[28]

At every point examination of the text of *Henry V* shows how, with the greatest deliberation, Shakespeare called in question the ideal of the warrior-prince of chivalry leading an English patriot army to a victory divinely ordained as part of national destiny. However, knowing that he could not change an audience, Shakespeare's structure contrived seemingly to do just that, while at the same time his argument with jingoistic historiography and art provided for the discerning auditor who could mind true things by what their mockeries be.[29]

7
Julius Caesar

The record of antiquity, whether in chronicle or biography, romance or poetry, offered Shakespeare the most momentous of actions which shaped history: the fall of Troy and the movement of the Roman republic to empire with the death of Julius Caesar. Unencumbered by Christian metaphysics, the Roman world presented the conflict between civic *virtù* and power politics. The citizen-Stoic acted upon ideals of conduct enshrined in the history of Rome in war and peace.[1]

On the plains of Philippi, both sides, Brutus and Cassius, Antony and Octavius, seek a parley. This is doubly odd since neither party seems to have any particular proposal or plan to put to the other. The incident is not to be found in Plutarch, but Kittredge has drawn attention to the conventional nature of such 'flyting' matches before battle in Elizabethan drama.[2] Here, in *Julius Caesar*, however, there is a singularly metadramatic emphasis since the parley turns out to be actually about argument and action. The parley itself suspends the action of battle with talk, and the talk is about the action of killing Caesar and Brutus's arguments concerning that event:

> Brutus   Words before blows; is it so, countrymen?
> Octavius Not that we love words better, as you do.

Brutus rallies against Octavius, but Antony turns his words against him:

> Brutus   Good words are better than bad strokes, Octavius.
> Antony   In your bad strokes, Brutus, you give good words; Witness the hole you made in Caesar's heart, Crying, 'Long live! hail, Caesar!'

                                                                (5.1.27–32)

The exchanges concerning past action and argument continue until Octavius' growing impatience puts a stop to them by insisting on the present battle which will resolve the dispute.

> Come, come, the cause. If arguing make us sweat,
> The proof of it will turn to redder drops.
> Look,
> I draw a sword against conspirators;
> When think you that the sword goes up again?
> Never, till Caesar's three and thirty wounds
> Be well aveng'd . . .
>
> (5.1.48–54)

The 'cause' is both the verbal and physical arguments of conspiracy, assassination and civil war, about to be tested by the present battle, the 'proof' of an argument of action. Editors point out that the thirty-three wounds here seem to be a misremembering of the twenty-three of Plutarch and Seutonius. It is important to note the increase rather than decrease in Shakespeare's mind when transposing words from the pages of North to actions performed live on stage before an audience, which are then recollected with a sense of growing enormity. This is crucial later.

The 'parley' epitomises the fundamental dramaturgy of the play which develops from the opening series of arguments concerning conspiracy, to the argument of action enacted before us with Caesar's assassination, and the arguments in the Forum justifying and condemning the death. The long-drawn-out coda of civil war follows in which blunt political realities provide 'proof' for an argument that Brutus has only just become aware of – the disjunction between words and things, political idealism and political reality.

The reality of Cassius' political motivation is immediately obvious to the audience. Countering Brutus' relative introspection, Cassius' chiding confounds flattery and respect in 'your hidden worthiness' (1.2.57), and Brutus himself is seen to be as susceptible as any would-be tyrant to such ingratiation, though his appeal to 'the general good' (1.2.85) might be taken as a provisional form of impersonalised exoneration. As with 'honour' Brutus has a powerful sense of meaning as inherent in words, the exact opposite to Falstaff. For Brutus 'honour' and 'Rome' are neither hypostatised entities nor mere rhetorical abstracts to be bandied about for ulterior purposes. In contrast, Cassius' use of the first-person pronoun in his recollection of saving Caesar from drowning in the

Tiber reveal his highly personal rancour, resentment and jealousy. Whereas Brutus argues what he believes as truth, Cassius chooses an argument to persuade rather than because he believes it, thus a Stoic emphasis for Brutus, 'The fault, dear Brutus, is not in our stars...' (1.2.140), but reinforced superstition for Casca:

> ...you shall find
> That heaven hath infus'd them with these spirits
> To make them instruments of fear and warning
> Unto some monstrous state.

> (1.3.68–71)

Alone, Cassius indicates the basis for his strategy with Brutus; that unbending conviction and principle, under certain circumstances, may become pliable: '...honourable mettle may be wrought / From that it is dispos'd' (1.2.309–10). What Cassius does not realise is how potentially self-destructive such honour can be, without any external provocation, as we might fear from Brutus's brooding disenchantment of act 1, before Cassius' approach, which is confirmed by the opening soliloquy of act 2. This is of such importance it needs to be quoted in full:

> It must be by his death; and for my part,
> I know no personal cause to spurn at him,
> But for the general. He would be crown'd:
> How that might change his nature, there's the question.
> It is the bright day that brings forth the adder,
> And that craves wary walking. Crown him that,
> And then I grant we put a sting in him
> That at his will he may do danger with.
> Th'abuse of greatness is when it disjoins
> Remorse from power; and to speak truth of Caesar,
> I have not known when his affections sway'd
> More than his reason. But 'tis a common proof
> That lowliness is young ambition's ladder,
> Whereto the climber-upward turns his face;
> But when he once attains the upmost round,
> He then unto the ladder turns his back,
> Looks in the clouds, scorning the base degrees
> By which he did ascend. So Caesar may;
> Then lest he may, prevent. And since the quarrel

Will bear no color for the thing he is,
Fashion it thus: that what he is, augmented,
Would run to these and these extremities;
And therefore think him as a serpent's egg,
Which, hatch'd, would, as his kind, grow mischievous,
And kill him in the shell.

(2.1.10–34)

Brutus' argument rests on one stated and one unstated premise drawn from inherited cultural commonplaces of politics and natural history: monarchy degenerates into tyranny; poisonous reptiles kill.[3] In arguing as he does, he attempts to convert a contingent into a necessary truth by allying laws of society and laws of nature, thereby converting the casuists' doubtful probabilism into a more certain probabiliorism. Probability that an action is lawful outweighs the probability that it is unlawful.[4] However, the ideological slide is reinforced by a culture which inherited the notion of nature reflecting society since both came about by the ordinances of divine creation. Yet the charge of the fallacy of the consequent can still be levelled at the argument:

the fallacy of thinking that, because if the hypothesis were true, certain facts would follow, therefore since those facts are found, the hypothesis is true.[5]

Yet the kind of verification Brutus mistakes for proof grasps only the shakiest of facts. Needless to say, Brutus' argument deconstructs itself in the deliberate exposure of its rhetoric and logic, an exposure only partially glimpsed by Brutus, who is largely unaware of his own tendentiousness.

Brutus' first words are categorical, urging a necessary conclusion at the outset to what in fact is acknowledged to be contingent at the close, 'Then lest he may, prevent' (l.28). Such prior insistence before an actually developed argument seems more emotional than logical and immediately raises the possibility that what follows is rationalisation rather than reason. The concessionary 'For my part . . . ', which follows, confers an anonymous and unquestionable judgement that Brutus is delivering rather than deciding. In contrasting 'personal cause' with the 'general [good]' (ll.11–12) Brutus invokes a conventional though false polarity which equivocates on the word 'personal'. Brutus finds a moral sanction in a professed lack of bias immediately following the most biased line in the whole speech, and evidently he is included in the supposed 'general' good which is not general at all but the Republican patrician class whose interests he represents, though his tragedy is that in reality he stands alone.[6] The naturalisation of tyranny follows: 'It is the bright day that brings forth the adder, / And that craves wary walking' (ll.14–15).

This would hardly constitute evidence in a court of law today, but it is most important to grasp how in Renaissance discourse this would have been conventionally permissible. In drawing from the *loci communes* Brutus is using an artistic proof deriving from the procedures of logic and rhetoric, as against the inartistic proofs of such things as testimony, portents, ghosts, etc., of which more shortly. Such artistic proofs are inclusive and deterministic. Whereas actual history and politics might raise the problem of exceptions, the general rule embodies a greater truth. But such 'proofs' should obviously be contributing to stronger forms of evidence otherwise the manifest *a priori* basis completely undermines any probative force. Brutus then generalises on the separation of conscience from power as an 'abuse of greatness' (l.18) but immediately recognises the opposite in Caesar: 'I have not known when his affections sway'd / More than his reason' (ll.120–1). This is triply ironic since it seems to defeat the argument both as an instance and as describing the very process at work in Brutus's own heart and mind, emotional insistence preceding rational discourse. Third, we have already heard that the tribunes Marullus and Flavius have been executed 'for pulling scarfs off Caesar's images' (1.2.285). Not a lot of 'remorse' seems to have gone into that demonstration of 'power' over Pompey's erstwhile supporters.

Virtue, Caesar's humility, is then shown to be an early stage of vice, ambition, and Brutus invokes another argument from commonplaces, the 'common proof' of 'ambition's ladder' (ll.21–2), spurned once climbed. Yet again, when Brutus turns to find evidence after rather than before argument, he finds the exact opposite: there are no grounds in Caesar's present behaviour to justify the course of action he is recommending: 'the quarrel / Will bear no color for the thing he is' (ll.28–9). That is to say, put bluntly, on *a posteriori* grounds Brutus has no argument whatsoever. Ironically, his final arguments (ll.30–4) are seen to work more against conspiracy than for tyranncide. The slain Caesar is 'augmented' by Antony's oration, which gives rise to the 'extremities' of civil war. Brutus finally resorts to the rhetoricians' proverb, an inartistic proof supposedly encapsulating the wisdom of generations, to kill the serpent or cockatrice in its shell. It will always remain a moot point whether Rome would have been better off had Brutus applied this to the conspiracy, rather than to Caesar's death. Thus the reasoning, on the gravest affairs of state, by a man who a few lines earlier could not even hazard a guess at the time of day.

Shakespeare chose to give Brutus such weak arguments at the same time as he chose not to weigh in heavily with the common Renaissance view of Caesar as the potential tyrannical destroyer of Roman liberty. In both instances Shakespeare qualifies a received idea: Brutus is less simply heroic, and Caesar less than the 'thrasonical' emperor of dramatic tradition.[7] The *a priori* basis of Brutus' reasoning reflects an abstract intellectual mind more ready to seize on the idea than the fact. The appeal to 'Rome' (2.1.47) in the covertly delivered letter is for Brutus the retrospectively idealised Rome of his ancestor Lucius Junius Brutus who expelled the Tarquin, not the contemporary Rome around him of public and private interest confounded, mob politics, senatorial manoeuvring and dormant Caesarism. Appeal to an heroic past has an ideal simplicity at odds with the complexity we have witnessed so far. The appearance shortly after of the aged and sick Caius Ligarius who shares Brutus' perspective in his appeal 'Soul of Rome!' (2.1.321) is almost farcical. If all the other conspirators, as Antony claims at the close, 'Did that they did in envy of great Caesar' (5.5.70), then Brutus and Caius Ligarius as exemplars of republican virtue, one disabled in mind the other in body, make a sorry pair – particularly following the actual evocation of murder, though of course this is hardly Brutus' word for it.

When Cassius urges an oath to seal the conspiracy, Brutus objects to any transcendant warrantee. He has a Stoic confidence in 'The even virtue of our enterprise' (2.1.133). For a Roman to break even part of a promise, let alone an oath, would mean that

> every drop of blood
> That every Roman bears, and nobly bears,
> Is guilty of a several bastardy . . .
>
> (2.1.136–8)

Blood here symbolises the natural legitimacy of virtue as a Roman birthright. Yet immediately following, when Brutus refuses Cassius' suggestion that Antony should die with Caesar, he contradicts the above rejection of religious sanction by insisting on the assassination of Caesar as a sacrifice 'for the gods' (2.1.173), and literal Roman blood is consequently ritualised into a symbolic purgation of the body politic. With the use and meaning of ritualistic words, as in an oath, Brutus is dismissive, but when it gets to the reality of an action behind the euphemism of 'our enterprise' (2.1.133), he is compelled to resort to metaphor, analogy and allusion.

At first, considering Cassius' proposal concerning Antony and Caesar, Brutus literalises the metaphorical by invoking the legal corporate notion of the state as a body politic: 'Our cause will seem too bloody, Caius Cassius, / To cut the head off and then hack the limbs...For Antony is but a limb of Caesar' (2.1.162–3, 165). Such literalisation of an organicist fiction quite blinds Brutus to the political reality of autonomous military reaction. It could be that on the death of his patron Antony's client fortunes might wane, but this does not necessarily incapacitate him politically. The reverse is true in fact. With dependence gone, power is up for grabs, Antony's hand is forced and he has to act one way or another. However, the resort to such imagery does serve to remind Brutus of the matter in hand, that Caesar is to be stabbed to death. He reacts to this by attempting to transform the bloodiness of the act by seeing it as sacrifice, not butchery. Brutus' intellectuality and abstraction seize on the preferred notion, both fatuous and ironic, of Caesar's bloodless spirit as the object of their conspiracy. This metaphysical entity parallels the idea of a 'soul' of Rome, but ironically it is the body of Caesar, as staged by Antony, which fires the body of Rome, the populace, who turn against the conspirators; though the final irony is that both the solid body of the triumvirate and the spirit of Caesar catch up with Brutus and Cassius at Philippi.

Faced with the ineluctability of blood, Brutus once more tries to transform it into the ceremonial of, as one editor suggests, killing the royal hart:[8] 'Let's carve him as a dish fit for the gods, / Not hew him as a carcass fit for hounds' (2.1.173–4). Whatever the distinction to be made between 'carve' and 'hew' the gruesome incongruousness is surely apparent to everyone, on stage and off stage, except Brutus. Yet again, as scholar and intellectual, he has a real belief in the distinctions he is making, a belief in verbal discrimination which the facts will totally belie. How is a stab to be sacrificial and not butchery? How, exactly, can Caesar be knifed 'boldly but not wrathfully' (l.172)? How, precisely, can he be carved but not hewn? Certain forms of execution can be ritualised to some extent, death before a firing squad for instance, and there are sufficient records to show that some forms of suicide, such as the Japanese *hara-kiri*, could be ceremonial. Most cultures have funeral rites for dead bodies, but what Brutus and the conspirators propose here is the impossible bloodbath of Shakespeare's 'three and thirty wounds'.

Some lines in the argument which have given editors difficulty bear witness to Brutus' inherent wish to distance himself from an actuality he cannot really contemplate.

> And let our hearts, as subtle masters do,
> Stir up their servants to an act of rage,
> And after seem to chide 'em.
>
> (2.1.175–7)

These lines were often cut from late eighteenth- and nineteenth-century productions as embarrassingly hypocritical and also incompatible with the view of Brutus as an idealist.[9] Looking more closely it is possible to see their consistency, however paradoxical, with the argument as a whole. Immediately following the hunt allusions it appears that Brutus is developing an argument through a suppressed pun of a conventional kind – [hart] / 'heart'. Antony gives the pun full rein in his grief before the conspirators in the next act:

> Pardon me, Julius! Here wast thou bay'd, brave hart,
> Here didst thou fall, and here thy hunters stand,
> Sign'd in thy spoil, and crimson'd in thy lethe.
> O world, thou wast the forest to this hart;
> And this indeed, O world, the heart of thee.
> How like a deer, stroocken by many princes,
> Dost thou here lie!
>
> (3.1.204–10)

Brutus' silent pun reverses the situation. Instead of the 'hart' which is hunted, the 'hearts' now hunt; unlike Antony's language, perhaps a slightly baroque moment for the poetry of *Julius Caesar*. Brutus' language moves from the external picture of the hunt with its masters looking on and servants carving the royal beast to the internalised evocation of 'our hearts', 'masters' and 'their servants'. That is, the passions as servants of the heart are urged on to the 'act of rage' (l.176) to be chided thereafter. Brutus' humanist compunction, however faint, impels him to distance himself from the thought of the act by dividing the administrative and executive faculties of mind and body into master and servants, as if the killers were somehow misguided emissaries. Possibly an added irony that seems directly relevant is that after victory at Pharsalia, when Pompey's head was brought to Caesar, he turned away in tears, and had the murderers executed. The attitude of Brutus is not conscious hypocrisy but unconscious self-deception. With this addition to Shakespeare's source, the purgation Brutus insists on becomes a barbarous atrocity defiling the Roman ideals he stands for.

However, a sense of outrage at such horror, though not displaced, is qualified by evidence of a sort which Shakespeare builds into the drama. As we have seen, the arguments of Brutus and Cassius are weak and thus in rational terms justification is poor. But following this scene, from act 2, scene 2 to the point of Caesar's assassination, there are sufficiently cumulative details to warrant some genuine doubt about Caesar's future conduct if elevated further. Perhaps Brutus was right, but for the wrong reasons. Before this sequence, in Shakespeare's selection of material, the grounds for seeing Caesar as tyrant are slight. The execution of Marullus and Flavius could possibly be seen as necessary *realpolitik*, their action forcing Caesar to respond. Shakespeare does not particularly stress the triumphal entry following victory over Pompey's sons as contrary to the Roman practice of triumphing only over external enemies. Beyond this there is little but the revelation of Caesar's short- and long-term physical disabilities. Exhausted in the Tiber, recurrent epilepsy and the deafness which Shakespeare added for an almost farcical debunking effect – ' . . . for always I am Caesar. / Come on my right hand, for this ear is deaf' (2.1.212–13). The actor having to move from left to right brings out a touch of almost Shavian comedy.

More seriously, from act 2, scene 2, following Brutus' arguments, the audience is put in the position of witness for whom evidence provides testimony. An important division takes place here between verbal argument and the argument of action. We have heard how Brutus' arguments have largely failed in their deployment of artistic logical and rhetorical proof. Inartistic proofs, the evidence of witnesses and their testimony, ghosts, dreams, portents and such-like, provide another perspective. The irony of the prodigies summarised by Calphurnia (2.2.13–26) is that they do not portend the disasters brought about by the tyrannic destroyer of the state, but the disasters brought about by the patriot saviours of the country. What is of direct relevance is Caesar's behaviour in relation to these and other matters right up to the point of his death.

Though Cassius claims that Caesar has recently turned from his Epicurean beliefs and 'is superstitious grown of late' (2.1.195), he appears unaffected by the omens and decides that he will 'go forth' (2.2.28) with a Stoic's indifference to death. The augurs' examination of a beast without a heart is interpreted by Caesar as a comment on such cowardice. Then on grounds no stronger than Calphurnia's plea, he decides to remain at home on the pretence of sickness. With the entry of Decius, a conspirator, this decision is put more emphatically:

> ... tell them that I will not come today.
> Cannot, is false; and that I dare not, falser:
> I will not come to-day.

>> (2.2.62–4)

This assertive and dictatorial language becomes bluntly contemptuous in response to Calphurnia's 'Say he is sick' (l.65), as Caesar reverses his earlier decision.

> Shall Caesar send a lie?
> Have I in conquest stretch'd mine arm so far,
> To be afeard to tell greybeards the truth?
> Decius, go tell them Caesar will not come.

>> (ll.65–8)

Decius asks for a 'cause' (l.69). The gory details of Calphurnia's dream which Caesar relates should not distract us from his immediate reply: 'The cause is in my will' (l.71). This offers no less than the most concise self-definition of the tyrant to be found in Renaissance literature. Absolute, arbitrary and answerable to no one, with the automatic assumption of might and right, the tyrant stands exposed in naked 'will'. Not the ranting tyrant of a miracle play or florid Senecan villain, but something much more subtle. Not something from the phantasmagoric worlds of mythologising imagination, not larger than life, but life itself, a credible, realised, fallible human being enacted before us.

Caesar is superstitious, then not superstitious; resolute, then irresolute; he will go, he will not go; he will pretend sickness, he will not pretend sickness. Deferring to his wife before the expectations of the senate indicates further his dangerous partiality. The senate will be denied a reason, but Decius as a favourite – 'Because I love you' (2.2.74) – is told of Calphurnia's dream. Personal bias here comes before the impersonal responsibilities of office. Then, tempted by Decius' favourable interpretation of the dream, his suggestion of the offered crown and clever facetiousness at the initial capitulation to Calphurnia, Caesar vacillates once again, 'for I will go' (l.107). The would-be *imperator* shows manifest lack of judgement, further vitiated by credulousness. At the outset he defers to his wife but shows no deference for the gods since, in his arrogance, he sees himself as a more potent earthly phenomenon than that of the heavens: 'Danger knows full well / That Caesar is more dangerous than he' (2.2.44–5). Before the Capitol, surrounded by those he believes will shortly be urging a crown upon him, quite inconsistent with what we have just witnessed in the privacy of his home, he affects what he feels to be an appropriate magnanimity which seals his doom: Artemidorus' warning petition is deferred: 'What touches us ourself shall be last serv'd' (3.1.8).

These details have been stressed since the dialogue which follows, up to Caesar's death (3.1.13–77), usually receives most critical attention, though perhaps without seeing it as part of a calculatedly developed sequence as suggested here. For example, when Caesar spurns the petition of Metellus Cimber, not only does he take inflexibility to be a virtue, running directly counter to Renaissance commonplaces on clemency and justice, but in his language he condemns himself: ' . . . I am constant as the northern star' (3.1.60). That 'constant', which is insisted on (3.1.72–3), should be weighed against the vacillation we have noted.[10] Inviting petitioners, Caesar had asked, 'What is now amiss / That Caesar and his senate must redress?' (3.1.31–2). The imperious arrogation of the possessive pronoun has always been noted for its abuse of Roman sovereignty and legislature and it should be added that the senate is not seen to play any part whatsoever in the decision that Caesar refuses to rescind. The senate – *c'est moi*, to adapt a later instance. Finally, Caesar's god-like boast 'Wilt thou lift up Olympus?' (3.1.74) reminds us of the man helped from the floor of the market-place because of the 'falling sickness' (1.2.254). Two forms of evidence then, the arguments of Brutus and Cassius and the evidence of witness-auditors as testimony, precede Shakespeare's provision of one of the most powerful arguments of action to be found in his *oeuvre*.

The sour yet sychophantic Casca, whose first words of command and deference, 'Peace, ho, Caesar speaks' (1.2.1) in retrospect encapsulate resentful subordination, is the first to strike, 'Speak hands for me!' (3.1.76). The next line of dialogue is Caesar's '*Et tu, Brute*? – Then fall Caesar!' Accompanying these two lines are usually found the original two stage directions reading *They stab Caesar. Dies*. A consequence of reading the play is that these two lines are read successively without the reader stopping to take into account the nature of the action. In recent years there has been a critical shift from text-based study of poetic drama, deriving from the practice of new criticism, to study of the text in performance, whether actual or hypothetical. Further developments have taken place with what is called audience reception theory which has been touched on above in consideration of audience engagement as 'witnesses', and is of even greater importance in *Troilus and Cressida*. Here Caesar's death and what immediately follows provides an argument of action which directly comments on all the arguments we have examined. When Casca cries 'Speak hands for me!' he has little idea of what this is a prologue to.

Let us assume that the three and thirty wounds are conscious or unconscious exaggeration of the twenty-three found in the sources. Among those listed as entering in act 3, scene 1, Publius is a senator who remains on stage, Lepidus is a future triumvir , and Popilius a sympathiser with the conspiracy. Though he returns later, Trebonius the conspirator acts as a decoy to lead off Antony. That leaves the conspirators Brutus, Cassius, Casca, Decius, Metellus and Cinna who carry out the assassination. Six men, twenty-three wounds; that is, approximately four each if they are distributed equally. A moot point, which to a large extent will depend on the director. How many productions have actually shown all strikes being delivered? The issue is an important one. If a director does his homework he will come across a cue in Plutarch:

> the conspirators thronging one upon another, because every man was desirous to have a cut at him, so many swords and daggers lighting upon one body, one of them hurt another, and among them Brutus caught a blow on his hand, because he would make one in murthering of him, and all the rest also were every man of them bloodied.[11]

In standard martial art training it is acknowledged that it is not possible for more than three people at once to successfully attack an individual. Where there are more than three attackers they get in each others' way. Plutarch's representation indicates two things. At the beginning all the conspirators tried to get in a blow, inadvertently wounding each other. It would seem unlikely that thereafter one group of three were allowed to finish their four blows then allowing the other three their turn. Therefore it appears more likely that the blows would have been delivered haphazardly, under the passion of the moment, presumably at no more than two at a time. If this were the case then the staging has to be quite protracted, if, that is, each had more or less the same number of blows, each returning at least once. But if they are unequally distributed then the staging would have to reflect degrees of what only can be called the savagery of some of the attackers delivering as many as six stabs. Whichever bloody permutation a director decides on, the spectacle will be nasty, brutish and long-drawn out. As he found in the sources, following *Et tu Brute*, Shakespeare desisted from the final ignominy of Brutus's last strike – in the 'privities'.[12]

Twenty-three wounds means a great deal of blood, and if the killing is staged fully, as it should be, then the gruesome spectacle of one bloody corpse and six bloodied men presents an argument that the possible tyranny of one has been replaced by the actual tyranny of the few.[13] The tyrant's greatest power is over life and death and that has been meted out by the conspirators. The background deaths of Marullus and Flavius fade away beside the reality of the argument of action, what the conspirators have done as against what Caesar might have done, which render Brutus' arguments nugatory. If tyranny is a relationship between words and things then, given the materials Shakespeare chose to dramatise, Brutus and the conspirators are more dangerous than Caesar. Caesar's words are arrogant but as far as stage action is concerned he does very little apart from turning down Metellus' petition, whereas Brutus' words appeal to such things as the noble history of republican Rome, virtue, liberty and honour, but in contrast his action realises all the horror of the foreboding of 'a hideous dream' (2.1.65), rather than the 'Liberty! Freedom! Tyranny is dead!' (3.1.78) which Cinna acclaims. Perhaps this might seem closer to Antony's view of 'these butchers' (3.1.255)?

Brutus persists in his notion of a cleansing ritual in a piece of stage business which adds a further macabre dimension to Antony's view (and ours?). Shakespeare added Brutus' ceremony to what he found in Plutarch:

> Stoop, Romans, stoop,
> And let us bathe our hands in Caesar's blood
> Up to the elbows, and besmear our swords;
> Then walk we forth, even to the market-place,
> And waving our red weapons o'er our heads,
> Let's all cry, 'Peace, freedom, and liberty!'
>
> (3.1.105–10)

Though there are no stage directions it appears that the communal blooding is carried out since Cassius refers to the second half of the proposal – 'Ay, every man away. / Brutus shall lead . . . ' (3.1.119–20) and Antony explicitly refers to the goriness, ' . . . whilst your purpled hands do reek and smoke' (3.1.58), which Brutus acknowledges:

> Though now we must appear bloody and cruel
> As by our hands and this our present act

You see we do, yet see you but our hands
And this the bleeding business they have done.

(3.1.165–8)

In his exchanges here with Antony, Brutus has to recognise that 'Or else were this a savage spectacle' were not 'Our reasons...so full of good regard' (ll.223–4). We know that the reasons are not of 'good regard' in the arguments we have examined: we see 'a savage spectacle'. In order to emphasise this relationship between verbal argument and argument of action, with the audience shift in perspective from Brutus to Antony, Shakespeare provides an epitome of his dramatic methods in the combination of the particular argument immediately preceding the action of 'Stoop, Romans, stoop'. Brutus and Casca engage in an argument on fate, life and death.

> *Casca*   Why, he that cuts off twenty years of life
> Cuts off so many years of fearing death.

Brutus immediately follows this through:

> Grant that, and then is death a benefit;
> So are we Caesar's friends, that have abridg'd
> His time of fearing death. Stoop, Romans, stoop
>
> (3.1.101–5)

Blood has subverted Brutus' intellectual faculties. This is a glaring formal fallacy. The implied premise is 'life is fearing death' which is not only not necessarily the case but in the Stoic view expressed earlier by Caesar himself is explicitly denied:

> Of all the wonders that I have yet heard,
> It seems to me most strange that men should fear,
> Seeing that death, a necessary end,
> Will come when it will come.
>
> (2.2.34–7)

Brutus confuses the two notions, converting death as a necessary end to the necessity of life as fearing death. He stands self-condemned out of his own mouth, 'a savage spectacle' indeed. However, Cassius shares Brutus' view and envisages a different kind of spectacle:

> How many ages hence
> Shall this our lofty scene be acted over
> In states unborn, and accents yet unknown!

> (3.1.111–13)

Writing in the 1590s Shakespeare knew that this was true already, even before the success of his own play, but that is only ironically the point here, doubly so in the light of Cassius' argument which Antony seizes on for his immediate re-enactment in his Forum speech. This speech is duly famous as such, but it is also something of a play-within-a-play, or perhaps more accurately a Pirandellian rehearsal-within-a-play, with Antony as sole actor-manager. As Caesar has reminded us, Cassius '...loves no plays, / As thou dost, Antony' (1.2.203–4). In his performance Antony knows that he has one major advantage over Brutus. He has a prop, the body of Caesar, and as a soldier he has learned as much from the theatre of war as from the theatres of Rome – action speaks louder than words. The dead body of Caesar will be made eloquent. Those wounds, the 'dumb mouths', will be made to speak through Antony, 'To beg the voice and utterance of [his] tongue' (3.1.260–1). The conspirators' words will be weighed in the balance with their actions.

In discussion of *Julius Caesar* the Forum speeches of Brutus and Antony invariably receive critical comment, particularly concerning the contrast in rhetoric between Attic and Asiatic styles, the intellectualism of Brutus, the emotional appeal of Antony, and so on.[14] One of the most subtle aspects of the placing of Brutus' speech, however, is the way that it realises the proleptic parody Antony had asked his servant to deliver in the preceding scene. This can be brought out by paralleling relevant passages:

> *Servant* Thus, Brutus, did my master bid me kneel;
> Thus did Mark Antony bid me fall down;
> And, being prostrate, thus he bade me say . . .

> (3.1.123–5)

> *Brutus* . . . hear me for my cause and be silent, that you
> may hear. Believe me for mine honor, and have
> respect to mine honor, that you may believe.

> (3.2.13–14)

Both passages are marked by tautology and redundance. The idea of kneeling in the first appears in three forms, 'kneel...fall down... prostrate' with three 'thus's'. Brutus asks 'hear me for my cause', which necessarily means being silent, though he goes on to ask for this as well, needlessly tagging on a second clause repeating the substance of the first. Further, the parallelism in the servant's lines '...did my master bid me kneel...did Mark Antony bid me fall down' has a circular counterpart in Brutus' 'Believe me...may believe?' Again

> *Servant* ...Mark Antony shall not love Caesar dead
> So well as Brutus living
>
> (3.1.133–4)

> *Brutus* ...Had you rather Caesar were living, and die
> all slaves, than that Caesar were dead, to live all free men?
>
> (3.2.24–5)

Parallelism and antithesis mark both speeches here, but whereas Antony's is quite clear, Brutus allows an enthymeme to obscure his unacceptable premise. The excluded middle proposition in Brutus' speech is something like [Caesar living would be] 'a tyrant enslaving the people'. There are other echoes of language and structure as if Antony, knowing of Brutus' style of public oratory, has sedulously included characteristics of it to ensure his admittance in order to achieve his ulterior purpose, to obtain Caesar's body for the political strategy of his funeral oration. In his servant's speech Antony presents himself as another kind of Brutus, a subtle move intimating that he knows that intellectuals are often incapable of seeing things in anything but their own self-reflecting terms – for example, Brutus' 'If there be any in this assembly, any dear friend of Caesar's, to him I say, that Brutus' love to Caesar was no less than his' (3.2.17–19). Brutus' argument is to Rome and the Romans. We have touched on his idealised view of Rome above, and here we find the complementary view of 'Romans'. The plebeians are elevated to an all-inclusive '*Romanitas*' alongside republican patriots like Brutus, in effect. The most forceful answer to this argument is the argument of action of the anarchic mob, which in the next scene tears to pieces Cinna the poet, a mob earlier perceived by Casca as 'the rabblement... the tag-rag people...the common herd' (1.2.244, 258, 264). Brutus' parallelism is a syntactic approximation to the social posture he adopts but the antithesis of dead/live runs the risk of exposing his sleight-of-hand enthymeme, were it not for the fact that the conditional 'If...If'

(3.2.17–20) and the rhetorical questions would probably bemuse an illiterate crowd. Unfortunately, Brutus puts everything at risk by attempting to move from intellectuality with an emotional heightening:

> As Caesar lov'd me, I weep for him; as he was
> fortunate, I rejoice at it; as he was valiant, I honor him;
> but, as he was ambitious, I slew him. There is tears, for his
> love; joy for his fortune; honor, for his valor; and
> death for his ambition.

> (3.1.24–9)

Brutus spells out Caesar's proved virtues as against his unproved vice and inadvertently tips the argument against himself. The crowd applauds Brutus not for his argument but for what the plebeians perceive to be some dimly apprehended compliment to themselves from a Roman renowned for honesty. One pin-prick bursts the rhetorical bubble, 'Let him be Caesar' (3.1.51) cries the third plebeian.

Brutus' abstract argument lacks evidence, it deploys the ideas of Rome and ambition but allows words alone to persuade. Antony understands the common people, the materialism of whose lives leaves them open to the persuasion of things – objects, events, anything concrete and physical, not least of which is a corpse: *Enter* MARK ANTONY ... *with Caesar's body* (3.2.40). Antony's overall strategy, which Falstaff would have appreciated, is to juxtapose the verbal and the physical, cause and effect, honour and a mutilated body. In his exponential performance Antony restages the assassination by rehearsing the principle of the arguments gradually introducing concrete contradictory instances of Caesar's behaviour. Intermittently, for increasingly emotional effect he draws attention to the body in a patterned use of withheld climaxes to wind up the fury of the crowd to its highest pitch. To bring out the references to, and use of, the body, sometimes overlooked because of the fame of the first speech, they are listed below in their emotionally incremental form.

> I come to bury Caesar (l.74)
>
> My heart is in the coffin there with Caesar (l.106)
>
> ... now lies he there (l.119)
>
> ... dead Caesar's wounds (l.132)
>
> Whose daggers have stabb'd Caesar (l.153)
>
> Then make a ring around the corpse of Caesar (l.158)

Look, in this place ran Cassius dagger through;
See what a rent the envious Casca made;
Through this the well-beloved Brutus stabb'd (ll.174–6)

... Look you here,
Here is himself, marr'd as you see, with traitors (ll.196–7)

Even when Antony makes a full disclaimer for his oratorical abilities (a rhetorical ploy in itself), he takes the opportunity to recapitulate the method he has used throughout:

For I have neither wit, nor words, nor worth,
Action, nor utterance, nor the power of speech
To stir men's blood; I only speak right on.
I tell you that which you yourselves do know,
Show you sweet Caesar's wounds, poor, poor, dumb mouths,
And bid them speak for me.

(3.2.221–6)

Antony works on his audience over four main speeches, (ll.73–107; ll.118–60; ll.169–97; ll.210–30), knowing that having chosen to stay in Rome rather than flee to join Octavius, anything but success would mean his arrest and execution for defying the conditions laid down by Brutus. The first part of the opening speech brings to the fore Brutus' honour and Caesar's ambition as unsubstantiated opinions rather than fact. Then Antony reminds his audience not of opinion but the facts of Caesar's service to Rome, the 'captives' and 'ransomes' from conquests by which all have been beneficiaries. Caesar's concrete, physical act of thrice refusing 'a kingly crown', witnessed by thousands, is then measured against ambition. The speech closes with the seemingly distraught Antony directing the crowd to the body of Caesar, 'my heart is in the coffin there with Caesar'. The facts of Caesar's life and death are weighed against a word, that repeated 'honourable' – how could one possibly be commensurate with another is the unstated question.

With the evidence of the crowd taking his side Antony's second speech redirects attention to the body and emotionally heightens the gathering by introducing the idea of 'mutiny and rage' and six times the idea of 'wrong' without once saying that Brutus and Cassius wronged Caesar, though getting as close to it as possible. Then swiftly moving from such unspecified 'wrong' Antony introduces Caesar's will, giving it emphatic concrete force by showing it on stage and describing its discovery.

Holding aloft the will, at the same time as he intimates that again they would be beneficiaries, Antony redirects his audience's attention not just to the body of Caesar, but to the martyrdom of wounds as if Caesar had suffered for his goodness to the people '['the commons'] . . . would go and kiss dead Caesar's wounds / And dip their napkins in his sacred blood' (3.2.132–3). Thus provoking his listeners with Caesar's love and the intention of the will, though withholding its contents, Antony brings together the body of Caesar, the wounds, and honour, in the graphic juxtaposition of the verbal argument and the argument of action.

> I fear I wrong the honourable men
> Whose daggers have stabb'd Caesar
>
> (3.2.151–2)

The latent accusation is now made explicit and Antony knows that the die is cast, he must win. To do so, in his third speech he takes the theatrical element one step further by narrowing the distinction between audience and actor. He descends to the body to share grief and rage with the audience. The whole of the speech directs attention to the specific wounds, playing on the fortuitous fact that Caesar died wearing a mantle worn against the Nervii in one of the most arduous of the Gallic campaigns. Knowing that actions speak louder than words Antony urges audience participation in the examination of each wound, 'Look . . . See', dwelling on Brutus' betrayal and using the word 'treason' for the first time, as his audience weeps, but reserving his *coup de théâtre* for the most emotional climax of all. Having focused his listeners' eyes on the rent vestments of Caesar, he removes the garments to reveal the mangled torso and disfigured face of Caesar, ' . . . Look you here, / Here is himself, marr'd, as you see, with traitors' (ll.196–7). Antony closes the spatial and temporal gap between 'there' (ll.106, 119) and 'here', forcing his audience to become as close as possible actual witnesses of the slaughter. With the response to this it is evident to Antony that the day is his.

The fourth speech is a coda that begins and ends with 'mutiny', which was the precise beginning of Antony's earlier prophecy (3.1.259). He has indeed

> . . . put a tongue
> In every wound of Caesar, that should move
> The stones of Rome to rise and mutiny
>
> (3.2.228–30)

Antony's mastery is such that he hardly needs the will, but he adds it as fuel to the fire, and Caesar's public-spirited magnanimity is revealed. It would be cynical to say that Caesar's seventy-five drachmas outweigh Brutus' endowment of republican virtue. Brutus' compliments offered the crowd the brotherhood of patriotism, but Antony returns to them their real identity in mob power licensed by temporary anarchy, and restores their martyred *pater patriae*.

The aftermath of the assassination brings with it the base actualities of mob violence, political division, civil war and corruption. Such realities have little to do with Brutus' conception of 'Rome' and 'honour'. Act 4 opens with the death sentence being cynically meted out to political rivals and enemies. Antony appropriates Caesar's will to meet the cost of war – so much for the plebeians' inheritance. Later division in the unity of the triumvirate is foreshadowed. Shortly, we hear that a hundred senators have been put to death, including Cicero. Brutus' inept political sense – he would not allow the execution of Antony and permitted him to make his funeral address – now extends to the field of battle. At Philippi he forces a wrong decision on Cassius and the battle is lost. In the world of practical expediency, of compromise and action in the heat of the moment, Brutus has no place. In his quarrel with Cassius (4.3) Brutus cannot see that his charges of minor corruption before a major battle are misplaced. Military unity and morale should come before such divisive moral scrupulousness over officer corps perks and the patronage of seniority.

> *Cassius*   You have condemn'd and noted Lucius Pella
> For taking bribes here of the Sardians;
> Wherein my letters, praying on his side,
> Because I knew the man, was slighted off.
>
> (4.3.2–5)

Cassius' worldly standards cannot see that for Brutus there is only one inflexible criterion for all conduct: Roman honour. Therefore, Brutus '…had rather be a dog, and bay the moon, / Than such a Roman' (4.3.27–8) as Lucius Pella. To condone an instance of corruption cannot for Brutus be anything less than to call in question the validity of their whole enterprise.

> Did not great Julius bleed for justice' sake?
> What villain touch'd his body, that did stab
> And not for justice?
>
> (4.3.19–21)

For Brutus that word 'justice' is absolute and uncompromising. A primary reality inheres in words before things. In his essentialist idealism Brutus assumes that his view of the world, and his language which represents it, is shared by everyone else. Whereas we, the audience, have been made to see the nominalist reality of concrete, particular things – not least actions.[15] Ironically, the only person who uses language in such an absolutist fashion is Caesar, who apotheosises the source of all meaning in his name.[16] 'Caesar' to Caesar is what 'honour' is to Brutus. Otherwise, all around Brutus language is used contingently within a given situation for ulterior purposes, in a Wittgensteinian sense meaning residing in the *function* words and sentences have at any given moment, as Antony well realises. It was not the army of the triumvirate, Caesar's ghost or his own sword that brought Brutus down. Once the unified conception of reality and of meaning founded on the integrity of words and ideas, language and actions, was divided, Brutus' reason was defeated, and his end a matter of time. Strato's judgement, 'For Brutus only overcame himself' (5.5.56), was truer than he could ever know.

8
Antony and Cleopatra

In one of the most distinguished studies of *Antony and Cleopatra* Janet Adelman writes, 'the play consists of a few actions and almost endless discussion of them'.[1] Eventually we have the suicides of Antony and Cleopatra, but the battles of Actium and Alexandria take place off-stage. This leaves the hoisting aloft of Antony to the Monument (4.15) as the most protracted on-stage action which has produced 'endless discussion' by editors and theatre historians: how, exactly, was it carried out?[2] What does it mean? I wish to examine the argument of this action in relation to the many arguments concerning another, future action – Caesar's triumph.

The triumph of Caesar is a representation within a play full of representations deriving from the representation of history, the main source we know as Plutarch's 'Life of Marcus Antonius'. The opening representation of Antony as degenerated from a Mars to an effeminised minion establishes the critically long-familiar analysis of the play in moralistic terms of Roman and Egyptian points of view, the dialectic of discipline and debauchery, reason and sensuality. The dialectic develops in complex ways as the main characters vacillate in reciprocal representations of each other, of an extreme kind, from apotheosis to abasement: Hercules and Isis, drunk and trollop; Venus and Mars, liar and fool. And these representations are found again in the comments of other characters, the two most famous being Enobarbus' *ekphrasis* of Cleopatra 'O'er-picturing... Venus' (2.2.200), on the river Cydnus and Octavius' recollection of Antony 'so like a soldier' (1.4.70), enduring the hardship of military campaign. In a sense nothing escapes representation since we are reminded of actors dressing up as characters: at a crucial point this is emphasised with the line 'Some squeaking Cleopatra [will] boy my greatness' (5.2.220). On the other hand, Shakespeare cannot resist parodying the idea of representation in Antony's account of the crocodile which is neither fabulous beast nor zoological specimen, but 'shap'd...like itself' (2.7.42). A humorous rebuff for Lepidus certainly, but also a proleptic reflection on Antony's travesty of Stoic constancy, 'Here I am Antony, / Yet cannot hold this visible shape' (4.14.14).[3]

Towards the close of the play a dualistic point of view is suggested which we have encountered several times in this study: Maecenas says of Antony, 'His taints and honors / Wag'd equal with him' (5.1.30–1). The *laus–vituperatio*, praise–blame trope of 'taints and honors' recalls that of Prince Hal's words over the dead Hotspur, 'praise' and 'ignominy' (*1 Henry IV*, 5.4.99–100). The dualistic reading of the play as either a critique or celebration of sexuality and romantic love divides into the classical and medieval representations of the story, and romantic and modern responses to the play. On the one hand, Antony is a great figure brought down by lust and Cleopatra the witchlike seductress, on the other, Antony and Cleopatra ultimately realise an apocalyptic transcendence in love. Conventional criticism usually comes down on one side or another, whereas it appears that Shakespeare deliberately chose to emphasise such extremes in order to walk a dramatic tightrope, shifting balance from lust to love, glory to shame, and vice versa. Presumably this is why the dramatist chose to entitle the play *Antony **and** Cleopatra* unlike the Senecan predecessors known to him for whom it was either the tragedy of Antony or Cleopatra, but not both.[4] For the educated part of the audience trained to think on both sides of the question, *in utramque partem*, it is as if Shakespeare provided a work designed to challenge such disjunctive reductionism, since the either/or approach is manifestly inadequate when confronted with the overwhelming richness of such a play. Response to Roman moralism discounts dramatic poetry and response to Cleopatra's poetry discounts the carefully constructed ironies of the drama.

The procedure here will be to re-examine the issues by consideration of argument and action, Caesar's triumph[5] and the hoisting to the monument. Preceding this, it will be argued that Shakespeare's portrayal is partly in reaction to other representations where Caesar's triumph becomes an issue, from Horace to Samuel Daniel's *The Tragedie of Cleopatra*. Finally, the theory of the carnivalesque will provide the means of overcoming the impasse of criticism in Shakespeare's Parthian shot at Caesarism.

For his patron Augustus, after the battle of Actium, Horace celebrates Cleopatra's defeat (*Odes* 1.37), castigating her loathsome gang, yet recognising her steadfastness in resolving on a premeditated suicide to evade the ignominy of being carried off to Caesar's triumph. There is no mention of Antony or any passion, high or low, just the evasion of the triumph. In North's Plutarch, whatever Cleopatra's gifts of mind and beauty, when it comes to her relationship with Antony, 'Thus began this pestilent plague and mischief of Cleopatra's love', and it is consistently seen as 'poison'.[6] Yet when Plutarch gets to the triumph there is a different emphasis. The first mention occurs very late when it is observed that Octavius 'thought that if he could take Cleopatra and bring her alive to Rome, she would marvellously beautify and set out his triumph'.[7] When we get to Cleopatra's consideration of the triumph it is quite different from Shakespeare's. Shakespeare did dramatise Dolabella's warning in Plutarch that Octavius intended to send Cleopatra and her children ahead of him through Syria. Cleopatra then gains access to Antony's tomb on the pretext of offering last oblations. In her long speech to the spirit of Antony a particular distinction is made: 'I am forbidden and kept from tearing and murdering this captive body of mine with blows, which they carefully guard and keep, only to triumph of thee.' What this last phrase means is made clearer immediately after when Cleopatra implores Antony's spirit again: 'suffer not thy true friend and lover to be carried away alive, that in me they triumph of thee.'[8] The speech ends with Cleopatra's avowal that the greatest of all her griefs has been the brief separation from Antony which she will now end in 'one self tombe with thee'. In short, Plutarch's Cleopatra here, her 'poison' seemingly forgotten, wishes to prevent Octavius' use of her to triumph over Antony. We do not find any egotistical motives of her shame at the thought of her ignominy in the triumph. Her death here, in her own terms, is an affirmation of romantic love, in spite of Plutarch's strongly censorious moralism elsewhere.

Though this striking view anticipates some Renaissance Senecan portrayals, it is none the less exceptional. Lucan, on the contrary, in *The Pharsalia*, believed that Cleopatra's charms almost claimed Octavius's heart, 'she nearly headed an Egyptian triumph and led Augustus Caesar a chained captive behind her'.[9] In Shakespeare's play the idea of Cleopatra seeking a liaison with Octavius plagues Antony's imagination. Possibly Shakespeare took the idea from the Roman histories of Lucius Florus where, after Actium, 'The Queene kneeling at the feete of *Caesar*, laid baits for his eyes'. Unsuccessful with this, Cleopatra seeing 'her selfe reserved for triumph'[10] chooses suicide beside Antony: a rather different sequence to that of Plutarch. These two views, of Lucan and of Florus, reappear, respectively, in Petrarch's *Trionfi* and

Boccaccio's *De Claris Mulieribus*. In Lord Morley's sixteenth-century translation of Petrarch, Lucan's surmise is realised:

> Hym that thou seest that so lordly doth go
> And leadeth wyth hym his love also,
> It is the valeaunte Cesar, Julius.
> Wyth him is quene Cleopatra the beutiouse;
> She tryumphes of hym, and that is good righte
> That he that overcame the worlde by myght
> Should hymself over commen be
> By his love, even as thou mayest se.[11]

Needless to say, this is found as part of the triumph of Cupid. In Boccaccio's work, translated as *Concerning Famous Women*, we hear echoes of Florus:

> When Alexandria had been captured, Cleopatra tried in vain with her old wiles to make young Octavian desire her, as she had done with Caesar and Antony. Angry at hearing that she was being reserved for the conqueror's triumph, and without hope of safety, Cleopatra, dressed in royal garments, followed her Antony.[12]

In Chaucer's *Legend of Good Women* Cleopatra dies as a martyr to love, but this medieval view of her death, like that of Plutarch in antiquity, is exceptional. By and large Cleopatra was seen as the cunning and lascivious destroyer of a great man, Antony, whose lust contributed to his fall. Summarising the Elizabethan view, outside the Senecans, of Antony and Cleopatra's career in general, Franklin M. Dickey writes: 'Instead of seeing Antony and Cleopatra as patterns of nobility and of a deathless love, the Elizabethan reader must have seen them as patterns of lust, of cruelty, of prodigality, of drunkenness, of vanity, and, in the end, of despair. Nowhere does an author hint that their love enriched their lives.'[13] Dickey's study, though rather old now, is still cited, but for all his scholarship he overlooked the disjunction in Plutarch's representations, as we have seen, between his view of their lives, and his view of their deaths.

With the advent of Senecan tragedy as a germinal form in Renaissance Europe, we find in Italy, France and England the subject of Antony and Cleopatra taken up by aspiring neoclassical imitators. Shakespeare knew Sir Philip Sidney's sister Mary Herbert, the Countess of Pembroke's translation *The Tragedy of Antonie* (1595) by Robert Garnier, and

Samuel Daniel's *The Tragedy of Cleopatra* (1594) which will be the main focus of attention here, but a brief glance at Octavius' triumph in their predecessors will provide a more precise historical focus. The 'argument' to Cinthio's *Cleopatra* (*c.* 1542), which suggests that Cleopatra's suicide is a direct result of her dread of appearing in Octavius' triumph, is misleading. Though in act 1, scene 1 Cleopatra fears that defeat in battle will result in her being carried to Rome, thereafter it is largely others, not herself, who anticipate the triumph. The nurse imagines her 'in servile yoke / Under the power of Roman women' (3.5); Mecenas, who pleads for her pardon, imagines that 'insane for glory / He'll want her to adorn his Roman triumph' (3.4); Olimpus, her doctor, dwells on 'the anguish she will have to endure / When she is led in bonds to the Capitol' (5.1). In act 5, scene 6 Proculeius relates a waiting lady's account of Cleopatra's death, '"Tis done" she said, "in order to escape / Servitude and deep shame".'[14] However, this is a one-sided view since Cleopatra had decided on suicide and ordered poison on hearing of Antony's death. For all the Stoical pondering on Fortune and excessive passion, the lovers are reunited in death. Yet a qualm remains. Is Cinthio inconsistent, or is he suggesting that others saw more clearly a motive Cleopatra kept from herself? As we shall see, Shakespeare shifted the balance on this issue, making it perfectly clear, yet finally problematising that clarity.

In the structural development of Cesare di Cesari's *Cleopatra* (1552) Octavius' triumph takes on a telling centrality.[15] In act 1 Cleopatra wishes for death to release her from her suffering. Act 2 stresses Octavius' intentions for a Roman triumph. Act 3 confronts Octavius and Cleopatra in their respective pursuit of fame, and fear of shame, in the debate on the triumph. To evade Octavius' victory Cleopatra resolves on death, an action which will simultaneously diminish Octavius' plans for his immortal name and indemnify her suffering and shame with tragic nobility, thereby eclipsing the emperor. The romantic motif is entirely secondary.

The motive for Cleopatra's suicide in Etienne Jodelle's *Cleopatra Captive* (1552) is a matter of some debate. Franklin M. Dickey finds that following the vengeful Antony's summons from hell, Cleopatra 'after trying to deceive Octavius . . . dies to avoid his triumph rather than because Antony has called'.[16] Slightly modifying this, Geoffrey Bullough states, 'Cleopatra still loves him but her suicide is also caused by her fear of servitude'.[17] Contesting these views Marilyn Williamson argues the case that this position rests too singularly on the premise of romantic love creating an either/or situation – to evade triumph, /to join Antony. If, as Williamson insists, the dramatisation here of the Antony and Cleopatra story involves more than love, then the motivation is more complex: 'If Cleopatra is thought of as a queen as well as a lover, quite as Antony is an emperor as well as a lover, the balance of motivation falls into better perspective.'[18] Thus Cleopatra's suicide can be seen as a response to Antony's ghostly plea for an eternal equity in suffering, to atone for the harms she brought him in life. This may be 'balance' of one sort, but equally, of another kind is the fact that she triumphs over Octavius by evading his triumph. There is no evidence that Shakespeare knew Jodelle, whereas it is accepted that he knew Garnier and Daniel.

The prose 'Argument' to Garnier's play concludes of Cleopatra in the monument – 'Which she not daring to open least she should be made a prisoner to the Romaines, and carried in Caesar's triumph, cast downe a cord from an high window ... ',[19] etc. Thus placed this would seem to anticipate the view that Cleopatra's suicide here is more to evade the triumph than to join Antony in death. But as in Cinthio's argument above, this would be misleading. Act 1 opens with a lengthy Senecan soliloquy by Antonius in which he sees himself as betrayed by Cleopatra to Octavius at Actium. While bearing arms still he will resist Octavius' 'triumph', but Cleopatra's 'sweet baites' have 'vanquisht' him in her 'triumph' (ll.28–34). Honour and empire have been betrayed by the 'foule sinke' (l.121) of his passion. And what is more, Antonius believes Cleopatra seeks 'to please' Octavius. Evidently, in this speech we find the staple anti-feminism of antiquity and the Middle Ages.[20]

Then, in act 2, we find not a licentious sorceress, but a dignified noble Cleopatra who is absolute for death. Denying betrayal though accepting responsibility for the flight at Actium, rejecting destiny or the gods' influence, this Cleopatra takes everything upon herself – conspicuously opposite to Antonius who blames everything and everybody but himself. In a purely romantic gesture she declares of Antonius, 'He is my selfe' (l.373), and finally, 'I will die. I will die' (l.651). Not once here is the triumph mentioned. Thus her resolution, it is implied, is to evade the triumph in order to die with Antonius, not to die with Antonius in order to evade the triumph.

When Dircetas, the soldier who takes Antonius' sword to Octavius, describes Cleopatra's entombment, 'For she who feared captive to be made, / And that she should to *Rome* in triumph goe' (ll.1631–2), it provides a Roman perspective, but does not cancel the dramatically emphatic position of Cleopatra we have just heard. In the last act, when Cleopatra approaches the point of suicide, she bemoans not her own fate but what she brought on Antonius. Her servant Euphron, trying to dissuade her, evokes the image of her children as objects of scorn in Octavius' triumph, provoking the reply, 'Never on us, good Gods, such mischiefe send' (l.1829), but this is the merest aside as she builds to an exhausting emotional climax and dies without any asps by some sort of spontaneous evacuation of the spirit.

As with Garnier, the argument to Daniel's *The Tragedie of Cleopatra* (1599) immediately draws attention to the triumphal theme. Octavius 'thought it would bee a great Ornament to his Triumphes, to get her alive to Rome'. In the opening soliloquy Cleopatra reflects on this

> And I, t' adorne their triumphs am reserv'd
> A captive, kept to honour others spoils
> ... That Rome should see my scepter-bearing hands
> Behind me bound, and glory in my teares,
> That I should passe whereas *Octavia* stands,
> To view my miserie that purchas'd hers[21]
>
> (ll.47–8, 67–70)

But in a sense these considerations are ancillary since the burden of her speech is quite remarkable. Hardly mentioning Antony at all, this Cleopatra, unlike the self-sacrificing heroine of Garnier's play, seeks a Stoical re-integration of selfhood. Now stripped of the trappings of greatness, she experiences the possibility of a kind of existential freedom, 'I must die free, / And die my selfe uncaptur'd, and unwonne. / Bloud, Children, Nature, all must pardon me' (ll.92–4). Suicide will bring 'Honour', the Stoic warrantee of authenticity. She and Antony are equally to blame, she insists, thus 'faith and love' will exact an equal penalty from her in suicide. In contrast to the similarity with Jodelle, here it is Cleopatra, not Antony, who provides the motives for action. In this extraordinary speech Cleopatra even goes as far as to admit that in his life she never really loved Antony 'sincerely'. Only now, with his death, is this the case.

In Cleopatra's second soliloquy Daniel in part echoes Plutarch:

> Thou knowest these hands intomb'd thee here of late,
> Free and unforc'd, which now must servile be,
> Reserv'd for bands to grace proud Caesar's state
> Who seekes in me to triumph over thee ...
>
> (ll.1122–5)

That is, she sees herself as being used by Octavius in a triumphal tableau depicting Antony. This is brought out in the following lines where Cleopatra invokes the aid of any available divine powers:

> Do not permit she should in triumph show
> The blush of her reproach, joynd with thy shame:
> But (rather) let that hateful tyrant know,
> That thou and I had powre t'avoyde the same.

(ll.1134–7)

Here Cleopatra chooses death to avoid triumph, but not on her own behalf. As she had insisted on equal blame for their fall, so she insists on eventual mutuality in death to avoid mutuality of shame. Redemptive honour in both cases prevails over romantic love.

The Senecan tragedies considerably enlarged the range of responses to the story of Antony and Cleopatra well beyond the narrow moralism generally found elsewhere. As tragic heroine, statuesque and dignified, the tendency was to idealise Cleopatra in the widest sense – for her to embody the ideals of honour, self-sacrifice and queenliness in the declamatory soliloquies of the Senecan mode, final tragic probity always dramatically indemnifying moral waywardness. This was the dramatic tradition when Shakespeare turned to the subject and provided the most comprehensive and the most challenging series of viewpoints of all.

In *Antony and Cleopatra* Shakespeare carefully patterns the allusions to, and development of, the idea of Octavius' triumph. In act 3, scene 13 Antony has the insolent servant of Octavius whipped, and in an almost subliminal way reveals his real fears:

> and be thou sorry
> To follow Caesar in his triumph, since
> Thou has been whipt for following him.

(ll.135–7)

After the defeat of Actium, Antony blames Cleopatra for the surrender of his fleet and in doing so evokes Octavius' triumph in a particularly graphic way:

> Vanish, or I shall give thee thy deserving,
> And blemish Caesar's triumph. Let him take thee
> And hoist thee up to the shouting plebeians!

Follow his chariot, like the greatest spot
Of all thy sex; most monster-like, be shown
For poor'st diminutives, for dolts, and let
Patient Octavia plough thy visage up
With her prepared nails.

(4.12.32–9)

Cleopatra re-evokes this kind of detail shortly, but before examining this a crucial further instance of Antony's must be noted. After the confrontation Cleopatra retreats to the monument and sends word that she is dead. Antony resolves on death to join her and holds his reluctant servant Eros to his oath that he will carry out his duty and kill him. To persuade Eros, again he reverts to the argument of the triumph:

Would'st thou be window'd in great Rome, and see
Thy master thus with pleach'd arms, bending down
His corrigible neck, his face subdu'd
To penetrative shame; whilst the wheel'd seat
Of fortunate Caesar, drawn before him, branded
His baseness that ensued?

(4.14.72–7)

Consideration of this argument needs careful placing. Ernest Schanzer drew attention to 'the extraordinary likeness, the near-identity of Antony and Cleopatra, in feeling, in imagination, in tastes, in their responses to people and events, and in their modes of expressing these responses'.[22] Ironically, for all the detailed illustration provided, the issue of their responses to Octavius' triumph is not touched on. This is doubly ironic since it would have been the exception to Schanzer's case, if the following argument is allowed. Believing Cleopatra is dead, Antony uses the image of the triumph to persuade Eros to kill him in order to join her. Here the 'news' of her death and his decision is immediate and unequivocal. It will be demonstrated that exactly the reverse is true of Cleopatra in her consideration of the triumph.

Eros kills himself, Antony fails to kill himself outright and with the refusal of others to finish him off, on hearing that Cleopatra is alive, asks to be taken to the monument where he asks for one thing – a last kiss. Evidently, with Antony on the brink of death, the scene is set for a romantic climax of the kind we find in *Romeo and Juliet* and *Othello*.

In *Romeo and Juliet* 'Thus with a kiss I die' (5.3.120). In *Othello* 'I kiss'd thee ere I kill'd thee. No way but this, / Killing myself, to die upon a kiss' (5.2.358–9). Garnier's Cleopatra indeed dies upon a thousand kisses, closing the tragedy, 'A thousand kisses, thousand thousand more / Let you my mouth for honors farewell give'. And Daniel's Cleopatra, determining on death, uses an expression Shakespeare borrowed for Othello, or at least an expression used by the Nuncio in relating her death, '... she knew there was no way / But this' (ll.1551–2). Yet instead of the romantic *liebestod*, Shakespeare's Cleopatra refuses to descend from the monument and we hear:

> I dare not, dear –
> Dear my lord, pardon – I dare not,
> Lest I be taken. Not th' imperious show
> Of the full-fortun'd Caesar ever shall
> Be brooch'd with me, if knife, drugs, serpents have
> Edge, sting, or operation. I am safe:
> Your wife Octavia, with her modest eyes
> And still conclusion, shall acquire no honor
> Demuring upon me.
>
> (4.15.21–9)

As we have just seen, Antony evoked the triumph in order to join Cleopatra in death, she now evokes the triumph to keep her distance from the dying Antony. '*I* dare not, / Lest *I* be taken ... *I* am safe'. Cleopatra's immediate priorities are quite clear. Her security first, love a poor second, since she accepts the chance that Antony might die before he can be hauled up the side of the monument, which is in marked contrast to the Cleopatras of the Senecans. Shakespeare's Cleopatra had decided to haul Antony up, knowing he was near death, even before his request. This element of calculation jarrs somewhat with the poetry of Cleopatra's invocation on seeing the dying Antony, 'O sun, / Burn the great sphere thou mov'st in! darkling stand / The varying shore o' th' world!' (4.15.9–11).

In Garnier's play Antony does not request a kiss and is hauled up the monument by Cleopatra and others. However, Dircetas relates the story, reported Senecan action again, and in doing so provides a rhetorical *ekphrasis*, or heightened verbal picture-painting, very expressive of the pathos of the scene. Shakespeare's argument of action has the audience witness the scene on stage and there are sufficient verbal cues to warrant direction which would bring out the burlesque elements of this physically awkward feat of staging.[23] Shakespeare's language stresses the weight:

> Here's sport indeed! How heavy weighs my lord!
> Our strength is all gone into heaviness,
> That makes the weight.
>
> (4.15.32–4)

First, Antony fails to kill himself, and then Cleopatra has evident difficulty hoisting him up the monument. This incipient burlesque is brought out by the almost comic references which immediately follow the preceding quote:

> Had I great Juno's power,
> The strong-wing'd Mercury should fetch thee up,
> And set thee by Jove's side.
>
> (4.15.34–6)

But Cleopatra debunks the allusions herself, 'Wishers were ever fools' (4.15.37), she says. Commentators have suggested that the action here ironically recalls Cleopatra's earlier remarks on fishing

> my bended hook shall pierce
> Their slimy jaws; and as I draw them up,
> I'll think them every one an Antony,
> And say 'Ah, ha! Y'are caught'.
>
> (2.5.12–15)

The argument of action which demonstrates the disparity between love language and the motive for action (or inaction) takes on an emblematic overlay here. Garnier recalls the commonplace:

> Like as the cunning fisher takes the fishe
> By traitor baite whereby the hooke is hid:
> So *Pleasure* serves to vice in steede of foode
> To baite our soules thereon too liquorishe.
>
> (ll.1176–9)

An English example would be Wyatt's 'Farewell, Love, and all thy laws forever. / Thy baited hooks shall tangle me no more'. A graphic example, in every sense, is the literalised portrait of female beauty in *The Extravagant Shepherd* (1654) where, as well as literal roses in the cheeks and suns as eyes, no less than ten fishing rods baited with hearts, spring out from netted coils of hair.[24]

In the same scene, with Antony's demise Cleopatra certainly thinks on death, but yet again, with the entry of Proculeius and the soldiers, her mind turns to the triumph:

> Know, sir that I
> Will not wait pinion'd at your master's court,
> Nor once be chastis'd with the sober eye
> Of dull Octavia. Shall they hoist me up,
> And show me to the shouting varlotry
> Of censuring Rome?
>
> (5.2.52–7)

With Dolabella's entry we have one of the most sustained poetic passages in which Cleopatra celebrates Antony in relating her dream of him as a transcendental Colossus, Jupiter and cosmic king beyond all conceptions of imagination, nature and art. For the Renaissance dreams could be either visionary or delusive. Yet if we allow this sublimity, evidently beneath it is the question to which Cleopatra knows the answer, and she gives voice to both, 'Know you what Caesar means to do with me? . . . He'll lead me then in triumph?' (5.2, 106, 109). At the beginning of act 5 Octavius spelt this out to Proculeius, and Dolabella now confirms it for Cleopatra.

It would be timely here to introduce a further, complicating factor. When did Cleopatra order the asps? After her interview with Octavius in act 5, where Shakespeare uses the details in Plutarch concerning the trick to persuade him that her withholding of jewels indicates an intention to live, Cleopatra sends Charmian off-stage to check on the asps. If they were ordered *before* Antony's death then it would indicate that her suicide was planned solely to evade Octavius' triumph. In Plutarch Cleopatra is something of an expert on the effects of different poisons. At the close this appears in Shakespeare as 'her physician tells me / She hath pursu'd conclusions infinite / Of easy ways to die' (5.2.354–6). Her earlier words in the monument when she spoke of 'knife, drugs' and 'serpents' having 'Edge, sting, or operation' (4.15.25–6) showed that after defeat in the sea battle she anticipated suicide as the only way to evade Octavius' triumph. Presumably either she decided on the asps immediately after this, or had ordered them already, taking the precaution of further means, knife and drugs, just in case – in fact, when she is seized in the monument she is only just prevented from stabbing herself (5.2.39).

When Dolabella confirms Octavius' intention to send Cleopatra and her children through Syria three days before him, note again what is primary and what is secondary in her mind when left alone with her servants. In fact, at this point Cleopatra's evocation of the triumph is the most thoroughgoing in the play as a whole. Addressing Iras she begins:

> Thou, an Egyptian puppet, shall be shown
> In Rome as well as I. Mechanic slaves
> With greasy aprons, rules, and hammers shall
> Uplift us to the view. In their thick breaths,
> Rank of gross diet, shall we be encluded,
> And forc'd to drink their vapor.
>   ... Saucy lictors
> Will catch at us like strumpets, and scald rhymers
> Ballad's out a' tune. The quick comedians
> Extemporally will stage us, and present
> Our Alexandrian revels: Antony
> Shall be brought drunken forth, and I shall see
> Some squeaking Cleopatra boy my greatness
> I' th' posture of a whore.
>
>   (5.2.208–13, 15–22)

Only then does Cleopatra turn her attention to the dead Antony. She imagines joining him in mutual contempt for Octavius, receives the bite of the asps, and realises that if Iras gets to Antony first it might be her rather than she who receives his kiss, which is somewhat ironic since that is just what she had denied Antony at the base of the monument. This dialectical irony, found throughout the play, continues in act 5, pre-empting unalloyed recognition of romantic transcendence or reintegrated Stoic selfhood. The boy actor of Cleopatra, having just reminded the audience of that fact, claims 'I am marble-constant' after again acknowledging, 'I have nothing / Of women in me' (5.2.238–40). Inconstancy is the anti-feminist stereotype, just as Cleopatra's claim 'I am fire, and air' (5.2.289) recalls the opposite stereotype, women as cold and wet and thus 'changeable, deceptive, and [of a] tricky temperament'.[25] Yet the paradox remains that neither detached scepticism nor neoplatonic affirmation seem adequate or appropriate to the mixed modes of the play.[26]

The mixed mode is primarily dualistic, the much discussed Roman and Alexandrian points of view, but a significant dimension is added to Shakespeare's argument with history in the reversal of his source: this may be called the Parthian view. In Plutarch's 'Life' many pages are taken up with Antony and the protracted Parthian campaign, whereas in the play it is reduced to just a few mentions and the brief thirty-eight-line scene of act 3, scene 1. Why did Shakespeare bother to include it at all many seem to have asked, since a study of acting editions of the play shows that of thirty-six texts, thirty-four omitted this scene.[27] Unlike Jodelle, who included material making plain that Antony's Parthian defeat derived from his eagerness to be with Cleopatra for the winter, Shakespeare chose to include the basis for the discussion between Antony's lieutenants, Ventidius and Silius, while leaving out facts which would directly controvert what is said. Generally speaking, Shakespeare chose to emphasise Antony's ultimate disgrace at Actium. We hear of something like Antony's early campaigning in Octavius's eulogy (1.4.56–71), but only in one remark is Antony's extensive engagement in the Parthian campaign after Ventidius' victory referred to. This is when Eros answers Antony's charge that he kill him:

> The gods withhold me!
> Shall I do that which all the Parthian darts,
> Though enemy, lost aim and could not?

> (4.14.69–71)

Elsewhere, fleetingly, Shakespeare presents Antony as peripheral and disengaged from the actual fighting, merely delegating from afar. Yet in this we are made aware of the magnitude of the merest aside on which the fate of legions spread throughout Asia minor depend. The messenger of act 1, scene 2 brings news not just of Fulvia's wars, but, to Antony's confessed shame, of Labienus who ' ... hath with his Parthian force / Extended Asia' (ll.100–1). In the scene where marriage with Octavia brings temporary reconciliation, Antony enters with Ventidius in the midst of, again, peripheral negotiations, 'if we compose well here, to Parthia' (2.2.15), which are finalised in the following scene, 'You must to Parthia. Your commission's ready' (2.3.42).

In act 3, scene 1, Ventidius enters *as it were in triumph* with the body of Pacorus the son of Orodes, King of the Parthians, slain in revenge for the death of Marcus Crassus. This scene of thirty-seven lines largely consists of Ventidius' reply to Silius' congratulations which anticipates that

> ... thy grand captain, Antony,
> Shall set thee on triumphant chariots, and
> Put garlands on thy head.
>
> (3.1.9–11)

Ventidius' argument in reply gives another meaning to discretion as the better part of valour. That is, too great a success by a junior officer, in completely routing the Parthians, could put his commander's nose out of joint. One reputation would inevitably challenge the other. Thus it is actually best to achieve less. In his letters to Antony, Ventidius will stress how it was 'in his name ... with his banners, and his well-paid ranks' (ll.30, 32) that victory was won. In Plutarch not only do we find extensive details of Antony's fighting the Parthians in person, at the same time as Ventidius, but when he hears of his lieutenant's victory he acts in an altogether different fashion from that suggested by Shakespeare's Ventidius. The grounds for Ventidius' apprehension about too great a victory are certainly there in Plutarch, yet when the Parthian campaign is (temporarily) finished, we find that Antony 'having given Ventidius such honours as he deserved, he sent him to Rome, to triumph for the Parthians. Ventidius was the only man that ever triumphed of the Parthians until this present day.'[28] Obviously, Shakespeare left this out because it went directly against what he wished to use the material for, namely, 'Caesar and Antony have ever won / More in their officer than person' (3.1.16–17).

Shakespeare's reshaping of this Parthian argument offers a corrective readjustment in the middle of the play, midway between the dramatised worlds of Rome and Alexandria, and the principals therein. The Parthian scene gains immediate point in the structural contrast with the preceding scene of the triumvirs' Bacchic boozing on Pompey's galley (2.7). Earlier, Pompey had referred to the triumvirs as 'Chief factors for the gods' (2.6.10) and, when a servant carries out the drunken Lepidus Enobarbus, remarks, ''A bears the third part of the world, man; seest not?' (2.7.90). Genial derision here but decorous solemnity (and a greater portion) for the dead Antony, in whose 'name lay / A moi'ty of the world' (5.1.18–19). Pompey's galley scene offers a travesty of this imperial aggrandisement in the reality of the world dependent on the power and judgement of three men, one slightly drunk, one habitually drunk and the third in a state of drunken collapse, all oblivious to their near assassination. In the following scene of Ventidius and Silius we have an inverse reality of the power behind the 'name' with the anonymous legions in the theatre of war. Shakespeare's argument by selection and scenic juxtaposition is very marked here since Plutarch records several times how, on campaign, Antony shared all hardships, comforted the sick and wounded, and was dearly loved by his troops: this is just hinted at in the play as an implicit reminder of his decline (see 4.2.10–23). Another point of view implicit throughout, rather than explicit like the foregoing, which offers a subversive synthesis of the Rome/Alexandria dichotomy, is that of the carnivalesque.[29]

The carnivalesque in *Antony and Cleopatra* has several elements which combine to burlesque Roman power and authority. Excess of food, drink and sex in the 'rioting' (2.2.72) of 'lascivious wassails' (1.4.56), 'Egyptian bacchanals' (2.7.104) and 'Alexandrian revels' (5.2.218), emphasise the carnival body which is symbolised in the frequently observed identification of Cleopatra's sexuality with the fecundity of the Nile: Cleopatra embodies the carnival renewal of Nature.[30] The carnivalesque mode formally inheres in the generic struggle between tragedy and comedy, the comic uncrowning of the high reduced to low when emperor and queen dress down as slave and maid to go slumming in Alexandria.[31] In the eyes of Rome greatness is made familiar and ridiculous.[32] Cleopatra envisages depiction of those 'Alexandrian revels' on a triumphal carriage or adjacent *tableau vivant*. As Antony and Cleopatra had displayed their triumph in love, so Octavius will re-display it in kind. The conduct of Antony and Cleopatra offered to any onlooker, patrician or plebeian, slave or burgess, a counter-triumph of Mars and Venus, Hercules and Isis. And in doing so they burlesqued the power and authority they were supposed to embody. To decline from a moral standard is one thing but to collapse it in laughter is another. Rome cannot be laughed at so Octavius's triumph will turn the tables.

Antony and Cleopatra's conduct in their metaphorical counter-triumph of love, re-enacted before the populace, offered a burlesque of regal power. From this point of view, Cleopatra's crown was always 'awry'. After envisaging all the splendours of 'the barge she sat in' (2.2.191ff) speech, we hear of Cleopatra hopping 'forty paces through the public street' (2.2.229). Moments after claiming 'We stand up peerless' (1.1.40) Antony plans an egalitarian outing, 'Tonight we'll wander through the streets and note / The qualities of people' (l.l.53–4). The play *Antony and Cleopatra* re-enacts this irony every time it is played before the populace. Plutarch several times refers to the populist element in their display. As a matter of fact at one stage he remarks that their 'foolish sports' were so many that he will limit himself to two stories. One is the angling incident which Shakespeare used (Cleopatra has a salted fish surreptiously placed on Antony's fishing line, 2.5.15–18), the other is as follows:

> And sometime also when [Antonius] would go up and down the city disguised like a slave in the night, and would peer into poor men's windows and their shops, and scold and brawl with them within the house, Cleopatra would be also in a chambermaid's array, and amble up and down the streets with him, so that / often times Antonius bare away both mocks and blows.[33]

Plutarch's note on the Alexandrians' response to this japery is highly significant for the argument here concerning carnivalisation of genre:

> ...the Alexandrians were commonly glad of this jollity and like it well, saying very gallantly and wisely that Antonius showed them a comical face, to wit, a merry countenance; and the Romans a tragical face, to say, a grim look.[34]

Shakespeare carefully leaves out the fact that Antony was a dissolute reveller long before he met Cleopatra, implying that his conduct derives solely from his infatuation. Octavius records his drunken populism: 'To reel the streets at noon, and stand the buffet / With knaves that smells of sweat' (1.4.20–1). Antony himself claims after victory that were the palace big enough 'To camp this host', 'we all would sup together' (4.8.33). Octavius is horrified by precisely this egalitarian populist element, 'publicly enthron'd' in Alexandria. Maecenas, aghast, asks 'This in the pubic eye?', to which Octavius answers, 'I' th' common show-place, where they exercise' (3.6.5, 11–12). Cleopatra is Isis, Thetis, Venus, and so on, but she also knows that she is 'No more but e'en a women' (4.15.73). The lovers' passion is both exclusive and inclusive, earthy and poetic, patrician and plebeian, and thus its potential carnivalesque anarchism.

The counter-triumph of Antony and Cleopatra's love is completed in death but in a rather complex way which alters Cleopatra's motivation, subsumes the carnivalesque within the theatrical, and finally transmutes comedy to tragedy: the triumph of Antony and Cleopatra is the triumph of a squeaking boy.[35] In Cleopatra's reference to the Roman boy actor Shakespeare destabilises illusion by exposing his Jacobean counterpart, the boy actor of the queen, to the contemporary audience. But instead of conceding comedy, which the metatheatrical moment anticipates, an uncompromising reversal takes place as the boy dresses for the tragic finale. Shakespeare now, in effect, reveals the tiring house as the actor is robed, as Enobarbus recalled, 'o'erpicturing Venus' on Cydnus to meet Antony.[36] After the interlude of the clown's comic insistence on the feminine, actor and audience are mutually absorbed in the complexity of performance, willing the transformation and rein-statement of the tragic boy–queen–goddess, subsuming irony in the absoluteness of death. Greatness made familiar and ridiculous is now reversed as the actor's virtuosity reinvests queenly beauty and godlike magnificence. The final meeting will be in the theatre of the mind for each member of the audience as art triumphs over history. Caesar's tri-umph, Plutarch tells us, 'carried Cleopatra's image with an aspic biting of her arm',[37] whereas each member of Shakespeare's audience carries away the paradox of an incarnation that becomes transcendent, the image of the boy becoming queen to unite with Antony not ultimately to evade the triumph, but to join in mockery of the 'ass / unpolicied' (5.2.307–8), for ''Tis paltry to be Caesar' (5.2.2).

9
Coriolanus

Action and argument in *Coriolanus* culminate in the Roman hero's march on Rome and Volumnia's plea to her son, which saves the city. The assault on the *patria* is in direct contrast to the action of Coriolanus virtually singlehandedly capturing the city of Corioles, from which he gained his honorific name-attribute.[1] In one action he is apparently a traitor and betrayer of the civic and martial honour of the patrician leadership class, in the other he fulfils the ideal of the self-sacrificing hero-patriot offering his life in war on behalf of his country. Here we have the contrast of a seemingly realised ideal brought into question by the reversal of a paradoxical reality.

The play begins with a reality of another order, the class friction between the patricians and the plebeians, reflected in a specific historical argument concerning politics and economics at the beginning of the Roman Republic.[2] Plutarch records two disturbances, first the plebeian revolt against state-sponsored usury: second, the protest against the dearth of corn and the high prices charged for what little there was.[3] Shakespeare gives pre-eminence to the latter, but combines it with the former in the addition of a line: the First Citizen protests that the patricians 'make edicts for usury, to support usurers' (1.1.81–2). This remark follows Menenius' explanation that the patricians, the 'fathers', have only 'charitable care' and it is the gods in fact who have created the famine, not them (1.1.65–78). Unfortunately, Menenius undermines his argument in several ways. If we at least attribute to the gods of what Coriolanus accuses the plebeians, 'It is a purpos'd thing' (3.1.38), then its intention appears to be to profit the patricians at the expense of plebeian starvation. This is made even more emphatic by Menenius' argument paralleling the heavens and the state:

> For your wants,
> Your suffering in this dearth, you may as well
> Strike at the heaven with your staves as lift them
> Against the Roman state, whose course will on
> The way it takes, cracking ten thousand curbs
> Of more strong link asunder than can ever
> Appear in your impediment.
>
> (1.1.66–72)

Coriolanus in effect repeats this identification of religion and state: 'You cry against the noble Senate, who / Under the gods keep you in awe' (1.1.186–7). Coriolanus' language recalls the scepticism of such figures as Polybius, Machiavelli and Marlowe.[4] A sceptical response to such a view was available to early modern England in Cicero's *De legibus* where he recognises the mutual self-interest of state and religion whereby a priesthood drawn from the patrician class administered to the superstitious needs of the lower orders.[5] A radical though unobtrusive aspect of Shakespeare's presentation of the plebeians here, as Brecht noted, is that in their response to Menenius they ignore the religious dimension and directly attribute the dearth to patrician hoarding of grain, promotion of usury and the repealing and creation of statutes to consolidate their domination (1.1.79–86).[6]

Menenius' immediate argument in defence is 'a pretty tale', the famous fable of the belly taken from Plutarch and Livy. The corporate state is figured as the body politic with rebellious 'members' accusing the idle belly of hoarding. Initially, the plebeians are sharply sceptical but appear to be won over since, eventually, Menenius claims that 'these are almost thoroughly persuaded' (1.1.201). Such a claim is almost laughable since Shakespeare's presentation of the argument is both deliberately unconvincing and deconstructive. Menenius argues through the belly's speech that its function is to distribute food to the body (1.1.130–46). The analogy with the 'senators of Rome' (l.147) and the plebeians is then spelt out. Such a parallel rather glaringly brings home the fact that this is just what the senators are not doing. The plebeians are being starved by them, not nourished. Furthermore, Shakespeare adds a subversive element to his sources by elaborating on the analogy; 'I am the store-house and the shop / Of the whole body' (ll.133–4) says the belly, who continues the commercial image with:

> Yet I can make my audit up, that all
> From me do back receive the flour of all,
> And leave me but the bran.

> (1.1.144–6)

The concrete economic and social reality of 'store-house', 'shop' and 'audit', and the corn-grinding production process of 'flour' and 'bran', associate the civic authorities with the grain merchants, the *frumenta-tores*, who are profiteering, which implies the mutual activity of the landowning classes, the merchants and the distributors, in the patron–client network beginning with the patricians in the senate.[7] The patron-ising ventriloquial state speaks through its representative, Menenius, but the argument reveals what it intends to conceal. Eventually, the state will speak again through the 'belly', the womb of Volumnia, when the voice of patrician ideology overwhelms its opponent.[8]

The voice of Comenius in his encomium on Coriolanus as victor at Corioles gives perfect expression to what is otherwise deeply problematic in the play, the correlation, the decorum, between words and deeds. Comenius' celebration of martial valour gives honorific expression to the ideology of the Roman state driven to feed itself by the conquest and pacification of client-state suppliers of grain. Both in Comenius' speech and in the immediate action of the play Coriolanus' valour is foremost, but the economic objectives of the politics of Roman war are just hinted at before and after the battle: 'The Volsces have much corn' (1.1.249), Coriolanus observes. When Aufidius expostulates at the 'con-dition' upon which Corioles will be handed back, 'What good condi-tion can a treaty find / I' th' part that is at mercy?' (1.10.6–7), he then throws in a final reference to the 'city mills' (1.10.31). Editors point out that this alludes to the London corn mills built beside the Globe theatre after 1588, but in the play they will presumably be part of that Roman 'condition'.

Robert S. Miola details the way in which Comenius' panegyric closely conforms to the specifications of epideictic oratory as laid down in such a well-used handbook as the *Rhetorica ad Herennium* (usually attributed to Cicero) and in Quintilian's *Institutes of the Orator*.[9] The speaker acknowledges the challenge to match words with deeds, 'I shall lack voice: the deeds of Coriolanus / Should not be utter'd feebly' (2.2.82–3).

Immediate consensus may be established by celebrating what is common to the hero and society, the worship of valour 'the chiefest virtue' (2.2.84) which Plutarch celebrated at the opening of his *Life* of Coriolanus:

> Now in those days valiantness was honoured in
> Rome above all other virtues; which they call *virtus*,
> by the name of virtue itself, as including in that
> general name all other special virtues besides.[10]

A summary of deeds follows, the 'statement of facts' particularly bringing out any disadvantage that was overcome. The fact that Coriolanus fought against the last tyrant king, Tarquin, when just a boy of sixteen fits the bill exactly (2.2.87–99). Finally, Coriolanus' repudiation of spoil points to admirable selflessness. What he did he did for Rome.

A further general point needs to be added to Miola's account. The twin ideals of ancient Rome were valour and eloquence. Eloquence gave expression to the God-given gift of reason, which differentiated man from beast. Valour, deriving largely from hand-to-hand combat, derived from the near-bestial barbarism of slaughter, repeatedly emphasised in the play, for example when Coriolanus appears, completely covered in blood 'as he were flea'd' (1.6.22), as if he were flayed like a skinned beast. The assumption of the essential reason of man has to rationalise the horrors of war by converting the bloody reality of deeds into the language of fame and glory, the panegyrical voice of the state which sublimates dehumanisation with heroism. Coriolanus' personal integrity in Shakespeare's portrayal derives from his impulse to reject words and to insist on the self-validation of deeds. When Comenius delivers his encomium, Coriolanus cannot listen, and he leaves – 'When blows have made me stay, I fled from words' (2.2.72), he says. His tragedy is that he cannot finally flee from Volumnia's words which expose the most fatal wound of all – feeling.

It is often claimed that Coriolanus is inarticulate, in direct contrast to Plutarch's attribution of an 'eloquent tongue' to him,[11] but the characteristics and limitation of his speech and arguments arise from two quite different situations – arguing with his mother and arguing with the plebeians.[12] The former is a special case which will be confronted, as it must, with Volumnia's plea at the gates of Rome. Elsewhere, Coriolanus' aristocratic contempt for all things plebeian leads to a choleric disdain for any discussion or argument with them. But when amongst his noble peers, the senators and patricians (*'all the* GENTRY', 3.1.OSD) and goaded by the tribunes Sicinius and Brutus, his arguments are powerful and protracted enough (3.1.62–170) to risk arrest by the aediles. Though vehement, Coriolanus is graphically articulate. He attacks the immediate political issues of the creation of the tribunate; the danger of free corn distribution; the debasement of the senate, and so on, but there is one basic premise that underpins all his arguments as an unconditional absolute – the superiority of the patrician class. The nature of its exclusiveness emerges a little later in the confrontation, following Sicinius's provocative question, 'What is the city but the people?' and the plebeians' reply, 'The people are the city' (3.1.198–9). Sicinius' question is in answer to the First Senator's fear that rebellion would 'unbuild the city and lay all flat' (3.1.197). Brockbank notes the probability that the tribune twists an allusion to a legal maxim to his own advantage, 'A city and town differ in this, that the inhabitants are called the city, but the town comprises the building'. For 'people' read plebeians, i.e. the majority.[13]

Coriolanus' reply to this, linking Rome, people and buildings, sharply bursts out just before his exit:

> I would they were barbarians, as they are,
> Though in Rome litter'd: not Romans, as they are not,
> Though calved i' th' porch o' th' Capitol!

> (3.1.237–9)

In Coriolanus' words (the exact opposite of Brutus' and Mark Antony's appeals to the plebeians at the Forum in *Julius Caesar*) there is an absolute difference in kind not just degree. The plebeians are virtually animals, 'litter'd', whereas the patricians are near-gods, like the victorious Coriolanus of whom Brutus grudgingly admits, 'As if that whatsoever god who leads him / Were slyly crept into his human powers' (2.1.219–20).

At times Coriolanus conceives of himself as above the gods, for example when Menenius urges him to 'Repent what you have spoke' (3.2.37), his insults to the plebeians. Coriolanus replies, 'For them? I cannot do it to the gods' (3.2.38). This draws a much discussed comment from Volumnia which begins her argument to persuade Coriolanus on the necessity of compromise, in terms of honour and policy:

> You are too absolute,
> Though therein you can never be too noble,
> But when extremities speak. I have heard you say
> Honor and policy, like unsever'd friends,

> I' th' war do grow together; grant that, and tell me
> In peace what each of them by th' other lose
> That they combine not there.

(3.2.39–45)

One of the problems editors discuss here is the seeming contradiction of lines 40–1: uncompromising nobility seems to be praised, then it is recognised that extreme situations necessitate compromise. The issue is furthered by the fact that heretofore Volumnia herself has been totally uncompromising in the upbringing of her son and, in addition, the combination of honour and policy she recalls Coriolanus recommending is nowhere found in the play or in Plutarch.[14] However, perhaps contradiction is more apparent than real. The glimpses we have had of Volumnia's stern education are always of a military kind. Circumstances have changed and the military victor is now in reach of a consulship, the highest civic position in the republic. In part the 'too absolute' refers immediately to Coriolanus' refusal of deference before the gods. Furthermore, the claim concerning honour and policy in war is perfectly acceptable when we recall that a military manoeuvre designed to mislead the enemy is a commonplace tactic of strategy: it is hardly dishonourable. However, the ideological complexity of honour and policy in the cultural contexts of ethics and action in the early modern period can be rather more involved than this as the following incident, taken from the invaluable work of Mervyn James, shows.

Riding north in October 1536 to put down the Pilgrimage of Grace, the Duke of Norfolk felt it prudent to write to his master, Henry VIII, 'I beseech you to take in good part what so ever promise I shall make unto the rebels...for surely I shall observe no part thereof for any respect of that what other might call honour distained'; 'thinking and reputing', he added, 'that none oath nor promise made for policy to serve you mine only master and sovereign can distain me'.[15] As servant of Henry, Norfolk's personal honour, giving his word, is subsumed by that of the king's. With the growing centralisation of honour under the Tudor regime, the state prevails over the individual.

Volumnia continues her argument by going to the heart of the matter – the relationship of honour to one's word.[16] She urges Coriolanus to address the plebeians,

> not by your own instruction,
> Nor by th' matter which your heart prompts you,

> But with such words that are but roted in
> Your tongue, though but bastards, and syllables
> Of no allowance, to your bosom's truth.
>
> (3.2.53–7)

Volumnia claims that this would no more dishonour Coriolanus than to capture a town in siege warfare by 'gentle words' (3.2.59) rather than force of arms.[17] This argument raises a further complication, the issue of intention in relation to honour. Before examining this, in contrast let us turn to another incident in the Pilgrimage of Grace in James's study. Lord Darcy, captain of the royal castle of Pontefract, surrendered to the rebel leader Robert Aske in 1536, subsequently appearing to join with him. When asked by a royal herald about his honour and the possibility of seizing Aske and killing him, or delivering him to the king, Darcy replied that it would be lawful for the herald, 'but not for me, for he that promiseth to be true to one, and deceiveth him, may be called a traitor, for what is a man but his promise?' This statement was used as evidence towards his execution. Darcy, like Coriolanus, was 'too absolute': his personal honour is primary but not private since in situations where a solemn oath, promise or word is given it is made public. This consideration was beyond the Duke of Norfolk with whom policy prevails over honour.

Coriolanus' situation is not quite the same. His speech to the plebeians does not necessarily involve a promise or an oath of honour, and the plebeians were by definition outside the aristocratic community of honour. If, however, whatever Coriolanus says is quite unrelated to what he feels there would be no dishonour since he is not betraying his intention. Moreover, in honour transactions it is recognised that '[t]he moral commitment to tell the truth derives ... from the social commitment to persons to whom it is due'.[18] Thus the discourse of honour allows a casuistic situation to arise in which a person can be both a man of honour and a liar: even more casuistically, a lie could not be considered as impugning a man's honour unless it were exposed in public accusation by a peer.

Ironically, Coriolanus' integrity is so absolute he has completely internalised the discourse and code of honour severing the link between selfhood and society, honour thereby becoming an existential rather than a social modality. Thus when Volumnia reminds her son of the public dimension, 'I am in this / Your wife, your son, these senators, the nobles' (3.2.64–5) it must fail since for Coriolanus a lie would be not to the plebeians but to himself: 'Must I / With my base tongue give to my noble heart / A lie that it must bear?' (3.2.99–101). When, momentarily, he imagines self-betrayal, it strengthens his resolve: 'I will not do't, / Lest I surcease to honor mine own truth' (3.2.120–1). Even though he seemingly is prepared to comply with Volumnia's persuasion that 'Action is eloquence' (3.2.76), what follows is inevitable. Autarkic narcissism responds to the sentence of banishment not with a lament on the loss of the *patria*, the fatherland, but with 'I banish you!' (3.3.123).

Volumnia is called upon to put her own principles into practice in her plea to Coriolanus at the gates of Rome. Here we have the most protracted sequence of argument and action at the climax of the whole play: action in the sense of the gestures of the suppliants and an action which eloquence must dissuade Coriolanus from, the sack of Rome. With the entry of Volumnia, Virgilia, Valeria and Coriolanus' young son, accompanying the verbal argument are a number of visual signs and gestures which realize action as eloquence. The nobles are poorly dressed (5.3.94–5); we have Virgilia's 'curtsy' (l.27), Volumnia's bow (l.29), young Martius's appealing 'aspect' (l.32), the kiss with Virgilia (l.44), the kneeling of Volumnia (l.56) and Martius (l.75). Finally, they all kneel to 'shame' Coriolanus (l.169) and reinforce the verbal argument.

Volumnia's argument gives voice to the centralising ideology of the Roman state, patriotism, but she knows that she cannot make this appeal directly since the former saviour of his country is about to become the conqueror of Rome.[19] In seeking revenge Coriolanus has betrayed the ideals of Rome in war and peace. These ideals were congenial to the centralising Tudor state, and schoolboys like Shakespeare at Stratford Grammar school absorbed them at an early age in Cicero's *Offices*, commonly in the translation by Nicholas Grimald of 1556.[20] The core concepts of Cicero's civic ethics outlined here from a few works are found throughout his writings and were absorbed by humanist education into the commonplace thought of Tudor England.[21]

As T.W. Baldwin demonstrates, the schoolboy at Stratford would have come across these passages:

> But if question, or comparison be made, to whome the greatest dutie ought to be yeelded: our countrie, and parents be the chief, by whose benefites we ar moste bounde: our children, and all our holle familie be the next: which hang al vpon vs alone, and can haue none other refuge: then be our kinsfolke, that agree well with vs: which commonlie stand in the like estate.[22]

ther be degrees of duties ... the first ... be due to the godds immor-
tall: the seconde, to our countrie: the third, to our parents[23]

What if ones father will go aboute to vsurpe, as a tyrant, or to betray
his countrie: shall the sonne conceale it? Nay he shall desire his
father, not to doo it: if he nothing preuaile, he shall blame him, and
threaten him also. And last of all, if the mater tend to the destruction
of his countrie: he shall preferre the safetie of his countrie before the
safetie of his father.[24]

Grimald is faithful to Cicero's Latin in the last clause – *patriae salutem
anteponet saluti patris* – but the Loeb translator prefers to bring out the
implication of that *anteponet* ('place before'): 'he will sacrifice his father
to the safety of his country'.[25] Conversely, we find in *De finibus* that
'praise is owed to one who dies for the commonwealth, because it
becomes us to love our country more than ourselves'.[26] *Patria* in Cicero
is variously translated as 'country', 'native country', 'fatherland' and
'state'. Country and native country are distinguished in *De legibus*
where the translator prefers the word fatherland:

so we consider both the place where we were born our fatherland,
and also the city into which we have been adopted. But that fatherland must stand first in our affection in which the name of republic
signifies the common citizenship of us all. For her it is our duty to
die, to her to give ourselves entirely, to place on her altar, and, as it
were, to dedicate to her service, all that we possess. But the fatherland which was our parent is not much less dear to us than the one
which adopted us. Thus I shall never deny that my fatherland is
here, though my other fatherland is greater and includes this
within it.[27]

In passing, note here how the translation brings out the gender anomaly
of *patria* as a substantive which takes the feminine case: the fatherland
appears to incorporate the female.[28] Reserved until last is probably the
most repeated pronouncement of Cicero on the *patria*, recalling Plato,
as much of his thought is characterised by the influence of the Greek,
Panaetius of Rhodes: 'man was not born for self alone, but for country
and for kindred'.[29]

So the Ciceronian order of duties is towards gods, country, parents,
family and kindred at the cost of self-sacrifice or sacrifice of others in
extreme circumstances. As we see in Sir John Hayward, Tudor England

converted Ciceronian republicanism to monarchist absolutism by placing the *pater patriae* before the *patria*:

> But our country is dearer unto us then our parentes, and the prince is *pater patriae*, the father of our country, and therefore more sacred and deere unto us then our parentes by nature, and must not be violated, how imperious, how impious soever hee bee.[30]

Cicero's duties receive a considerable emphasis in Volumnia's argument, both directly and indirectly, as indeed they have been stressed throughout the play. Annabel Patterson notes that the word 'power' is found more times in *Coriolanus* than in any other play, often connoting, she argues, a structural political usage which anticipates radical developments in the seventeenth century.[31] 'Power' needs to be linked with 'country' and the 'gods', the ideological state apparatus of the republic which permeates the play.[32] The word 'country' occurs many more times (37) in *Coriolanus* than in *Julius Caesar* (6), or *Antony and Cleopatra* (3), and more times than in any other of Shakespeare's plays. Volumnia's plea draws very closely on North's Plutarch, where 'country' occurs nine times: in her argument (5.3.94–186) we find seven occurrences. The Ciceronian values may be found on virtually every page of the play and in one place particularly they are grouped together – in Comenius' attempt to defend Coriolanus against the sentence of banishment. Comenius is not allowed to get very far, but in beginning his argument with a presentation of *ethos*, the speaker's credentials, we hear:

> I have been consul and do show for Rome
> Her enemies marks upon me. I do love
> My country's good with a respect more tender,
> More holy and profound, than mine own life,
> My dear wives' estimate, her womb's increase
> And treasure of my loins; then if I would
> Speak that –

> (3.3.110–16)

Here the *patria* which has been served ('service' is another crucial term in the play) both in war and peace, is placed before life and family. The respect, the Roman *pietas*, for the *patria* is 'holy': pieties towards gods and country are identified.

Upon the entry of the supplicants Coriolanus finds, in Ciceronian terms, standing before him parent (Volumnia), family (wife and son) and kindred (Virgilia). With their gestures, outlined above, his resistance vacillates – 'out, affection', 'I melt', 'I'll never / Be such a gosling to obey instinct' (5.3.24, 28, 34–5) – and he then resolves to 'stand / As if a man were author of himself, / And knew no other kin' (5.3.35–7). The content of Volumnia's argument is found in the source, but not this last-quoted remark of Coriolanus. In North's Plutarch Volumnia does argue that if the resolution she suggests is accepted, 'thyself is the only author', but this meaning of 'author' is quite different from that of Shakespeare's text where the phrase 'author of himself' means 'self-begotten'. Shakespeare's expression reads like a conscious rejoinder to the commonplace from De finibus, quoted above, 'man was not born for self alone, but for country and for kindred' (*non sibi se soli natum meminerit sed patriae, sed suis*) which functions as an anticipatory prologue to Volumnia's argument. I conjecture that when Shakespeare studied Volumnia's speech in Plutarch he recognised the Ciceronian categories and alluded to the one which was missing and was so relevant to Coriolanus. As critics have observed, that word 'alone' is almost an epithet for the choleric antagonist.[33] Shakespeare thus heightened the conflict between Roman altruism and Greek autarky, the self-sufficiency which resists pity that Cicero had rejected.[34]

The consciousness of Ciceronian ethics is then brought out as *pietas*, if not pity, overcomes Coriolanus in the 'deep duty' (5.3.51) to a parent, as he kneels. To indicate the paradox of such an act, given the overall situation, Volumnia reverses Ciceronian decorum in the priority of duties:

> I kneel before thee, and unproperly
> Show duty as mistaken all this while
> Between the child and parent
>
> (5.3.54–6)

However, Volumnia's acknowledgement that she and the others are there as 'suitors' (5.3.78) on behalf of Rome makes Coriolanus insist on the intransigence of his action and allegiance, and he preempts her argument with, 'desire not / T' allay my rages and revenges with / Your colder reasons' (5.3.54–6). Volumnia's argument is hardly 'cold': she begins emotionally with an appeal to the pathetic spectacle they present and immediately reemphasises duties and relationship, graphically introducing the first reference to the *patria*, 'tearing... / His country's bowels out' (5.3.102–3). Then by way of a dilemma she introduces the first duty, to the gods. She and the women cannot offer 'prayers to the gods' (5.3.105) both for their country and for Coriolanus' victory. The Roman sense of fatherland is then shifted to the feminine, 'The country, our dear nurse...' (6.3.110). The relationship between the country and the feminine is repeated with a punitive emphasis:

> thou shalt no sooner
> March to assault thy country than to tread
> (Trust to't, thou shalt not) on thy mother's womb
> That brought thee to this world.

> (5.3.122–5)

The syntax of North's Plutarch is clearer: 'thou shalt no sooner march forward to assault thy country but thy foot shall tread upon thy mother's womb, that brought thee first into this world'.[35] The body politic has become a feminine body. Volumnia's imagery combines maternity and barbarity, the process of motherhood and the practice of rape and slaughter in war.

Coriolanus' reply partly reflects this feminity, 'Not of a woman's tenderness to be' (5.3.129). Earlier, Coriolanus has easily dismissed Menenius' appeals to him as 'son' from a 'father' (5.2.70–1) because the father to him is the abstract state at war, not a person of feelings and affection. Volumnia then shifts her ground by offering a solution to a dilemma from Coriolanus' point of view. How can he act for both the Volsces and the Romans and preserve his honour? The giving and receiving of mercy will reconcile both. To reinforce this position Shakespeare continues with an argument from Plutarch:

> ... but this [is] certain,
> That, if thou conquer Rome, the benefit
> Which thou shalt thereby reap is such a name
> Whose repetition will be dogg'd with curses;
> Whose chronicle thus writ: 'The man was noble,
> But with his last attempt he wip'd it out,
> Destroy'd his country, and his name remains
> To th' ensuing age abhorr'd.'

> (5.3.141–8)

Ethically and politically this point is rather obvious, but Coriolanus seems somewhat stunned by it since he cannot bring himself to reply: 'Speak to me, son...Why dost not speak?' (5.3.148, 153). Still Coriolanus cannot bring himself to answer. Always 'too absolute', has Coriolanus' pride become so obsessed with the wrong done him by Rome that he simply has not grasped the wrong he does himself, his name, by marching on Rome? Volumnia, consciously reserving her most powerful weapon until the last, then resorts to the emotional appeal of weeping, kneeling and asserting her recriminating motherhood: 'There's no man in the world / More bound to 's mother . . . Thou hast never in thy life / Show'd thy dear mother any courtesy . . . thou restrain'st from me the duty which / To a mother's part belongs' (5.3.158–9, 160–1, 167–8). Coriolanus is defenceless before emotion and feeling disarms him. The joint appeal to fame and affections destroys Coriolanus because they are incompatible, as Volumnia well knows. Her life-long tutelage has ensured that kindness, compassion and pity were expunged from Coriolanus' upbringing.

Modern criticism inevitably focuses on Volumnia and Coriolanus in terms of feminism and gender theory. Indeed, it is difficult now, when considering such a work, to imagine the limitation of any approach without the insights into the politics of sexuality provided by these approaches. Janet Adelman refines new criticism's discussion of imagery[36] by correlating the idea of starvation and maternal deprivation with a psychoanalytic approach which sees eating as signalling oral vulnerability and need. Volumnia's deprivation creates heroic masculinity in the form of Coriolanus' phallic aggression.[37] For Adelman, Volumnia's failure to feed is the centre of the play's concern with the starving condition of the plebeians. Three quotations are essential for her argument: Volumnia's 'Anger's my meat; I sup upon myself, / And so shall starve with feeding' (4.2.50–1); the claim to her son, 'Thy valiantness was mine, thou suck'st it from me' (3.2.129); and Menenius' remark that 'there is no more mercy in [Coriolanus] than there is milk in a male tiger' (5.4.26–7). The conflation of literal and metaphorical in an argument that rests on a vulnerable methodology (not quite 'how many children had Lady Macbeth?' but 'how often did Volumnia feed her baby?') seems questionable, yet the direction taken is fitting for such perverse psychology.

In another psychoanalytical approach, drawing on pre-oedipal object-relations theory, Madelon Sprengnether sees the Freudian patriarchal theory of ascendant masculinity as permanently threatened by the primary bond with the mother.[38] This for Sprengnether is what is found in the relationship of Volumnia and Coriolanus, in which the hero flees from femininity to the warrior ethos of masculinity pursued by the fantasy of annihilating female omnipotence that tragically complements his own self-destructiveness.

In considering these gender approaches Lisa Lowe makes an important distinction. Whereas Adelman had seen the failure of mothering as causal, Lowe sees Roman patriarchy as the fundamental shaping power. That is, the issue of gender, femininity and Volumnia needs to be linked to the political situation of the city.[39] Lowe's own argument then rather back-tracks from this position by pursuing the conflict between public and private identity: the social, political and ideological is subsumed by the psychological. Lowe's point may be redirected to the historicised ideological context of ethical and political discourse I have begun above. Commentators always quote Volumnia's revelatory account of her education of Coriolanus since it offers a basis for understanding both character and society. I follow suit.

Volumnia took the place of Coriolanus' dead father, suppressing the feminine in herself and her son to instil in the youth the masculine Roman military virtues of strength, asceticism and hardihood, joined with the skills of weaponry and patrician leadership. Coriolanus' childhood is epitomised in the recollection prompted by young Martius' behaviour in tearing apart a butterfly – 'One on 's father's moods' (1.3.66). Roman manhood is valour, victory in conquest, killing rather than being killed, which Coriolanus fulfilled encouraged by Volumnia: 'I tell thee, daughter, I sprang not more in joy at first hearing he was a man-child than now in first seeing he had prov'd himself a man' (1.3.15–17). As a consequence, the procreative experience of love and generation undergoes a transvaluation and reversal. Glorious death in war and posthumous reputation would be like a growing child, 'Then his good report should have been my son; I therein would have found issue' (1.3.20–1). Then, in a quotation central to most arguments on the play, grotesquely the suckling of an infant is compared to wounds in war:

> The breasts of Hecuba
> When she did suckle Hector, look'd not lovelier
> Than Hector's forehead when it spit forth blood
> At Grecian sword contemning.

> (1.3.40–3)

Affection, tenderness and nurture are specifically seen in terms of their reverse, 'Thy valiantness was mine, thou suck'st it from me' (3.2.129).[40] In sum, the formation of Coriolanus' being derives from a division of masculine and feminine (note how Virgilia's part is downplayed) inimical to each other in circumstances of war. Comenius unwittingly rehearses this in his account of the sixteen-year-old Caius Martius' defeat of Tarquin. Girl-like with 'Amazonian chin', he overcame the enemy:

> When he might act the woman in the scene,
> He prov'd best man i' th' field . . .
> . . . His pupil age
> Man-ent'red thus

(2.2.96–9)

The masculinity and femininity which Sprengnether discusses in the abstract terms of oedipal and pre-oedipal theory are deeply inscribed within classical and humanist culture, within the mind of Coriolanus as a boy, and eventually in the wounds of his body. Volumnia's empowering accommodation of femininity and masculinity completely overwhelms the all-masculine warrior. I have outlined above Ciceronian patriarchalism and patriotism with their dominant male modes. Let us now consider further the gender implications of Volumnia's appeal in her argument for the country as nurse and womb. The early modern use of nurse always signifies the wet-nurse suckling a baby. Thus nurse and womb connote the symbolic centres of female sexuality and motherhood. Critics commonly regard Volumnia as symbolic of Rome itself. Adelman, for example, says 'Coriolanus turns his rage towards his own feeding mother, Rome', '[f]or Rome and his mother are finally one'.[41] The *patria* and gender have been touched on, attention to Rome and femininity is revealing.

The mythological origin of Rome is a source of gender contention. The name Rome is commonly attributed to Romulus but the feminine figure of Roma is a close second. Roma, the presiding goddess of the city, was worshipped from early times and is linked to two other mythological Roma figures: the female Trojan who advised fellow captives to burn the Greek fleet and escape to Italy: the daughter of Italus and Lucania – in some traditions said to be the wife of Aeneas or Ascanius. In sixteenth-century English 'Rome' and 'room' were homophones ('Now is it Rome indeed and room enough', *Julius Caesar*, 1.2.156), therefore it would appear that Roma was pronounced *ruma*, the old Latin word (collateral with *rumis*) for the suckling breast.[42] Rumia, Rumilia or Rumina were the various names deriving from *ruma*, for the Roman goddess of nursing mothers. She was worshipped in a separate temple, where milk not wine was offered as a libation, near the fig tree (*ficus ruminalis*[43]) under which Romulus and Remus had sucked the breast (*rumis*) of the she-wolf.[44] These details are found in one of the most well known of Renaissance reference works, Carolus Stephanus' (Charles Estienne's) *Dictionarium Historicum, Geographicum, Poeticum*.[45]

This information lends a greater complexity to the function of gender in Volumnia's argument before Coriolanus. 'The country, our dear nurse' is both metaphorical and mythological, invoking the breast of the she-wolf and the breast of Roma, the greater *patria*. The controlling strategy of Volumnia's argument is to move from the masculine to the feminine (Coriolanus' response of five 'mothers' [5.3.182–93] surpasses Volumnia's four [5.3.159–78]). The ventiloquial voice of the patriarchal state speaks through Volumnia, just as the male actor speaks through the female part. Earlier, in response to Sicinius' 'Are you mankind?', Volumnia replies 'was not a man my father?' (4.2.16, 18). Cicero's *Offices*, as we have seen, affirmed that for the *patria* the son would sacrifice his father. Here the mother sacrifices her son, fulfilling Menenius'

> Now the gods forbid
> That our renowned Rome, whose gratitude
> Towards her deserved children is enroll'd
> In Jove's own book, like an unnatural dam
> Should now eat up her own!
>
> (3.1.288–92)

In order to achieve her end Volumnia has to revive the one spark of humanity she didn't smother in his youth. As Coriolanus' actions realised the image of the bloody breast in the Hecuba–Hector speech (1.3.40–3), 'I have ... [d]rawn tuns of blood out of thy country's breast' (4.5.98–9), so the argument of Volumnia–Roma–ruma will exact a blood sacrifice on her nurse's breast.

The sadomasochistic transvaluation of love and war reaches its homoerotic conclusion in Aufidius' slaughter of Coriolanus.[46] Whatever emphasis a director may bring to the short scene of Volumnia's triumphal entry as 'patroness, the life of Rome' (5.5.1), past productions indicate the inevitability of her recognition of what she has done.[47] Yet in another sense she had killed her son long before, as the anecdote of young Martius killing a butterfly in 'One on 's father's moods' (1.3.66) indicates. The Greek word *psyche* is the same for butterfly and the soul. Volumnia's regimen killed the soul. Consequently, Coriolanus became a deathly reification ('a thing of blood', 2.2.109), an accumulation of public attributes – fame, glory, reputation – which must be renewed by action. 'He was a kind of nothing, titleless' (5.1.13), Comenius reports, but the greater truth is that he is a kind of nothing, warless. And that kind of nothing is, in the existential terms of Sartre's early philosophy, his facticity. Bred for war, Coriolanus' being is coextensive with the external public image. He has no soul, he is a hollow reflector of Roman *virtus*. It is this that he fulfils, he cannot do otherwise, in response to Volumnia's reminder of the ultimate facticity of 'chronicle thus writ', the fixity of history. Coriolanus knows that he goes to his death amid the Volsces ('But let it come', 5.3.189), and here Shakespeare added a detail not found in Plutarch. The hero reverts to historicity, re-enacting the past, to confirm his facticity forever:

> Cut me to pieces, Volsces, men and lads,
> Stain all your edges on me . . .
> If you have writ your anuals true, 'tis there
> That, like a eagle in a dove-cote, I
> Flutter'd your Volscians in Corioles.

> (5.6.111–15)

Following Volumnia's argument occurs possibly the most quietly powerful of all Shakespeare's arguments of action when Coriolanus *holds her by the hand, silent* (5.3.182.1). 'O mother, mother!' he asks, 'What have you done?' (5.3.182–3). Understanding, as Shakespeare understood, the vital dramatic relationship between words and actions, that 'Action is eloquence', Volumnia knows what she has done. To save Rome Volumnia sacrifices her son, using motherhood to ensure the continuance of the fatherland, 'the Roman state, whose course will on / The way it takes' (1.1.69–70).

10
Troilus and Cressida

Homer's story of the fall of Troy always provoked polarised responses from those believing that an initial ambivalence derives from the poet himself, with such things as the less than godly behaviour of the gods and the seemingly mock-heroic similes,[1] to those who believed the Greek epics to be a source of wisdom and nobility. Even the wrath of Achilles could be converted from autarkic bloodlust to exemplary virtue, as it is found in de Sponde's Latin version, the source for Chapman's Homer.[2] Yet Chapman was also the translator of the primary text of mock-Homeric burlesque which survived from antiquity, the *Batrachomyomachia*, 'The Battle of the Frogs and Mice'. The most commonly cited view of the Greeks in early modern English culture is probably that of T.J.B. Spencer which presents the inherited Latin derogatory bias of the Greek as unscrupulous, dissipated and perfidious.[3] The author's own bias is apparent here with just a one-line aside on Chapman and nothing at all on the didactic cast of mind when confronted with the epic, as in Sir Philip Sidney:

> For as the image of each action styrreth and instructeth the mind, so the loftie image of such Worthies, most inflameth the mind with desire to be worthy, and informes with counsel how to be worthy.[4]

For the chivalric hero of the battle of Zutphen, Achilles embodied heroism and valour,[5] not the wrath and lust which were also part of the ambivalent inheritance.[6]

The chivalric versions of the Homeric narrative found in Shakespeare's principal sources for the siege of Troy, Caxton and Lydgate (with Chaucer as the primary source for the Troilus and Cressida romance), derived from the accounts of supposed eyewitnesses, Dares and Dictys. Both were antipathetic to Homeric heroism but Dictys was anti-Trojan and Dares, in reply, was anti-Greek, and thus another polarity was introduced into the tradition.[7]

In Robert Kimbrough's view, Caxton's *The Recuyell of the Histories of Troye* 'is a compilation of all the various attitudes toward and accounts of the fall of Troy',[8] favouring neither Greeks nor Trojans. There was, however, a separate ideological tradition fostered by nationalist chronicle which propounded the view (paralleled on the continent) that Brutus the fleeing Trojan was the founder of London which he called Troynovant. Such claims are found in the mythology of kingship given expression in royalist pageantry, such as King James' procession through the triumphal arches erected for his royal entry of 1604.[9] As a member of the retitled King's Men, Shakespeare and his colleagues were given new liveries to parade behind their royal patron. Another royalist endorsement of the heroic view of the Troy legend was that depicted in art on monumental tapestries, 'Large and imposing', their 'dignified presentation' 'recounts the tale ... with a sense of immensity and often of grandeur'.[10]

Grandeur of another kind was evoked in Chapman's Homer. Since Robert K. Presson's study, the striking fact that Shakespeare's choice of Homeric materials concerning the siege of Troy corresponds to that of Chapman's *Seaven Bookes of the Iliades* (1598) has been accepted as indicating a primary source the heroic tenor of which is subverted in *Troilus and Cressida*.[11] Focusing on Achilles, Richard S. Ide summarises: 'This is neither a Homeric nor a Renaissance Achilles Chapman is creating ... Achilles, who has tempered his wrath and sheathed his sword ... emerges from Chapman's translation as a wise and temperate man of honor, indeed, a patriotic defender of the public good',[12] and he emerges from Chapman's dedication as no other than the Earl of Essex, a somewhat ironic exemplar of contemporary Ciceronian civic virtue. From these introductory details we can see that the history of Homeric representation follows a dialectical pattern of praise and censure, both synchronic and diachronic, and Chapman and Shakespeare represent the extremes of *laus* and *vituperatio*.[13]

In *Troilus and Cressida*, more than in any other play, Shakespeare formalises both verbal argument and the argument of action. In doing so he structures the play around the complementary dramatic modalities of seeing and hearing and at the same time emphasises the former in a consistent metadramatic fashion. In this the play may be related dramaturgicallly to *Julius Caesar*, but here Shakespeare chose to stress much more thoroughgoingly the overlapping elements of stage identification and audience engagement. The actors are frequently made to ask elementary questions on behalf of an audience which knew the story and the names, but could not identify persons. The theatre could provide a specificity and life not possible in printed words: Nestor, for example, says of Hector, 'thy countenance ... I never saw till now' (4.5.195–6). Words heard and deeds seen are kept apart until the final dénouement of betrayal and slaughter when, indeed, 'The present eye praises the present object' (3.3.180).

The debates of the Greeks (1.2) and Trojans (2.2) are amongst the most extensive in Shakespeare's work and have always drawn critical attention in terms of the play's concern with love and war, as well as the question of their dramatic feasibility given their length and static nature. This is commonly accompanied by close attention to the all-pervasive reductive food imagery. This textual emphasis, though initially valuable, ultimately serves to discount the complementary dimension made apparent in performance, the visual, by which the actors of the Greeks and Trojans reconstruct the literary sources to re-invest, review and finally deconstruct their own mythic status.[14]

The intellectual nature of political, ethical and philosophical debate in a play thought to be originally staged for an Inns of Court audience of lawyers has led to the view of *Troilus and Cressida* as a play of ideas when, in fact, this is only half the drama.[15] The testimony of ideas is subjected to the evidence of action which is witnessed by the metajuristic audience. Consider, at the centre of the play, the much discussed argument of Ulysses persuading Achilles to re-establish his valorous reputation as a warrior. The sequence begins, more or less, with Ulysses' entry reading from a book, 'A strange fellow here / Writes me that man ... ' (3.3.95–6) and culminates in 'The present eye praises the present object' (3.3.180). The general context for the argument, as will be shown, is the play as a whole, no less, but the immediate context begins shortly before with Ulysses' stratagem to rouse Achilles from his egoistic lethargy. He instructs Agammemnon, Nestor and Ajax to 'pass strangely' (l.39) by Achilles to give him a taste of his own medicine, or in Ulysses' words 'derision medicinable' (l.44). Their behaviour will duplicate Achilles' demeanour. Ulysses introduces a familiar emblem, ' ... pride hath no other glass / To show itself but pride' (ll.47–8). Ironically, the narcissistic self-love of such pride is here 'mirrored' by others' aloofness, not by Achilles' self-reflexive egoism, which was usually mirrored by their former deference – 'They were us'd to bend, / To send their smiles before them to Achilles' (ll.71–2).

In his consideration of this event Shakespeare has Achilles continue the visual motif.

> ...What the declin'd is
> He shall as soon read in the eyes of others
> As feel in his own fall;
>
> (ll.76–8)

Following Achilles' speech Ulysses enters reading a volume coincidentally concerned with what 'a strange fellow' writes about, the necessity of external confirmation by others of an individual's virtues 'by reflection' (l.99). Achilles develops the argument, taking up the analogy of beauty. Beauty cannot see itself, but is seen by others. This is developed further by the example of 'the eye itself' (l.105) which can see itself only by reflection in another eye. Characteristically, Achilles' narcissism leads him to interpret Ulysses' metaphorical language literally in terms of the visual, presumably his own 'beauty'. Then by rhetorical amplification he reinforces his point by landing on a well worn commonplace of Renaissance literature.

> The beauty that is borne here in the face
> The bearer knows not, but commends itself
> To others' eyes; nor doth the eye itself,
> That most pure spirit of sense, behold itself,
> Not going from itself; but eye to eye opposed,
> Salutes each other with each other's form;
>
> (ll.103–8)

This has led to much editorial and critical comment. The Variorum editor discusses the nineteenth-century attribution to the *First Alcibiades* of Plato, which would make Socrates the 'strange fellow'. In Jowett's translation the passage develops the eye seeing itself reflected in the pupil of another eye as an analogy for self-knowledge, the soul looking into itself.[16] The analogy is perhaps not a just one since it seems to confuse reflection and introspection. However, commentators have suggested a more general source in commonplace books; have pointed out that only Achilles' reply is actually Platonic; have suggested Cicero's *Tusculan Disputations* as an alternative source; have suggested Montaigne's Stoic belief that man's virtues increase when shared.[17] Such critical debate is justified to a great extent since the compounded notions of mirror, sight, insight, self-knowledge and reflection permeate western culture, as Herbert Grabes has shown in his richly documented study, *The Mutable Glass*.[18] Before commenting on this we need to point up the relevant allusions in Ulysses' continuing argument.

Ulysses expands by rephrasing his earlier redaction of his author's argument. The scope of abilities and accomplishments are realised only in sharing them with others, dropping in a slight theatrical metaphor, 'Till he behold them form'd in th' applause / Where th'are extended' (ll.119–20), adding analogies of sound and heat. Then to rile Achilles he finds an example:

> . . . I was much rapt in this,
> And apprehended here immediately
> Th' unknown Ajax.

> (ll.123–5)

Achilles, bemused and affronted by the Grecian lords' behaviour, acknowledges Ulysses' argument, lamenting 'What, are my deeds forgot?' (l.144). In an elaborate reply Ulysses develops the notion that past deeds are forgotten, continuing unrivalled valour must be seen to be the case in the present.[19] This paraphrase is provided to hasten to the crucial quotation which Ulysses offers as summary, 'The present eye praises the present object' (l.180). As such it ties in with the visual allusions and would thus lend itself to the aforementioned debates of editors and critics. But this would be mistaken. However engrossing, this approach is very misleading for, in view of the total context of the play, not just the immediate context of this argument, this line and all the visual references have an ironic metadramatic function.

In 'The present eye praises the present object', predicate mirrors subject in a punning metadramatic joke with a serious purpose: 'present' here is spatial as well as temporal, the 'present eye' is the audience, while the 'present object' is the play itself, *Troilus and Cressida*: Shakespeare holding a mirror up to the ambivalances of a 'Tortive and errant' (1.3.9) legend. In Shakespeare's day 'praise' as an aphetic form was more often used than 'appraise'.[20] The Greeks may praise Ajax, but the theatre audience appraises the whole play, an appraisal determined by the relationship between argument and action, debate and deed, intellectual stasis and physical movement, 'Since things in motion sooner catch the eye / Than what stirs not' (3.3.183–4). Throughout the play 'things in motion' are mostly actors impersonating the warriors of antiquity, the incarnation of myth, but these superhuman descendants of gods are re-identified in terms of the mortal, fallible and corruptible, in great contrast to Nestor's recollection of Hector as 'Jupiter . . . yonder, dealing life!' (4.5.191).

On stage encounter and identification duplicate that of audience experience. Interrogatives, like those of Cressida's first lines, 'Who were those went by?' (1.2.1), 'Who comes here?' (1.2.37), permeate the play entirely. Indeed act 1, scene 2 suggests a paradigm for the whole work. Pandarus' 'Do you know a man if you see him?' (1.2.63–4) is a challenge for the audience as well as Cressida in its proleptic irony of vision and knowledge. In Pandarus' promotion of Troilus, with the procession of warriors returning from the battlefield, Shakespeare's metadramatic reconstruction gets under way. In Sam Mendes' 1990 production at the Pit theatre in the Barbican London, Pandarus and Cressida took up a vantage point *behind* the actual theatre audience thereby directly aligning the experience of character and auditor. The dramatic procedure here is quite different from Chaucer's poetic narrative. In the poet only Troilus is specified, on the return, 'With that came he and all his folk anoon . . . Lo, Troilus . . . with his tenthe som yfere'.[21] Shakespeare deliberately uses here and throughout the play a kind of stage version of slow motion. Here verbal confirmation of each identity slows down the actual appearance of each warrior – Aeneas, Antenor, Hector, Paris, Helenus and Troilus succeeded by the collective anonymity of the 'common soldiers', 'Asses, fools, dolts! chaff and bran' (1.2.241). The duplication of actual appearance and verbal reminder is at its most metadramatically emphatic with Hector; 'look you . . . look how he looks . . . Look you what hacks . . . Look you yonder, do you see? Look you there . . .' The burlesque possibilities inherent in the contrasts between reality and myth are heightened by Cressida's cue line for the portrayal of Troilus at this point, 'What sneaking fellow comes yonder?' (1.2.226). The world of Homeric magnitude implodes on that one word, 'sneaking'. Again, at this point Shakespeare applies the same slow motion technique as with Hector:

> Mark him, note him. O brave Troilus! Look well upon him, niece, look you how his sword is bloodied, and his helm more hacked than Hector's, and how he looks, and how he goes!
>
> (1.2.231–4)

A verbal statement clashes with a visual manifestation. For Cressida, as we have seen, Troilus is 'a sneaking fellow', for Pandarus Troilus is 'the prince of chivalry' (1.2.229), a view undercut by the opening scene in which Shakespeare invokes the commonplace incompatibility of Mars and

Venus, love and war. If the director takes his cue from Cressida, then we have a rather blunt contradiction between what is seen and what is heard.

This incongruity recurs in the Greek camp, after the debate, with Aeneas' arrival as herald seeking Agamemnon. Confronting the unknowing Aeneas and the Greek leader, Shakespeare with great deliberation delays identification, thereby simultaneously giving us the physical presence of Agamemnon on stage and Aeneas' verbal evocation. First we hear of 'great Agamemnon' and 'his kingly eyes' (1.3.216, 219); then 'those most imperial looks' (1.3.224); then 'that god in office ... the high and mighty Agamemnon' (1.3.231–2). Given the critical, anti-heroic tenor of the play, presumably the part of Agamemnon was originally given to one of the shorter members of the company, thus giving Aeneas' words a more than slight touch of comic absurdity in their misplaced inflation. At the end of the immediately preceding debate of the Greek council, Ulysses had spelt out with extensive detail Patroclus' mocking 'pageant' of Agamemnon and Nestor for the benefit of his sole auditor, Achilles. Here we find a triple mirror effect, Patroclus' performance for Achilles and Ulysses' verbal rendition for his two audiences, onstage and in the auditorium.

Similarly, in this play of mirrors the pageant is replicated by inversion in Thersites' 'pageant of Ajax' (3.3.272–99). The pageant is enacted on stage by Thersites, not narrated, and Ajax not the senior counsellors is its object, yet again with Achilles a chief auditor. The irony over and above the immediate burlesque is that the whole play as it unfolds develops into a mock 'pageant of Troy'. When Troilus too readily assures Cressida that 'in all Cupid's pageant there is prescribed no monster' (3.2.74–5) we have no need to point to the monstrousness of Spenser's depiction of Cupid's pageant in *The Faerie Queene* (III.xii, stanzas 7–25). In reply to Cressida's question, 'Nor nothing monstrous neither?' (3.2.76), we know that the answer is a resounding, proleptic 'Yes!'

As the returning Trojans had undergone re-identification for Cressida, and the audience, so conversely after his mock-battle with Ajax, on Achilles' invitation, Hector identifies the Greeks. Anticipating Nestor, Achilles wishes

> To see great Hector in his weeds of peace,
> To talk with him, and to behold his visage,
> Even to my full of view.

(3.3.239–41)

Note here how Achilles' meaning – to see Hector without his armour and helmet – has a triple visual emphasis ('To see ... to behold ... view').

Such verbal overstatement and redundance actually serves to call into question the status it affirms. What is the reality of such 'sight' when the last-quoted line so perfectly expresses Achilles' altruistic egoism, seeing himself seen seeing Hector who is a reflector of *his* greatness?

When Hector agrees to be feasted by the Grecians we have a scene mirroring that of act 1, scene 2 when Pandarus named the Trojans for Cressida. Hector asks Ajax, 'The worthiest of them tell me name by name' (4.5.159). Agamemnon and Menelaus are greeted and then, in Nestor's words, note the specific visual build-up to the line already quoted.

> I have ... seen thee oft, ... I have seen thee, ...
> I have seen thee ... This have I seen,
> But this thy countenance, still lock'd in steel,
> I never saw till now.
>
> (4.5.183–96)

Nestor in fact rehearses the audience's imaginative experience as readers of poetry while Shakespeare removes the helmet to show us the man beneath the panoply of chivalry, an image crucial for the argument of action. As an analogy with film, slow motion was suggested above, it is tempting in this scene to see Shakespeare as experimentally focusing the verbal and the visual in a fashion that suggests the close-up of the cinema. To demonstrate this it is necessary to quote a substantial sequence (4.5.231–43).

Achil	...Now, Hector, I have fed mine eyes on thee;
	I have with exact view perus'd thee, Hector,
	And quoted joint by joint.
Hect	Is this Achilles?
Achil	I am Achilles.
Hect	Stand fair, I pray thee, let me look on thee.
Achil	Behold thy fill.
Hect	Nay, I have done already.
Achil	Thou art too brief. I will the second time,
	As I would buy thee, view thee limb by limb.
Hect	O, like a book of sport, thou'lt read me o'er;
	But there's more in me than thou understand'st.
	Why dost thou so oppress me with thine eye?
Achil	Tell me, you heavens, in which part of his body
	Shall I destroy him – whether there, or there, or there? –

In this confrontation seeing is turned into an action, the act of seeing, which is made performative by finally rehearsing the act of slaughter as the audience is directed by this verbal lense to the limbs of Hector. The technique of proleptic delay prepares the ground for the argument of action thereby making the contrasts between word and eventual action all the greater.

'But there's more in me than thou understand'st', Hector says, sounding a note that is implicit in the manifold references to sight. Analogous to Hector's protest that there is more to him than Achilles sees is the challenge to the audience to ensure that they understand what they see. This has been rehearsed on stage earlier. Alexander, Cressida's servant, gives a derisory account of Ajax, which culminates in the description, 'a purblind Argus, all eyes and no sight' (1.2.29–30). The meaning of this becomes apparent when we meet the 'blockish' hero who, in his own eyes, is fully conscious of his public status, yet has no self-knowledge at all. This is pressed home by Thersites in another passage exemplary for the play as a whole.

> *Ther*   You see him there? Do you?
> *Achil*   Ay, what's the matter?
> *Ther*   Nay, look upon him.
> *Achil*   So I do. What's the matter?
> *Ther*   Nay, but regard him well.
> *Achil*   Well? why, so I do.
> *Ther*   But yet you look not well upon him, for
> whomsoever you take him to be, he is Ajax.
> *Achil*   I know that, fool.
> *Ther*   Ay, but that fool knows not himself.
>
> (2.1.57–66)

Thersites deliberately extends on the situation until he gets the locution he particularly wants in order to provide a comment, 'that fool', for Ajax, which barely conceals an equal contempt he can suggest, as 'a privileg'd man' (2.3.57), to the audience – 'as well as this fool', that is Achilles himself. (Compare the whole sequence 'what's Achilles?...' 2.3.45–68).

Thersites' phraseology, 'knows not himself', brings to the fore the question of self-knowledge in relation to public identity. In Renaissance terms *nosce te ipsum*, 'know thyself', was an injunction sufficiently difficult to have produced a counter-commonplace, here from the fifteenth-century *Ayenbite of Inwyt*, 'Pride blinds men so that they do not know or see themselves'.[22] 'Blind oblivion' may indeed have 'swallow'd . . . up' the city of Troy, as Cressida surmises (3.2.187), but the actions of the warriors survived in story and became inscribed in the human imagination in various ways. With Shakespeare's radical scepticism it is not simply time that is blind and forgetful but the personages themselves who are collectively deluded, seeing themselves as they believe others see them while we the audience see their blindness and hear their moral distortion – which brings us to the debates.[23]

In the Greek camp, act 1, scene 3, the war council assembles and is first addressed by Agamemnon. In his speech the Greek leader argues that what some have called 'shames' (1.3.19) are in fact 'the protractive trials of great Jove / To find persistive constancy in man' (1.3.20–1) which cannot be found in fortune's favours. 'Checks and disasters' (1.3.5) are thus seen in superhuman not human terms which enables Agamemnon to avoid the issue of military responsibility and judgment. This is effected by the simile from natural history:

> . . . Checks and disasters
> Grow in the veins of actions highest rear'd,
> As knots, by the conflux of meeting sap,
> Infects the sound pine, and diverts his grain
> Tortive and errant from his course of growth.

> (1.3.5–9)

But a tree cannot be said to be responsible for its growth as a general can be said to be responsible for an army under his command. Furthermore, in assuming that 'Checks and disasters' ultimately derive from Jove, Agamemnon converts extended failure into a virtue, namely 'constancy'. The human weaknesses of obstinacy and lack of judgement are converted to human strengths. 'Tortive', 'protractive' and 'persistive' appear to be Shakespearean coinages. That is, precisely at the weakest point in his argument, Agamemnon attempts logical legerdemain by means of tumid neologism. No wonder Patroclus sends him up, to the delight of Achilles. Nestor's support is equally damning. In demonstrating that 'In the reproof of chance / Lies the true proof of men' (1.3.33–4) he applies the analogy of a tempest dividing the men from the boys, and in doing so he collapses the distinction between valour and rashness, a distinction familiar in the Renaissance by way of Aristotle's *Nicomachean Ethics*, and crucial for the depiction of Hotspur, as we have seen. It would be tempting for a director to have the actor of Nestor here stroke his beard, as we are told he does in Patroclus's pageant, 'being dress'd to some oration' (1.3.166).

Ulysses' celebrated speech incorporating the commonplaces of Tudor orthodoxy, as we have been so often reminded, is, in dramatic rather than ideological terms, a massive circumlocutionary paradox. For Ulysses to have squarely faced Agamemnon with the shortcomings he clearly sees would have been insubordination of the 'degree' he is propounding. Instead, Ulysses with great deference invokes cosmological and social hierarchies in the correspondence of the heavens, men and nature, until he turns his argument to the immediate problem, 'The general's disdain'd / By him one step below ... ' (1.3.129–30). But even so his argument is taken by Nestor and Agamemnon in terms of a general condition, 'sickness' (1.3.140), rather than specific responsibility, and an effect – Achilles' pride – is blamed rather than the cause recognised, namely Agamemnon's failure in leadership. What we hear here has parallels in Troy.

The arguments in the Trojan camp begin with Hector's plea, 'Let Helen go' (2.2.17), since she has cost thousands of Trojan lives, each as dear as hers. Troilus objects to the mistaken implication that King Priam is being assessed, rather than those who have died, which is Hector's point, and thus avoids the direct issue of the cost in human lives in keeping Helen. Helenus jibes at Troilus' irrationality forcing him to retaliate that reason makes men cowards, leaving open the logical implication that valour and heroism derive from irrationality – of madness or animality. Hector's direct assertion that Helen is not worth the 'cost' in lives draws Troilus' 'What's aught but as 'tis valued?' (2.2.52) and Hector's famous reply in which he argues that value is not merely subjective, but is to some extent intrinsic as well as extrinsic. This has given rise to a considerable amount of philosophical, ethical and economic comment.[24] However, it is not directly answered by Troilus who instead offers an argument which amounts to the proposition that 'honour' consists in not recognizing an error of judgement, a form of obstinacy we have met in the Greek council.

The opening of Troilus' argument uses a disastrous analogy, 'I take today a wife ... ' (2.2.61). What could be more opposed than legal matrimony and illegal abduction of someone else's wife? As his argument proceeds, it becomes more and more incriminating since he admits to will in the matter of choice being led by the senses, 'My will enkindled by mine eyes and ears' (2.2.63) – that is, those senses which Shakespeare works on in a metadramatic way, as we have seen, throughout the play, towards a form of empirical not propositional truth, a truth that will force Troilus to acknowledge 'th'attest of eyes and ears' (5.2.122). Paris unwittingly offers the paradox that the dishonour of Helen's abduction can be reversed by the 'honourable keeping her' (2.2.149). That is, two wrongs make a right. Hector recognises the poor reasoning of Paris and Troilus, reasoning swayed by the biases of passion and thus incapable of ' . . . a free determination / 'Twixt right and wrong' (2.2.170–1). Hector then confronts his listeners with the full nature of Helen's abduction. It is a crime against ' . . . moral laws / Of nature and of nations' (2.2.184–5). And then occurs one of the most resounding turnabouts in Shakespearean argument. Hector continues:

> . . . yet ne'er the less,
> My spritely brethren, I propend to you
> In resolution to keep Helen still,
> For 'tis a cause that hath no mean dependence
> Upon our joint and several dignities.

(2.2.189–93)

Troilus identifies this further, 'She is a theme of honor and renown, / A spur to valiant and magnanimous deeds' (2.2.199–200). What she is actually seen to be, rather than heard about, this 'love's / invisible soul' (3.1.33),[25] is 'Nell' (3.1.52) another ale-houe drab, to adopt Thersites' Graeco-Jacobean view. Troilus separates honour from its cause and occasion, it is made an absolute separate from the relativity of circumstances which reason has demonstrated show, in fact, dishonour. If we rephrase Troilus' question thus, 'What's honor but as 'tis valued?', then Hector's reply has an ironic application borne out by the rest of the scene:[26]

> 'Tis mad idolatry
> To make the service greater than the god,
> And the will dotes that is attributive
> To what infectiously itself affects,
> Without some image of th'affected merit.

(2.2.56–60)

Ulysses apart, the Greeks and Trojans stand condemned by their own words, which flagrantly distort and abuse reason. Their arguments show that they are ethically confused and corrupt. And the final overpowering arguments of action reveal this corruption beneath the panoply of chivalric love and war.

However, before the act 5 dénouement, again structuring the play according to the mirror principle, Shakespeare offers a mock rehearsal in Cressida's admittance to the Greek camp and in the fight between Hector and Ajax. Twentieth-century debate for and against Cressida has been extensive, but perhaps the most informative discussion remains that of Hyder E. Rollins.[27] By the sixteenth century Rollins finds that there was one minor and one major way of seeing Cressida. Surprisingly, as is recorded in *Tottel's Miscellany*, she was seen as the symbol of love's fulfilment, as if the poets had closed Chaucer's narrative at the end of book three. And both poets, like Gascoigne and Turberville, and ballad-mongers in a popularising mode, similarly exalted Cressida. However, the most powerful and thoroughgoing image from Gavin Douglas onwards was that of faithless Cressida coarsely derided as 'wanton' and 'wicked'. The element of pathos and tragedy in Henryson's *The Testament of Cressid* was effaced by solely emphasising the merely punitive and didactic. As Rollins puts it, 'Shakespeare deserves our thanks for pulling Cressida partly out of the mire in which Henryson's followers had placed her' (p. 409). Ironically, the two ways of seeing Cressida – love's realisation, love's betrayal – are not contradictory but complementary in *Troilus and Cressida*. The mutuality of love is betrayed not just by Troilus's one-sided conviction of Cressida's guilt. Shakespeare dramatises the paradox that in seeming affective shallowness there was psychological authenticity and thus artistic depth.

Shakespeare's Cressida is not just an anti-feminist symbol, a didactic puppet to be handed around by the Greeks. When Cressida appeared on the Jacobean stage the proleptic ironies endowed by a moralising tradition could have paradoxically given everything she does a kind of guiltlessness. As if ultimately what she is and does comes from something outside herself; men, history, time, myth. Even her notorious worldliness seems acquired rather than inherent. Shakespeare realised that an actual person of flesh and blood, a boy actor, could jeopardise the imaginative investments of myth. Allowing a degree of love, not just sensuousness, allowing for fear as well as frivolity, Shakespeare sensed the crucial relationship between the limitations of Cressida's being and the contingencies of her circumstances. In effect Sam Mendes' production gave expression to this in the 'kissing scene' (4.5) by presenting a slightly bewildered Cressida acting out what was expected of her. Consequently, Ulysses' famous 'daughters of the game' (4.5.63) speech described not so much what she actually does but what it will come to be presented as, 'The Troyan's trumpet' / strumpet, heralded by '*All*' (4.5.64). In many respects Hector seems more culpable.

Hector's combat with Ajax follows the travesty of courtliness in the kissing scene. The combat is equally a charade in two ways. At the outset of the play we learn that Ajax 'cop'd' (1.2.33) Hector in the field, thus the challenge he subsequently makes to the Greeks appears more to enable him to re-establish his personal pre-eminence than to affirm chivalric values. Second, the duel itself barely gets underway before Hector refuses to continue fighting an adversary who is actually his cousin. In structurally aligning these two series of actions Shakespeare provides the first of 'a pair of spectacles' (4.4.14). This phrase is used by Pandarus of Troilus and Cressida on seeing their distress when they learn of the plans for an Antenor–Cressida exchange. Pandarus' pun goes to the heart of the play. The pair of spectacles in the immediate sense is apparent, but in a metaphorical sense Cressida's betrayal and Hector's death present a more exponential 'pair of spectacles'. Equally, the punning reference to glasses draws attention to the visual, seeing as re-vision with a new focus. Shakespeare did not have available to him the punning possibilities of the idea of 'bi-focal', but, as we shall see, he has a complementary neologism in '*Bifold* authority' (5.2.144).

Having succumbed to Diomedes' bullying love overtures and agreed on an assignation, Cressida's final words here are:

> Troilus, farewell! One eye yet looks on thee,
> But with my heart the other eye doth see.
> Ah, poor our sex! this fault in us I find,
> The error of our eye directs our mind.
> What error leads must err; O then conclude,
> Minds sway'd by eyes are full of turpitude.
>
> (5.2.107–12)

Leading up to this, the argument of action in Cressida's manifest betrayal has been protracted by the interpolated comments of the on-stage audience which is divided into two. Thersites' lewd comments appear not to be heard by Ulysses and Troilus who exchange asides. If we include the theatre audience here, then we have again the triple mirror effect noted above. Sexual betrayal is dramatised by small but momentous gestures. Far from being observed *flagrante delicto*, with the entry of

Cressida she merely whispers with Diomedes which continues as an action drawing Troilus' 'Yea, so familiar?' (5.2.8), thus inaugurating a series of comments from the onlookers. Diomedes threatens to leave after the whispering becomes bickering. His movement across the stage allows for more urgent interjections capped by Troilus' agonised words as Cressida attempts to mollify her lover with close whispering, yet again – 'O plague and madness!' (5.2.35). As stage business this allows for a sequence of exchanges between Troilus and Ulysses until further bickering as Diomedes strategy of seduction moves once more to departure, drawing from Cressida precisely what he is seeking, her assurance of love-making in an amatory gesture, 'She strokes his cheek' (5.2.51). We see this gesture and hear the stage auditors.

Sensing the completion of his love overtures in Cressida's moral surrender, Diomedes insists on an outward token which Cressida leaves the stage to find. From line 63 until shortly before Cressida's exit, Shakespeare makes the token, which is Troilus's sleeve, of course, the outward physical symbol of what is happening to Cressida as it is given to Diomedes, snatched back by Cressida, retrieved by Diomedes, and vainly grabbed at by Cressida until she finally gives up (5.2.87). The symbolic loss gives Cressida a real qualm which Diomedes quashes by adding the threat of separation to his former strategy at which Cressida's resistance crumbles, and an assignation is finally agreed. Before following Diomedes off stage Cressida's lament follows, 'Troilus, farewell! One eye yet looks on thee . . . ' (5.2.107). The irony of this is apparent to the on-stage auditors but even more so to the theatre audience since its experience is the precise opposite of Cressida's. She claims that 'The error of our eye directs our mind' (5.2.110), whereas the reverse is the case for the audience. The audience's 'eye' is fixed on what takes place on the stage and is explicitly urged to do so by way of that emphatic stress on the visual we have examined, and is immediately put before us again in Troilus's emotional impulse to 'invert th' attest of eyes and ears' (5.2.122). We do not, our eyes and ears have witnessed 'a truth' (5.2.119) which Troilus must deny. Needless to say, in these words, 'th' attest of eyes and ears' we have a superscription for the metadramatic and metajuristic thrust of the play as a whole. The 'pair of spectacles' is completed by the death of Hector, when we are finally faced with 'th' attest of eyes and ears'.

In studying the text of *Troilus and Cressida* it is not possible to skip quickly past the betrayal of Cressida since stage business and external comment are so protractedly intercut. With the death of Hector, as with so many Shakespearean 'fights', the action is often shunted into a stage direction parked beside a continuous text, whereas on stage there is often considerable business, an argument of action of great import in terms of the larger meaning of visual impact. In *Troilus and Cressida* Shakespeare provides a visual cue for the staging of Hector's death in Achilles' instruction, 'Empale him with your weapons round about' (5.7.5).

Hector was morally compromised in the combat with Ajax but to balance this, in Shakespeare's dualistic presentation, we need to recall Ulysses' comparison during the fight, between the reputations of the chivalric Hector and vindictive Troilus, ' . . . Hector in his blaze of wrath subscribes / To tender objects' (4.5.105–6). This betokens his knightly magnanimity which reappears at his demise. Shakespeare assiduously stresses the seemingly positive chivalric commitment in the language of act 5, scene 3 when we hear from Hector of 'honor', the 'vein of chivalry', of 'faith and valor', and of 'deeds worth praise' (ll.28, 32, 69, 93). Once again the comparative terms voiced earlier by Hector are raised:

> Tro   When many times the captive Grecian falls,
> Even in the fan and wind of your fair sword,
> You bid them rise and live.
>
> Hect   O, 'tis fair play.
>
> Tro   Fool's play, by heaven, Hector.
>
> (5.3.40–3)

For Hector, Troilus' assertion of 'venom'd vengeance' (5.3.47) is savagery. The disjunction here between chivalry and barbarism is compromised when we hear from Ulysses of Achilles' wrath on learning of Patroclus' death and

> his mangled Myrmidons,
> That noseless, handless, hack'd and chipp'd, come to him,
> Crying on Hector.
>
> (5.5.33–5)

This has to raise the question of the compatibility of Hector's noble words and the mutilation caused by his actions – are they 'deeds worth praise'? But the issue is partially deflected by the possibility of Ulysses' malicious exaggeration, and that the atrocity is reported rather than seen. The ambivalence recurs in the actual argument of action when the mighty combatants fight at last. Achilles tires and Hector allows him respite, 'Pause if thou wilt' (5.6.14), which is recognised but spurned, 'I do disdain thy courtesy . . .' (5.6.15). Presumably the Myrmidons did not qualify for 'pause' being allied with those who follow the warriors in act 1, scene 2: 'Asses, fools, dolts! chaff and bran! . . .' (1.241). This serves to remind us of a system of double values, like that already encountered in *1 & 2 Henry IV*, where, as we have seen, Shakespeare suggests that personal valour is realised at the cost of anonymous carnage. This is emphasised in another form in *Troilus and Cressida* with the mysterious entry of *one in armor* (5.6.26.1). What is important to grasp here is the structural movement in the argument of action between scenes 6 and 8.

In scene 6 the chivalric note is sounded and then undermined by Hector's ignoble pursuit of the armour, 'Wilt thou not, beast, abide? . . . I'll hunt thee for thy hide' (ll.30–1). Immediately following in scene 7 Achilles instructs his Myrmidons 'Empale him with your weapons round about, / In fellest manner execute your arms' (ll.5–6). (Shakespeare cannot resist pressing home the visual here with Achilles' 'my proceedings eye', l.7.) And then in scene 8 Hector returns with the armour and corpse (depending on the direction) declaring, notoriously, 'Most putrified core, so fair without, / Thy goodly armor thus hath cost thy life' (ll.1–2). According to the approach and arguments advanced in this chapter it is readily apparent how this falls into place. Achilles and the Myrmidons enter. Hector appeals to chivalry, 'I am unarm'd forego this vantage, Greek' (l.9). Then Hector is slaughtered. The action here is as extensive as the director makes it. Sam Mendes followed Achilles' instructions and had the Myrmidons 'empale' Hector with their spears and then kill him, thus combining the orchestrated and the ritualistic with the merely barbarous. In this the significance of the whole series from scene 6 to 8 was re-emphasised, namely the alternation between the chivalric and the atrocious in word and action. Clearly the armour and 'putrefied core' represent this. The sumptuous armour, the external manifestation of chivalry, is the equivalent to heroic language while the corrupt corpse is a metaphorical equivalent to the corruption of the actions we witness. The final ignominy for Hector follows when, Shakespeare drawing on Lydgate as source, Achilles has him tied to his horse's tail and dragged round the walls of Troy.

Shakespeare makes the impact of the arguments of action even more forceful by having relatively limited physical action up to this point, and then by cutting back on language and refusing to provide any real dénouement. In fact it is denied with Troilus' 'Hector is dead; there is no more to say' (5.10.22), just as an exchange of Ulysses and Troilus

following the betrayal seems to deny the possibility of speech expressing anything more than what action had made manifest: 'All's done
my lord'. 'It is' (5.2.115). But this is not quite the case for the audience-
witnesses. Shakespeare as dramatist-lawyer has provided two forms of
evidence, words and actions, and we are left to assess 'th' attest of eyes
and ears'. The strength of Troilus' feelings impels him to deny the
evidence of 'eyes and ears'. Instead he falls back on the testimony of
rhetoric.

> If beauty have a soul, this is not she;
> If souls guide vows, if vows be sanctimonies,
> If sanctimony be the gods' delight,
> If there be rule in unity itself,
> This was not she.

> (5.2.138–42)

The combination of *anaphora* and *gradatio*, akin to *sorites* ('soul', 'vows',
'sanctimony'), rehearses the commonplace Platonic truths of love, but
the evidence of witnesses, that is us, the audience, countermands this.
Troilus then turns desperately to logic and challenges one of the fundamental principles, the principle of contradiction, a thing cannot both
be and not be, 'This is, and is not Cressid' (1.146).

The fullness of human experience is more complex than that
allowed for by the laws of syllogistic reasoning. 'Bifold authority'
(5.2.144) applies more to the dualistic aspect of life than to logic.
Cressida does love, but betrays love and is betrayed by love. Hector is
seen to be chivalric but betrays chivalry, somewhat, and is savagely
betrayed by chivalry.

The arguments of action in *Troilus and Cressida* completely reject a
commonplace humanistic argument concerning the heroic literature of
antiquity and its continuity in Renaissance epic. Pandarus has the last
word, or rather the last song in which we hear 'Full merrily the humble-
bee doth sing, / Till he hath lost his honey and his sting'. Editors annotate
this in sexual terms of lewd innuendo. There was, however, the analogy
drawn between the bee extracting honey, even from plants otherwise
poisonous, and the moralised reading of otherwise dubious narratives:
as John Harington put it, for example, in the notes to canto XLIII of his
translation of the *Orlando Furioso*, 'there be two knavish tales that be
here in this booke, and yet the Bee will pyke out honny out of the worst
of them'. For William Fulbecke, in *Christian Ethics or Morall Philosophie*

(1587), 'the moral ambiguity of the Troy story was only too evident; he therefore warns the reader in the strongest terms that he is to emulate the bee and not the spider'.[28] On the contrary, satire was associated with 'bitter speaches', as Puttenham put it,[29] and at the heart of *Troilus and Cressida*, as we have seen and heard, is the bitter 'argument' of 'deadly gall', the 'theme of all our scorns' (4.5.29–30).[30]

11
Conclusion: Drama and Historiography

The approach to Shakespeare's dramatisation of history taken in the above chapters parallels the practice of humanist historiography itself. The arguments of speech and action central to early modern rhetorical culture were also at the heart of the humanist project to celebrate the words and deeds of great men, as an example for imitation and emulation, in the advice to princes mode or in actual histories (*Henry V* has been examined in this light). The alliance of classical rhetoric and history as part of renaissance historiography stimulated this but, in contrast, Shakespeare's history plays develop a radical pattern of reversal and rejection. The *Henry VI* plays draw on sixteenth-century chronicles yet calling into question, rather than openly confirming, Christian providentialism. (Though *Richard III* appears to do this, as we have seen it demonstrates orthodox theodicy as self-deconstructive[1].) *Richard II* and the *Henry IV* plays mark a development from the caricature 'Machevil' of Richard III to the distinct emergence of Machiavellian *realpolitik* in a contingent world of necessity and are thus closer to the late sixteenth-century appearance of 'politic', pragmatic history, represented by the figure of Tacitus, than to Ciceronian rhetoric and the teleology of the Tudor myth. This secularisation increases in the later Roman plays by drawing on Plutarch, the inheritor of that aspect of Graeco-Roman historiography which finds 'the cause of all historical events in the personality, whether individual or corporate, or human agents'.[2]

Humanist historiography was largely built upon just a few paragraphs of Cicero's *De oratore* (II, 9, 15) which included the frequently quoted definition of history as *testis temporum, lux veritatis, vita memoriae, magistra vitae, nuntia vetustatis*, loosely translated as history 'which bears witness to the passing of the ages, sheds light upon reality, gives life to recollection and guidance to human existence'. Crucially, Cicero continues by expostulating, 'whose voice, but the orator's, can entrust her to immortality'.[3] Consequently, history was regarded as a branch of rhetoric and thus subject to the same practices to achieve eloquence: pre-eminently, the praise of exemplary deeds as a model for the ideal ruler and the *ethopeia* (otherwise known as the *prosopopeia* or impersonation) in the invented speech.[4] Though in the *Poetics* Aristotle had claimed the superiority of poetry with its universal truth as against the lesser truth of history which is tied to the particulars of actuality, history was somewhat reinstated in his *Rhetoric* (I.ii.7–9) as the rich fund of examples for poet and orator.[5] As a short-cut for the renaissance schoolboy, like Shakespeare, collections of deeds and sayings culled from history – for example, Erasmus' *Apophthegmes*, translated by Nicholas Udall, 1542 – were available.[6]

Exemplarity derived its rhetorical and philosophic power from the belief in an hypostatised human nature, universal and unchanging, observable by patterns of repetition and thus predictable. Hence there was no problem in retrieving the past since it had never been lost. Histories reaffirm its continuity. This conviction is the foremost characteristic of pre-historicist thought and finds its most sustained advocacy in Dr Johnson's *Preface to Shakespeare*. Contemporary with Shakespeare is Samuel Daniel's letter defending his play *Philotas*, set in the period of Alexander the Great:

> the very Idea of those tymes, as they appeared vnto mee both by the cast of the storie and the vniuersall notions of the affayres of men, w^c in all ages beare the same resemblances, and are measured by one and the same foote of vnderstanding. No tyme but brought forth the like concurrencies, the like interstriuing for place and dignitie, the like supplantations, rysings & overthrowes, so y^t there is nothing new vnder the Sunne, nothing in theas tymes y^t is not in bookes, nor in bookes that is not in theas tymes.[7]

A contentious issue in the representation of times past was the practice of invention by both poet and historian. In classical and humanist history the invention of something like a battlefield oration was not simply an invention of what we would call a fiction (i.e. something that was not recorded and was thus unverifiable) but a truth arrived at by investigating the probable, what someone would have said, according to the principle of decorum and the transhistorical uniformity of human nature: the invented speech gave expression to a latent truth, the historian thereby enhancing the example.[8] Hall's invented speech of the Duke of York before parliament in 1460 is a good example of this.[9]

Needless to say, in practice the historian frequently adjusted his narrative, occasionally to fulfil not philosophical or ethical ends, but to satisfy the ideological pressures of patronage, as in the case of Machiavelli in his *History of Florence*.[10] An example of invention from Plutarch is most revealing of the licence that was taken. Shakespeare's interpretation of the *Life of Martius Coriolanus* is rooted in Volumnia's attitude to her son. Plutarch records:

> For he thought nothing made him so happy and honourable as that his mother might hear everybody praise and commend him; that she might always see him return with a crown upon his head; and that she might still embrace him with tears running down her cheeks for joy.[11]

In Shakespeare this is heightened and intensified:

> ...I...was pleas'd to let him seek danger where he was like to find fame. To a cruel war I sent him, from whence he return'd, his brows bound with oak. I tell thee, daughter, I sprung not more in joy at first hearing he was a man-child than in first seeing he had prov'd himself a man.
>
> (1.3.9–17)

Plutarch's source here was Dionysius of Halicarnassus, yet as C.B.R. Pelling shows, he chose to reverse what he found, namely:

> When have I ever been free of grief or fear from you, from the moment you reached manhood? When have I ever been able to rejoice, seeing you fighting war upon war, battle upon battle, gaining wound upon wound?[12]

Pelling argues that Plutarch re-invented by making this passage consistent with Volumnia's later behaviour at the close and thus psychologically plausible: some might say that such seeming inconsistency presents a fact of historiography but for the renaissance reader and auditor Plutarch and Shakespeare's invention is superior because it is consistent with decorum, the conformity of essentialist nature.[13]

At a simpler level it sometimes suits Shakespeare to follow the rhetorical invention of his source as, for example, in developing the Bishop of

Carlisle's speech (*Richard II* 4.1.114–49), worked up by Holinshed, but for his own ends as argued above. Similarly, in *Henry V* we find repeated the great commonplace of humanist historiography, the battlefield oration. Elsewhere, however, Shakespeare's invention is altogether of another order. To stay with *Henry V*, in the above chapter the lengthy encounter between the king and the common soldiers – Shakespeare's invention, not found in the sources – has been analysed in relation to the dramatic design of the play as a critique of nationalist historiography and the *res gestae* tradition of the mirror for princes. Elsewhere, above all with the comic subplot of the *Henry IV* plays, Shakespeare's artistry is not rhetorical in the sense discussed above but is part of a dramatic imagination which contests the ideology of Ciceronian and medieval historiography. In this respect Shakespeare may be compared with the self-conscious critique made by Machiavelli.

In *The Discourses* (3.xii) Machiavelli points out that in human actions necessity can lead to 'glorious achievements', noting that 'some moral philosophers have even maintained that without it neither the hand nor the tongue of man, the two noblest instruments of his glory, would have served his purpose perfectly, nor carried human works to that height of perfection which they have attained'.[14] A commentator suggests that the philosophers referred to are St Thomas Aquinas (*De regimine principum*, 1.1) and Aristotle (*Politics*, 1.2).[15] Hand and tongue refer to those deeds and words celebrated by epideictic history. The topics of *laus* and *vituperatio* are referred to in *The Prince* (XV), 'men ... are noted for various qualities which earn them either praise or condemnation'.[16] It is recognised that *The Prince* satirises the advice to princes genre by taking up the same topics but treating them realistically, rather than ideally. For example, conventionally the ruler should be praised for pity and condemned for cruelty.[17] (Shakespeare's introduction of 'mercy' into Henry V's speech at Harfleur, 3.3, problematises this, as I have discussed.) Conversely, for Machiavelli virtue can be condemned and vice praised, depending on how far, as a means, they either hinder or help to achieve the desired ends. Machiavelli's disjunctive mode, everything is either/or – a binary ultimatum to take unilateral action – shapes his political thinking with its rigid redaction of history into the bleak alternatives of a consequentialist ethic: ends justifying means.[18] Ironically, though condemned for his evil cynicism, from another point of view the devilish Florentine is not too far removed from the political utopians he scorns (*The Prince*, XV). The 'glory' Machiavelli insistently attributes to the Roman republic and the successful prince idealises the militaristic maintenance of the state by force and fraud with *virtù* triumphing over fortune and necessity. As in authoritarian monologism, the word glory deafens all opposition and inequity that is clearly heard, for example, in the dissonant voices of *Coriolanus*. Machiavelli is like Shakespeare's Brutus. As Brutus is blinded by the honour of *Romanitas* so Machiavelli is blinded by the glory of Rome as something like his blurred overview of the complex politics of the *lex agraria* and the Gracchi shows (*Discourses* I.xxxvii). Machiavelli's rhetoric of totalising glory homogenises history, whereas Shakespeare's dramatic vision is sharpened by heterogeneity and conflict. Shakespeare's understanding of history and his depiction of Rome are formally more challenging than the narratives of Livy, Plutarch and Machiavelli, or Tacitus for that matter.

In the course of the second half of the sixteenth century the historical writings of Cornelius Tacitus had become so widely read that modern historians commonly acknowledge the phenomenon as 'Tacitism'.[19] In his *Annals* and *History* Tacitus recorded, respectively, the decline of imperial Rome to the nadir of Tiberias, Caligula and Nero, and the tumultuous year of the four emperors, AD 69, the decline of Rome from civic humanism to absolutist self-interest. Sir Henry Savile and R. Greenway published most of Tacitus in English in a folio of 1598.[20] In his account of Tacitism, to which I am indebted, Richard Tuck characterises this movement as 'new humanism' as against the 'old humanism' of the first half of the sixteenth century, represented by Livy and Cicero.[21] I would prefer to use the expression counter-humanism rather than new humanism since this would indicate the scepticism, not to say pessimism, of such historiography which may be linked to the growing influence of Sextus Empiricus and Pyrrhonism as reflected pre-eminently in Montaigne in the late sixteenth century.[22]

There is a continuity, however. The writing of Tacitean 'politic' history is always linked to that of Machiavelli and Guicciardini, particularly in contemporary commentaries,[23] for example, in the key text of Justus Lipsius, *Six Bookes of Politickes or Civil Doctrine* (translated by William Jones, 1594) where Tacitus is the principal source.[24] In the fourth book, largely devoted to prudence, chapter 11 considers '*Whether mixed prudence, to wit, where there is deceit, ought to take place with a Prince?*' Lipsius is almost entirely Machiavellian in making the ends of 'publike profit' justify the means of deceit, etc. Lipsius cites the recommendation of Tacitus in the *Agricola* that the prince '*be able to intermingle that which is profitable, with that which is honest*' (p. 113). Professing horror at those who outrightly claim that whatever it takes to '*conserue authoritie*' is 'honest', he continues with the equivocation on that 'intermingle' in a vein not dissimilar to the casuistries of Shakespeare's Machiavel monarch and he concludes the chapter with a marginal note which reads like one of the Crookback's disingenuous asides – 'Some kinde of persons rage too much against Machiauell' (p. 114). What is of the greatest importance here is that in the course of his brief chapter Lipsius alludes in the marginal references to the main source of the useful and honest, the *utile* (profitable, advantageous, expedient) and *honestum* (honourable, moral, virtuous), of Cicero's *Offices* (3.viii), the core of old humanist ethics.[25] In his essay 'Of Profit and Honesty' (Florio's title), Montaigne recognises the necessity of reason of state determining that *utile* prevails over *honestum*.[26]

We find Machiavelli confronting Cicero on Pompey's barge, so to speak, in *Antony and Cleopatra*: Menas recommends to his leader that the vessel be cut adrift and the triumvirs assassinated – thus the empire could be seized. This is parallel to the Tudor situation adduced above in chapter 9 (p. 147) and to the situation Machiavelli considers in the *Discourses* (I.xxvii) when the tyrant Baglioni failed to take advantage of Pope Julius II's rashly putting himself in his hands, and killing him.[27] Pompey replies to Menas, 'Thou must know, / ... 'Tis not my profit that does lead mine honor; / Mine honor, it' (2.7.75–7). The response is a failure in the required Machiavellian *virtù* and Tacitean 'intermingling', rather than affirmation of a Ciceronian categorical imperative, as Pompey's following words make plain: 'Being done unknown, / I should have found it afterwards well done, / But must condemn it now' (2.7.78–80). Without Tacitean prudence his fate is sealed as one of Machiavelli's weak men.

To consider Shakespeare's arguments with history in relation to early modern historians influenced by Tacitean historiography I will glance at Paolo Sarpi (1552–1623), Arrigo Caterina Davila (1576–1631) and Sir John Hayward (1564?-1627): all contemporaries and inheritors of the Renaissance, Reformation and Counter-Reformation. Sarpi's *The Historie of the Councel of Trent* (translated by Nathanael Brent in 1640) and Davila's *The Historie of the Civill Warres of France* (translated by William Aylesbury in 1647) were very popular in Protestant England since both were read as exposing the devilish machinations of Catholicism. Milton called Sarpi 'the great unmasker of the *Trentine* Councel'.[28] To enter the pages of Sarpi is to enter a Kafkaesque labyrinth (a favourite word for Francis Bacon in his *History of the Reign of Henry VII*[29]) as if his history were a precursor of *The Castle* and *The Trial*. The accomplished historian was to explain events by causes and Sarpi's most powerful contribution to historiography was his recognition that cause goes beyond the individual to the institutional. Tacitean history explores self-interest and reason of state and Sarpi grasped that individual and group self-interest – of the Pope, the cardinals, diplomats and princes – were all trapped within the encompassing self-interest of the institution, the grinding mechanisms of papacy, empire and nation-state. Sarpi was influenced by English nominalism and believed that truth lay in particulars, but he tenaciously pursued the facts of history only to find the individual absorbed into the labyrinth of motive behind motive, the infrastructure of power politics behind the mask of religion.[30]

In this respect Davila's lengthy account of the Catholic–Huguenot civil wars entirely agrees. In fact, his words could almost be taken as a gloss on Sarpi's *Historie*, 'a colour of so specious and so necessary a cause as the defence and preservation of Their Religion . . . private interests . . . that honourable pretence .. the specious mask of Religion'.[31] Throughout Davila's *Historie* recur the same words: 'appearance', 'specious', 'colour' (as pretext), 'pretence', 'dissimulation', 'feigning', 'dissemble', 'interest'. In chapters 4 and 5, I have examined the politics of pretext in Boling-broke's return from France, his actions as king, and what may be called the 'politic pretext' of the Percies, a phrase taken from a poem of Ben Jonson of the 1590s in which he writes of the innocently imprisoned Earl of Desmond, puppet of Elizabeth's and Cecil's 'politic pretext, that wries a state'.[32] My interpretation of the argument and action of Boling-broke's return is precisely that recalled by Samuel Daniel in his account of the Wars of the Roses which Shakespeare had read. Of the oath at Ravenspurgh Daniel writes:

> . . . this pretence
> Was but a shadow to the intended act;
> Because th' euent doth argue the offence,
> And plainely seemes to manifest the fact.[33]

As in Sarpi, Davila's world is full of hinted secrets, private counsels and politic conjectures, all predicated on the assumption of Machiavellian deception to achieve power. The scene in 2 *Henry VI* where the necessity of Gloucester's death is recognised – 'That he should die is worthy policy, / But yet we want a color for his death' (3.1.235–6) – is like Davila's history brought to life: compare the following:

> . . . the King of Navar seeking to put a gloss upon the business with some specious reasonable colour . . . obtained a reasonable pretence (so necessary in Civil Warrs to feed the mindes of the people, and to palliate the interests of the parties . . .)[34]

Though feudal in subject matter, the politics of Shakespeare's histories parallels the court-centred absolutist histories of the Taciteans, though it is Ben Jonson's *Sejanus his Fall* (1605) that is usually discussed in this context. In Tacitus' *Annales* Sejanus, the leader of the Praetorian Guard, was the overreaching favourite, and rival in corruption and tyranny, of the Emperor Tiberias. Jonson's play gives expression to the barely concealed anxieties of the implied parallels of contemporary politics.[35]

Sir John Hayward is an interesting further parallel since it is likely that he saw some of Shakespeare's English histories before writing *The First Part of the Life and raigne of King Henrie IIII* (1599). Hayward's history was burnt and he was imprisoned for sedition, primarily because of his dedication to the Earl of Essex and the fact that the majority of the *First Part* was given to Richard II's defeat and deposition, such was the sensitivity of Elizabeth and her council. The queen asked Francis Bacon if there were any treason in the book, whereupon the famous reply was:

> 'For treason surely I found none, but for fellonie very many'. And when her Majesty hastily asked me 'Wherein?' I told her, the author had committed very apparent theft: for he had taken most of the sentences of Cornelius Tacitus, and translated them into English, and put them into his text.[36]

The *Second Part* of Hayward's history, covering the second, third and fourth year of Henry's reign, includes an account of the causes of the Percy rebellion which is most revealing in comparison with that of Shakespeare and Holinshed. In chapter 5 of this study I put forward an argument for Shakespeare's Machiavellian king provoking, and thus determining, the situation. Holinshed's brief and simple record attributes the rebellion to the Percies' 'envie' and 'malice';[37] Shakespeare elaborates on the Percies' 'honour' and 'debt' as I have developed at length above. F.J. Levy surmises that elsewhere Hayward was probably indebted to Shakespeare and here, I feel, the influence is quite strong.[38]

In the four pages he devotes to the narrative Hayward uses the events (the Scottish prisoners, the ransom for Mortimer) to interpolate a sententious disquisition full of politic aphorisms in the Tacitean mode. In fact, Hayward's interpretation takes the view that the Percies' insistence on Mortimer's ransom, etc., was because 'they required many things not soe much with care to obtaine as with purpose to picke occasion to revolte'.[39] (In my view Shakespeare's Henry is one step ahead.)

Hayward's specific interpretation of this example rests on the generalisation that such instrumental greatness feels that it can never be adequately rewarded, regards itself as indispensable and as in a position to control the prince. Conversely, the prince is always in fear of such power and cannot find security while others regard his kingship as their creation. Both Shakespeare and Hayward explore the ramifications of motive whereas Holinshed's understanding is limited to those two words, envy and malice. At Shrewsbury, in the parleying before the battle, Hayward supplies a line that encapsulates so much of politic history: 'all under couler of honest pretenses, having secrett instructions for underhand dealing.'[40] It is the world of Machiavelli's Florence, of Tiberias's Rome, of Shakespeare's English histories, and of the Tacitean historians.

Greek historiographical method relied on the testimony of eyewitnesses and the historian's own experience.[41] This mode was favoured in the early modern period and was one of the reasons for the popularity of Tacitus and Sallust. The strand of Renaissance neo-Aristotelianism which drew on the late medieval nominalist critique of Platonism, the *via moderna* opposed to the *via antiqua*, stressed induction, the role of observation and experience as a basis for knowledge, whether of nature or history.[42] For example, in his youth Davila had been a page in the French court of Catherine de' Medici and then a soldier serving Henry IV: as he points out in his introduction: 'I had the opportunity to observe, and be an eye-witnesse of the most secret and notable circumstances of so remarkable passages...I have learned of myself by Experience and Action.'[43] The commentaries of Machiavelli and the history of Guicciardini had particular force in that the authors had lived through the tempestuous misfortunes of Florence and Italy. Janet Coleman compares Machiavelli's 'eyewitness experience of the world' with today's eyewitness journalism.[44] In a sixteenth-century historian such as François Baudouin, observation took on an especially crucial function in that he was also a civil lawyer who wished to combine jurisprudence with history (as Shakespeare does in *Richard II* particularly, as I have shown). He believed that the historian was a judge of testimony and presumably the reader of such history also became a judge of evidence, above all of the argument of action.[45] For Baudouin, as for everybody, given the universality of the trope, history was the theatre of the world. In the introductory epistle to his lengthy poem on the civil wars of the fifteenth century, Samuel Daniel repeats the analogy:

Man is a creature of the same dimension he was; and how great and eminent soeuer he bee, his measure and height is easy to be taken.

And all these great actions are openly presented on the Stage of the World: where, there are euer Spectators, who will iudge and censure how men personate those parts, which they are set to performe; and so enter them in the Records of Memorie.[46]

In the light of this commonplace it is not difficult to recognise the metajuristic element I have stressed throughout *Troilus and Cressida*.[47]

More broadly, the above issues enable us to see that the advent of the stage history play recreated the empirical conditions of historiography, to witness the words and deeds of men in the arguments of speech and action. History is reconstituted by art in the dynamic present encounter with the proof of example, Shakespeare unmasking appearances in the revelation of causes. Shakespeare's understanding of causality goes beyond prediction by probability derived from exemplarity, universal human nature immanent within the individual whose particular character is then determined by the variations of *virtù*, fortune and necessity. Warwick's reply to Henry's recollection of Richard's prophecy of Northumberland's treachery ('There is a history in all men's lives' ..., *2 Henry IV* 3.1.80ff) illustrates this kind of knowledge. But Shakespeare's insights go deeper.

Shakespeare's history plays repeatedly dramatise an awareness of the dialectic of causality between society and the individual, both in feudal England and classical antiquity. Good and evil, represented by the virtues and vices, conventionally provided a taxonomy for individual behaviour both within the soul (the psychomachy) and society (the fallen world). In the secularised drama, however, the constitutive function of language as a defining feature of man and society is recognized but Shakespeare goes beyond the humanist commonplace of civilised self-compliment, such as 'societie of men is maintained by speech, as being the interpreter or rather expresser of the mind'.[48] Shakespeare's nominalism, as reflected in Falstaff, always tests the meaningfulness of the universal, such as honour, against the reality of its particular manifestation in speech and action.

In the feudal, early modern and ancient worlds honour shaped social structure. It provided a seemingly unifying belief system, an ideology: 'unifying' because its defensive principle was social and military obligation and interdependency in an hierarchic society. Consequently, society and the individual were mutually self-defining. Nobody of status (including Falstaff) could entirely escape, deny or abandon the claims of honour. Honour was a binding circle of cause and effect, the means and end of action according to the principal of feudal loyalty or civic *Romanitas*. To act according to honour was to fulfil the obligations of status and thus realise one's identity. Prince Hal and Falstaff attempt to escape into the world of the carnivalesque, but civil war and the death of the king end their saturnalia and they are reclaimed by the real world of duty, time and death. Coriolanus, his honour lost with his name, becomes 'a kind of nothing, titleless' (5.1.13). Antony claims, 'If I lose mine honor, / I lose myself' (3.4.22–3), but from a Roman point of view that honour has long since disappeared. Neither can sustain their being, with either revenge or romance, since they have denied its shaping source. Achilles and Troilus parallel Coriolanus and Antony in pride and passion, but when they return to the battlefield they enact the complete debasement of chivalric honour.

Yet in the various historical manifestations of honour dramatised by Shakespeare, whether Roman militarism, republican idealism or feudal chivalry, the very concept that had evolved to perpetuate the state and the common weal served to destroy them because of internal contradictions made manifest by civil war. In Shakespeare's depiction the Roman and English commonwealths existed in a state of tension between opposed forces, external and internal. Externally, Rome was constantly at war with immediately surrounding tribes as we see in *Coriolanus* and then, with conquest, at war with itself in patrician rivalries and with the world – Gaul, England, Germany, Parthia, and so on, as we see in *Julius Caesar* and *Antony and Cleopatra*. Furthermore, the internal threat of the plebeians remained a divisive factor. Parallel to this, Shakespeare depicts England as continually at war in Scotland, Ireland, and above all in France. Internally, England had inherited the civil strife of dynastic struggles, the inheritance of the ramifications of the Plantagenet line with the Houses of York and Lancaster, and the great families, the Nevilles, the Cliffords, the Percies. Further, the threat of peasant revolt paralleled that of the plebeians as we see so powerfully in the Jack Cade rebellion of *2 Henry VI*. Societies subsisting under such strains must inevitably collapse into the horrors of civil war, 'the centre cannot hold' as W.B. Yeats wrote, and 'mere anarchy is loosed upon the world'[49] and honour becomes both arbitrary and absolute: Coriolanus intends to destroy Rome; Brutus ensures the destruction of the republic; Hotspur rejoices in suicidal egoism. In Shakespeare's presentation the only survivor bathed in the dubious honour of Machiavellian 'glory' is Henry V. Shakespeare saw the essential paradox of cause within the structure of society and within the individual. Socially, honour becomes fissiparous, not unificatory, especially given the instability of legal succession and the privileges of aristocratic precedence. Subinfeudation gradually decentralised honour and empowered feudal might over right. This unique understanding of the interrelationship of society, politics and language is the major achievement of Shakespeare's arguments with history.

Notes

Introduction

1. Geoffrey Bullough (ed.), *The Narrative and Dramatic Sources of Shakespeare*, 8 vols (London: Routledge and Kegan Paul, 1958–75).

    The best single volume editions are those of the Arden series, the New Cambridge Shakespeare and the Oxford 'World's Classics' series. Of the three the Arden tends to have the fullest introduction, commentary and appendices, particularly the Arden Third Series which is completely re-editing the whole of Shakespeare. The following editions, in relation to the chapters of this book, are recommended:

    Edward Burns (ed.), *King Henry VI, Part One* (Walton-on-Thames: The Arden Shakespeare, 2000). Third series.

    Ronald Knowles (ed.), *King Henry VI, Part Two* (Walton-on-Thames: Thomas Nelson and Sons Ltd, 1999). Third series.

    Michael Hattaway (ed.), *The Third Part of King Henry VI* (The New Cambridge Shakespeare, Cambridge University Press, 1993).

    Antony Hammond (ed.), *King Richard III* (The Arden Shakespeare, London: Methuen, 1981). Second series.

    Peter Ure (ed.), *King Richard II* (The Arden Shakespeare, London: Methuen, 1956. Second series.

    Andrew Gurr (ed.), *King Richard II* (The New Cambridge Shakespeare, Cambridge University Press, 1984).

    A.R. Humphreys (ed.), *The First Part of King Henry IV* (The Arden Shakespeare, London: Methuen, 1960). Second series.

    A.R. Humphreys (ed.), *The Second Part of King Henry VI* (The Arden Shakespeare, London: Methuen, 1966). Second series.

    T.W. Craik (ed.), *King Henry V* (Walton-on-Thames: The Arden Shakespeare, 1995). Third series.

    David Daniell (ed.), *Julius Caesar* (Walton-on-Thames: The Arden Shakespeare, 1998). Third series.

    John Wilders (ed.), *Anthony and Cleopatra* (London: Routledge, The Arden Shakespeare, 1995). Third series.

    Philip Brockbank (ed.), *Coriolanus* (London: Methuen, The Arden Shakespeare, 1976). Second series.

    David Bevington (ed.), *Troilus and Cressida* (Walton-on-Thames: The Arden Shakespeare, 1998). Third series.

    Unless otherwise stated all references in this study will be to *The Riverside Shakespeare* edited by G. Blakemore Evans (Boston: Houghton Mifflin Company, 1974).
2. See Mario Praz, '"The Politic Brain": Machiavelli and the Elizabethans', in *The Flaming Heart* (New York: Doubleday Anchor Books, 1958), pp. 100–1.

3. See David Riggs, *Shakespeare's Heroical Histories: Henry VI and its Literary Tradition* (Cambridge, Mass.: Harvard University Press, 1971), pp. 34–61.
4. See A.M. Potter, '*Troilus and Cressida*: Deconstructing the Middle Ages?' *Theoria*, 72 (1988), pp. 23–35.

Chapter 1

1. Compare Alan C. Dessen, *Elizabethan Drama and the Viewer's Eye* (Chapel Hill: University of North Carolina Press, 1977), who is concerned with the visual aspects of staging and spectacle; and David Bevington, *Action is Eloquence. Shakespeare's Language of Gesture* (Cambridge, Mass.: Harvard University Press, 1984), in which all forms of stage gesture are categorised and examined.
2 T.W. Craik (ed.), *The Merry Wives of Windsor* (Oxford: Oxford University Press, 1990), p. 136.
3 'Shakespeare and Formal Logic', in Kemp Malone and Martin B. Ruud (eds), *Studies in English Philology: A Miscellany in Honor of Frederick Klaeber* (Minneapolis: Minnesota University Press, 1929), p. 387.
4 See Robert Miola, *Shakespeare and Classical Tragedy* (Oxford: Oxford University Press, 1992).
5 E.A.J. Honigmann (ed.), *King John* (London: Methuen, The Arden Shakespeare, 1954), p. ix.
6 This note may be added to the cultural complexity of the representation of Shylock as registered by James Shapiro in his *Shakespeare and the Jews* (New York: Columbia University Press, 1996).
7 *Shakespeare's Use of the Arts of Language* (New York: Columbia University Press, 1947).
8 T.W. Baldwin, *William Shakespeare's Small Latine and Lesse Greeke*, 2 vols (Urbana: University of Illinois University Press, 1944). Sister Joan Marie Lechner, *Renaissance Concepts of the Commonplaces* (New York: Pageant Press, 1962). Other earlier general studies consulted for this material are W.G. Crane, *Wit and Rhetoric in the Renaissance* (New York: Columbia University Press, 1937); Hardin Craig, *The Enchanted Glass* (Oxford: Basil Blackwell, 1960); Perry Miller, *The New England Mind: The Seventeenth Century* (New York: Macmillan, 1939); W.S. Howell, *Logic and Rhetoric in England 1500–1700* (Princeton: Princeton University Press, 1956). More recent studies examined are Lisa Jardine 'Humanist Logic', in Charles B. Schmitt, Quentin Skinner, Ekhart Kesslar and Jill Kray (eds), *The Cambridge History of Renaissance Philosophy* (Cambridge: Cambridge University Press, 1988), pp. 178–98; Lee A. Jacobus, *Shakespeare and the Dialectic of Certainty* (New York: St. Martin's Press, 1992); Peter Mack, *Renaissance Argument. Valla and Agricola in the Traditions of Rhetoric and Dialectic* (Leiden: E.J. Brill, 1993); Marion Trousdale, *Shakespeare and the Rhetoricians* (London: Scolar Press, 1982). An excellent collection is Wayne A. Rebhorn (ed.), *Renaissance Debates on Rhetoric* (Ithaca and London: Cornell University Press, 2000).
9. Trousdale, *Shakespeare and the Rhetoricians* gives some very good illustration from sixteenth-century rhetoricians of their own examples of applying the topics, see pp. 27–8.
10. See Jardine, 'Humanist Logic' and Mack, *Renaissance Argument*.

11. Harry Caplan provides a valuable introduction to his edition of the *Rhetorica ad Herennium,* formally known as *[Cicero] Ad C. Herennium De Ratione Dicendi* (The Loeb Classical Library, Cambridge, Mass.: Harvard University Press, 1954).

12. Thomas Ollive Mabbott and J. Milton French (eds), *The Works of John Milton* (New York: Columbia University Press, 1938), vol. xviii, pp. 128–220.

13. *The Adages, The Collected Works of Erasmus* (Toronto: University of Toronto Press, 1982–92), vols 31–4.

14. The enlarged version by Thomas Palfreyman is reproduced in a facsimile of the 1620 edition with an introduction by Robin Hood Bowers (Gainesville: Scholars Facsimiles and Reprints, 1967).

15. A very useful account of the *Progymnasmata* in education may be found in Donald Leman Clark, *John Milton at St Paul's School* (New York: Columbia University Press, 1948), pp. 230–49.

16. For consideration of Shakespeare's use of *laus* or praise topics, as recommended by Aphthonius, in *Romeo and Juliet* and *Twelfth Night*, see T.W. Baldwin, 'Shakespeare's Aphthonian Man', *Modern Language Notes*, 65 (1950), pp. 111–12.

17. The early chapters of Charles Osborne McDonald's *The Rhetoric of Tragedy: Form in Stuart Drama* (Amherst, Mass: University of Massachusetts Press, 1966) provide a good introduction to the classical material. 'The Technique of the Debate' is Madeleine Doran's relevant section on late medieval and Tudor drama in her celebrated *Endeavors of Art: a Study of Form in Elizabethan Drama* (Madison: University of Wisconsin Press, 1954), pp. 310–21. An outstanding specialist study is that of Joel B. Altman, *The Tudor Play of Mind. Rhetorical Enquiry and the Development of Elizabethan Drama* (Berkeley: University of California Press, 1978). More recently Neil Rhodes has related the *controversiae* to *Measure for Measure, The Merchant of Venice* and *Coriolanus* by way of Alexander Silvayn's *The Orator* (1596), see 'The Controversial Plot: Declamation and the Concept of the "Problem Play"', *MLR*, 95 (2000), pp. 609–22.

Chapter 2

1. Noted authorities include Malcolm Vale, *War and Chivalry* (London: Duckworth, 1981) and Maurice Keen, *Chivalry* (New Haven and London: Yale University Press, 1984), particularly ch. XII 'Chivalry and War', pp. 219–37.

2. See under 'Fealty' and 'Homage' in the invaluable reference work, Bradford B. Broughton, *Dictionary of Medieval Knighthood and Chivalry. Concepts and Terms* (New York: Greenwood Press, 1986).

3. See M.H. Keen's brilliantly even-handed essay, 'Chivalry, Nobility, and the Man-at-Arms', in C.T. Allmond (ed.), *War, Literature and Politics in the Late Middle Ages* (Liverpool: Liverpool University Press, 1976), pp. 32–45, particularly pp. 44–5. For illustration of how a campaign might be ultimately unsuccessful yet very profitable from payment of ransoms, see K.B. McFarlane, *The Nobility of Later Medieval England* (Oxford: Clarendon Press, 1973), pp. 19–40. The best general chapter on the ideals of chivalry and the reality of the knight at war is John Barnie's 'Aristocracy, Knighthood and Chivalry', in *War in Medieval Society. Social Values and the Hundred Years War 1337–99*

(London: Weidenfeld and Nicolson, 1974), pp. 56–96. Barnie's portrayal of Henry of Grosmont, first Duke of Lancaster, offers a telling corrective to those who follow the sceptical view influentially expressed by Johan Huizinga, *The Waning of the Middle Ages* (originally 1924; rep. New York: Anchor Books, 1954).

4. See Dean Loganbill, 'The Contrast between the Chevalier Bayard, a Chivalric Knight, and Giovanni de' Medici, a Pragmatic Captain', in Larry D. Benson and John Leyerle (eds), *Chivalric Literature. Essays on Relations between Literature and Life in the Later Middle Ages* (Kalamazoo: Medieval Institute Publications, Western Michigan University, 1980), pp. 117–30. For an analysis of the assumed 'dichotomy between the "real" world of politics and the "ideal" world of chivalry' which demonstrates 'the political character of . . . expressions of the ideal of chivalry', see David Morgan, 'From a Death to a View: Louis Robessart, Johan Huizinga, and the Political Significance of Chivalry', in Sydney Anglo (ed.), *Chivalry in the Renaissance* (Woodbridge: The Boydell Press, 1990), pp. 93–106.

5. After resistance, the city of Limoges was taken by storm in 1370 and its citizens massacred by the Black Prince. Froissart's account of the terror and pity of it is one of the most moving passages of his *Chronicles*. Other historians, however, pointed out that this reflected the rules of war when a siege was resisted. See John Barnie, *War in Medieval Society*, pp. 76–7. Similarly, Monstrelet records that in 1440 during the raid on Santerre, Lord Talbot massacred men, women and children sheltering in a church by burning the building down. Again, this was all within the laws of war. A contemporary, Honoré Bouvet, bemoaned such atrocities permitted by the chivalric code. See A.J. Pollard, *John Talbot and the War in France 1427–1453* (London: Royal Historical Society, 1983), pp. 125–6.

6. See A.B. Ferguson, *The Indian Summer of English Chivalry* (Durham: North Carolina University Press, 1965) for the thesis of decline: Benson and Leyerle *Chivalric Literature* concludes with 'The Major Themes of Chivalric Literature', pp. 131–47. Gordon Kipling, *The Triumph of Honour* (The Hague: Leiden University Press, 1977) considers the Burgundian element in Tudor revivals. Alan Young, *Tudor and Jacobean Tournaments* (London: George Philip, 1987) surveys the joust. 'Elizabethan Chivalry: the Romance of the Accession Day Tilts', Frances Yates's well-known article, is now found in the collection *Astraea. The Imperial Theme in the Sixteenth Century* (London and Boston: Routledge and Kegan Paul, 1975), pp. 88–111. Roy Strong examines the role of St George in *The Cult of Elizabeth* (London: Thames and Hudson, 1977), pp. 164–88. An important work, contemporary with Spenser, is *The Book of Honor and Arms* (1590) by Sir William Segar, eventually Garter King of Arms, now available with his *Honor Military and Civil* (1602) in 'Scholars' Facsimiles and Reprints' edition, ed. Diane Bornstein (New York, 1975). A.B. Ferguson picks up where his above book leaves off, in *The Chivalric Tradition of Renaissance England* (Washington: Folger Books, 1986). For a study which focuses on specific figures in the Elizabethan period, such as Spenser, Sir Philip Sidney and the Earl of Essex, see Richard C. McCoy, *The Rites of Knighthood. The Literature and Politics of Elizabethan Chivalry* (Berkeley: University of California Press, 1989).

7. For 'horror of treason' and 'open fact', see J.G. Bellamy, *The Law of Treason in the Later Middle Ages* (Cambridge: Cambridge University Press, 1970), pp. 89,

103: for the attainder of Henry VI and Richard III, see pp. 123–4. Details of Richard, Earl of Cambridge, taken from the parliamentary rolls, are found in the *Dictionary of National Biography* (Oxford: Oxford University Press, 1975), p. 1767.

8. See Mervyn James, *English Politics and the Concept of Honour 1485–1642* (Oxford: The Past and Present Society, 'Past and Present' Supplement 3, 1978), particularly pp. 2–4.

9. This might well have been included in the *chansons de geste* volume Talbot presented to King Henry's bride, Queen Margaret, as a welcoming gift, along with prose romances, treatises on war, chronicles and the statutes of the Order of the Garter. See Pollard, *John Talbot and the War in France 1427–1453*, p. 123.

10. From *Pierce Penilesse his Supplication to the Divell* (1592). See Thomas Nashe *Works*, ed. R.B. McKerrow (London: A.H. Bullen, 1958), I. p. 212.

11. Michael Hattaway (ed.), *The First Part of King Henry VI*, 'The New Cambridge Shakespeare' (Cambridge: Cambridge University Press, 1990), p. 105. Andrew S. Cairncross (ed.), *The First Part of King Henry VI*. 'The Arden Shakespeare' (London: Methuen, 1962), p. 44.

12. See Hattaway, *The First Part of King Henry VI*, p. 155.

13. See Julian Pitt-Rivers 'Honour and Social Status', in J.G. Peristiany (ed.), *Honour and Shame: The Values of Mediterranean Society* (London: Weidenfeld and Nicolson, 1965), p. 38.

14. For fuller treatment see my introduction to *King Henry VI, Part Two* (The Arden Shakespeare, 1999), pp. 73–105.

15. See Jean E. Howard and Phyllis Rackin, *Engendering a Nation* (London and New York: Routledge, 1997), p. 76.

16. *Divine Providence in the England of Shakespeare's Histories* (Cambridge, Mass.: Harvard University Press, 1970), p. 254.

17. See L.W. Cushman, *The Devil and the Vice in English Dramatic Literature before Shakespeare* (London: Frank Cass, 1900).

18. Josiah Pratt (ed.), *The Acts and Monuments of John Foxe* (London: The Religious Tract Society, 1877).

19. See Clifford Leech, *Shakespeare: The Chronicles*, 'Writers and their Work' 146 (London: Longmans Green, 1962), p. 17.

20. *Shakespearean Structures* (London: Macmillan, 1981), p. 6.

21. See Anthony Tuck, *Richard II and the English Nobility* (London: 1973), pp. 124, 198, and J.G. Bellamy, *The Law of Treason in England in the Later Middle Ages* (Cambridge: Cambridge University Press, 1970), p. 143.

22. *The Annales* (London, 1615), p. 381.

23. G. Neilson, *Trial by Combat* (Glasgow: Hodge & Co., 1890), p. 275.

24. Cited by Bellamy, *The Law of Treason*, pp. 145–6.

25. *The Faerie Queene*, vi.ii.7.

26. *The Book of Honor and Arms*, p. 30.

27. In the Arden edition quoted here Q's 'usurer' is preferred to F's 'usurper'.

28. *The Historical Collections of A Citizen of London in the Fifteenth Century*, Camden Society New Series XVII, ed. James Gairdner (London: Camden Society, 1875) John Nichols' *Illustrations of the Manners and Expenses of Ancient Times in England*, 1797 (New York: AMS Press, 1973), pp. 217, 220, prints the writ for the combat and the costs for disposal and execution.

29. See Neilson, *Trial by Combat*, pp. 188–9, for a detailed comparison.

30. *A Critical Enquiry into Antient Armour*, 3 vols (London: Henry G. Bohn, 1849), vol. 2, p. 125.

31. *The Second Part of King Henry the Sixth* (London: Methuen, 1909), p. 66.

32. *The Triumph of Maximilian I* (New York: Dover Publications, 1964). With a translation of descriptive text, introduction and notes by Stanley Appelbaum, p. 7.

33. Raphael Holinshed, *The Chronicles of England, Scotland and Ireland* (2nd edn, 1587; repr. London, 6 vols, 1808) vol. 3, p. 210. Robert Fabyan, *The New Chronicles of England and France* [1516], ed. H. Ellis (London, 1811) p. 168. *Grafton's Chronicle* [1569] (London: 2 vols, 1809), vol. 1, p. 628. Edward Hall, *The Union of the Two Noble and Illustre Families of Lancaster and York* [1548] (London, 1809), pp. 207–8.

34. *Certain Sermons or Homilies* (Oxford: The University Press, 1844), pp. 459–60. For a detailed commentary on all the Cade scenes, see my Arden edition.

35. See David Kunzle, 'World Upside Down: The Iconography of a European Broadsheet', in Barbara Babcock (ed.), *The Reversible World: Symbolic Inversion in Art and Society* (Ithaca and London: Cornell University Press, 1978), p. 51.

36. W.S. Holdsworth, *A History of English Law*, 17 vols (London: Methuen, 1903), vol. 3, pp. 294–302.

37. Leona C. Gabel, *Benefit of Clergy in England in the Later Middle Ages*, Smith College Studies in History, 14, nos 1–4 (October 1928–July 1929, Northampton, Mass.), p. 73.

38. For a summary, see Ronald Knowles (ed.), *Henry VI Part Two*, 'The Arden Shakespeare' (Walton-on-Thames: Thomas Nelson, 1999), pp. 92–5. Fuller discussion is found in N.B. Harte, 'State Control of Dress and Social Change in pre-Industrial England', in D.C. Coleman and A.H. John (eds), *Trade, Government and Economy in Pre-Industrial England* (London: Weidenfeld and Nicolson, 1976), pp. 132–65.

39. These details were spelt out in proclamations; see, for example, Paul L. Hughes and James F. Larkin (eds), *The Tudor Royal Proclamations*, vol. 2 (New Haven and London: Yale University Press, 1969), p. 280.

Chapter 3

1. Though actually seventeen years old, Hall (p. 251) records that he was twelve at the time of his death.

2. Recalled by Robert Greene on his deathbed, this line is at the heart of the authorial controversy. See D.A. Carroll, 'Greene's "vpstart crow" Passage: A Survey of Commentary', *Research Opportunities in Renaissance Drama*, 28 (1985), pp. 111–27.

3. *The Baronage of England* (1675), vol. I, p. 343.

4. Transl. G.W. Coopland (Liverpool: Liverpool University Press, 1949), p. 131.

5. Transl. George Bull (Harmondsworth: Penguin Books, 1961), p. 100.

6. The octavo reading adopted by Cairncross, not in the Folio or Riverside.

7. In a Declaration of 1308 that was quite unprecedented the magnates of Edward II argued that 'Homage and the oath of allegiance are stronger and bind more by reason of the crown than by reason of the person of the King'

(B. Wilkinson, *Constitutional History of Medieval England 1216–1399*, vol. 2, 'Politics and the Constitution 1307–1399' (London: Longmans Green, 1952), p. 111). See also pp. 100–7, 135–9. Thus the king was expected to fulfil obligations towards the crown and, to keep their oath, the barons in parliament could take action to ensure that he do so. This principle strengthened the two-way contractualism inherent in the coronation oath and provided the means of resistance to any signs of absolutism, as Richard II was to learn to his cost.

8. See A.R. Braunmuller's note on the rousing conclusion of *The Life and Death of King John*, 'Naught shall make us rue, / If England to itself do rest but true' (Oxford: Oxford University Press, 1994, p. 297).

9. See Patricia Parker, *Shakespeare from the Margins* (Chicago and London: Chicago University Press, 1996), ch. 1 'Preposterous Estates, Preposterous events: from Late to Early Shakespeare', p. 37.

10. This interpretation of all of Shakespeare's English histories in terms of the 'Tudor myth' ideology propounded by contemporary chroniclers which was most influentially argued by E.M.W. Tillyard in his *Shakespeare's History Plays* (London: Chatto and Windus, 1944) is now severely qualified, if not totally discredited and reversed in some quarters. Probably the best way into the subject is Robin Headlam Wells's 'The Fortunes of Tillyard: Twentieth Century Critical Debate in Shakespeare's History Plays', *English Studies* 66 (1985), pp. 391–403. Alternatively, see my introduction to the Arden *2 Henry VI*, pp. 41–54.

11. See Antony Hammond (ed.), *King Richard III*, The Arden Shakespeare (London: Methuen, 1981), pp. 102–3.

12. I am indebted here to Louis E. Dollarhide, 'The Logic of Villainy: Shakespeare's Use of the Fallacies', *University of Mississipi Studies in English*, 10 (1969), p. 51.

13. Henry Walter (ed.), *Doctrinal Treatises* (Cambridge: The University Press, The Parker Society, 1848), p. 332.

14. For the more complex significance of the word in theory and practice, see Lisa Jardine, *Francis Bacon. Discovery and the Art of Discourse* (Cambridge: Cambridge University Press, 1974), pp. 29–47.

15. See Julie Hankey (ed.), *Richard III*, 'Plays in Performance' (Bristol: Bristol Classical Press, 1988), pp. 210–29.

16. See George A. Kennedy, *A New History of Classical Rhetoric* (Princeton, NY: Princeton University Press, 1994), pp. 7–8, 17–18.

17. See Leah Scragg, 'Iago – Vice or Devil', *Shakespeare Survey*, 21 (1968), pp. 53–65 and John D. Cox, *The Devil and the Sacred in English Drama 1350–1642* (Cambridge: Cambridge University Press, 2000), pp. 76–81.

18. See Stuart Clark, *Thinking with Demons. The Idea of Witchcraft in Early Modern England* (Oxford: Clarendon Press, 1997), pp. 80–3, 94–8.

19. For conscience and Richard generally, see John S. Wilks, *The Idea of Conscience in Renaissance Tragedy* (Routledge: London and New York, 1990), pp. 78–99. For conscience, Richard and early modern discourse, see Camille Wells Slights, *The Casuistical Tradition in Shakespeare, Donne, Herbert, and Milton* (Princeton, NY: Princeton University Press, 1981), pp. 68–78.

20. *Endeavours of Art*, p. 316.

21. *King Lear and the Gods* (San Marino: The Huntington Library, 1966), pp. 22–3. Elton's study of scepticism may be read against Keith Thomas's outline of

popular providential beliefs in *Religion and the Decline of Magic* (London: Weidenfeld and Nicolson, 1971), pp. 78–113.

22. See A.L. French, 'The Mills of God and Shakespeare's Early History Plays', *English Studies*, 55 (1974), pp. 313–24.

23. *The City of God*, transl. John Healey (London: Dent, 1945) vol. I, Bk I, ch. VII, p. 9.

24. *Idem*.

25. For Calvin's dismissal of 'permission' and insistence on God's will directly implicated in evil, see *Institutes of the Christian Religion* I, xviii. 1 and 4 (*Calvin's Institutes*, Grand Rapids, Michigan, n.d.) pp. 111, 114–15. As with all these arguments, the further distinction which Calvin draws between God's will and his 'precept' in man's evil actions simply turns providential order into captious and devious prevarication. Compare Bullinger's 'Sermon X', 'On Sin and the Kinds Thereof', *The Decades of Henry Bullinger*, ed. Thomas Harding, 'The Third Decade' (Cambridge, The University Press, 1850), pp. 373ff; *The Writings of John Bradford*, ed. Aubrey Townsend (Cambridge: The University Press, 1848), p. 213; William Fulke, *A Defence of the Sincere and The Translations of the Holy Scriptures into the English Tongue*, ed. Charles Henry Hartshorne (Cambridge: The University Press, 1843), pp. 562–3.

26. *The City of God*, vol. 2, Bk XX, ch. II, p. 270.

Chapter 4

1. See Holinshed, pp. 837–46. For a modern appraisal of Richard's reign, see Nigel Saul, *Richard II* (New Haven and London: Yale University Press, 1997).

2. For a succinct account, see Anthony Tuck, *Crown and Nobility 1272–1461* (London: Fontana, 1985), pp. 218–23.

3. The authorative study for details of the combat drawn on here is G. Neilson, *Trial by Combat* (Glasgow: Hodge & Co., 1890). For Woodstock, see p. 260.

4. Sir John Bourchier, Lord Berners (transl.), *The Chronicle of Froissart* (London: David Nutt, 6 vols, 1903), vol. VI, p. 312. On the question of regal inheritance, the story that Bolingbroke's ancestor Edmund, first Duke of Lancaster, was the first-born son of Henry III and therefore older than Edward I, was spread by Lancastrian supporters. See F.W. Maitland, *The Constitutional History of England* (Cambridge: Cambridge University Press, 1926), pp. 192–3. In 1594 the Jesuit agitator Robert Parsons cited the view of those who believed that John of Gaunt should have succeeded Edward III, his father, before Richard. See Edna Zwick Boris, *Shakespeare's English Kings, the People, and the Law* (London: Associated University Presses, 1978), pp. 193–4.

5. In *Shakespearean Politics. Government and Misgovernment in the Great Histories* (Athens and London: Ohio University Press, 1983) C.G. Thayer analyses this scene in a reading of 'The Death of Divine Kingship: *Richard II*' which builds upon Gaunt's words at 1.2.37–41.

6. See J.G. Bellamy, *The Law of Treason in England in the Later Middle Ages* (Cambridge: Cambridge University Press, 1970), p. 143.

7. See Mervyn James, *English Politics and the Concept of Honour 1485–1642*, Past and Present Supplement 3 (Oxford: The Past and Present Society, 1978), pp. 15–17.

8. See J.G. Bellamy on the Act of Attainder (*The Law of Treason in England*, pp. 177–205) which, in effect, pre-empted any judicial process in parliament. The king's declaration that someone was a traitor was judgment in itself, a procedure Richard frequently used.
9. See Neilson, *Trial by Combat*, pp. 189, 270, 273.
10. In Peter Ure's edition a lengthy note is supplied outlining the differing accounts of Holinshed and Froissart. In Holinshed, as in the play, the combat procedure is halted and the king withdraws: in Froissart details of taking counsel well before the date of the combat (which does not appear in his record) are given, (*King Richard II*, 'The Arden Shakespeare', London: Methuen, 1956, pp. 28–9). My point remains: Richard went to Coventry knowing what he would do. The counsel merely rubber stamps his decision.
11. See Paul Gaudet, 'Northumberland's "persuasion": Reflections on *Richard II* II.1.224–300', *Upstart Crow* 4 (Fall 1982), pp. 73–85.
12. An excellent introduction to these issues is 'Law' by Donald R. Kelley, in H.J. Burns (ed.), *The Cambridge History of Political Thought 1450–1700* (Cambridge: Cambridge University Press, 1991) pp. 66–94.
13. For the place of these absolutist ideas within medieval political thought and for detailed reference to manuscript sources, see Otto Gierke, *Political Theories of the Middle Age* (Cambridge: Cambridge University Press, 1900), particularly ch. V, 'The Idea of Monarchy', and ch. VI, 'The Idea of Popular Sovereignty'.
14. *De legibus* Bk 3, 3, 8. For natural law, see R.S. White, *Natural Law in English Renaissance Literature* (Cambridge: Cambridge University Press, 1996), ch. 3 'The reception of Natural Law in Renaissance England'.
15. See R.W.K. Hinton, 'English Constitutional Doctrines from the Fifteenth Century to the Seventeenth', I English Constitutional Theories from Sir John Fortescue to Sir John Eliot, *English Historical Review* 75, no. 296 (1960), pp. 410–13.
16. Maitland, *Constitutional History*, p. 99.
17. Maitland, *Constitutional History*, pp. 99–100.
18. Leopold G. Wickham Legg (ed.), *English Coronation Records* (Westminster: Archibald Constable & Co. Ltd, 1901), p. 88. This volume includes the Latin of *Liber Regalis*, the text used for the coronation, pp. 81–112, and an English translation, pp. 112–30. To save space, however, the translation frequently refers forward to the English text of Charles I's coronation order, without pointing out the amendments made to that translation.
19. Wickham Legg, *English Coronation Records*, p. 116. See Ronald Knowles, 'The Political Contexts of Deposition and Election in *Edward II*', *Medieval and Renaissance Drama in England*, 14 (forthcoming).
20. See Percy Ernst Schramm, *A History of the English Coronation* (Oxford: The Clarendon Press, 1937), ch. VII 'The King and the Law: the Coronation Oath', pp. 203–13.
21. See Schramm, *A History of the English Coronation*, pp. 134–6, and Wickham Legg, *English Coronation Records*, p. 125.
22. Wickham Legg, *English Coronation Records*, p. 92.
23. ' . . . perhaps the most important words ever written for the history of political thought' (J.W. Allen, *A History of Political Thought in the Sixteenth Century*, London: Methuen, rep. 1961, p. 132).
24. *Certain Sermons or Homilies* (Oxford: Oxford University Press, 1844), pp. 100–3.

25. See J.W. Allen, *A History of Political Thought in the Sixteenth Century*, p. 128.
26. See William Huse Dunham, Jr. and Charles T. Wood, 'The Right to Rule in England: Depositions and the Kingdom's Authority, 1327–1485', *The American Historical Review*, 81 (1976), pp. 742–7.
27. The principal chronicles were Thomas Walsingham's *Historia Anglicana*, the *Ypodigma Neustriae*, the *Annales Ricardi Secundi et Henrici Quarti*, and Thomas Otterbourne's *Chronica Regum Angliae*. See Louisa De Saussure Duls, *Richard II in the Early Chronicles* (The Hague and Paris: Mouton, 1975), p. 118.
28. I use the formulation of the medieval legist Bartolus who distinguished between the tyrant *absque titulo* (without title, and the tyrant *ex parte exercitii*, by 'practice' or 'exercise' of oppression). See Roland Mousnier's very helpful summary of the legal, political and theological history of the problem, 'It is Permissible to Kill a Tyrant', in *The Assassination of Henry IV*, transl. Joan Spencer (London: Faber and Faber, 1973) pp. 65–105. King Richard acknowledged his 'insufficiencie' (Holinshed, II, 864) as *rex inutilis*, the canonical doctrine of the inept, incompetent king who must be removed from office, but clearly Shakespeare was drawn by the drama of more criminal kingship. See Edward Peters, *The Shadow King. 'Rex Inutilis' in Medieval Law and Literature, 751–1327* (New Haven and London: Yale University Press, 1970), pp. 116–34.
29. See Saul, *Richard II*, p. 419.
30. See Donald R. Kelley, 'Ideas of Resistance before Elizabeth', in Gordon J. Schochet (ed.), *Law, Literature and the Settlement of Regimes*. Proceedings of the Folger Institute Centre for the History of British Political Thought, vol. 2 (Washington: The Folger Institute, 1990), p. 7. For the importance of John of Salisbury's *Policratus* in this regard, see Richard H. Rouse and Mary A. Rouse, 'John of Salisbury and the Doctrine of Tyrannicide', *Speculum* 42 (1967), pp. 693–79.
31. See Knowles, 'The Political Contexts of Deposition and Election in *Edward II*' (forthcoming).
32. See Peter Holmes, *Resistance and Compromise. The Political Thought of the English Catholics* (Cambridge: Cambridge University Press, 1982), pp. 129–35.
33. The *Declaration* is published as Appendix No. XII (pp. xliv–xlviii) in M.A. Tierney (ed.), *Dodd's Church History of England* (London: Charles Dolman, 1840. Rep. Farnborough: Gregg International, 1972), vol. III.
34. I quote from the London edition of 1712, p. 36. See also pp. 13–19 on John Knox, Calvin and other Huguenots.
35. I assume that this is why Shakespeare left out any reference to the historical incident of Northumberland ambushing Richard and taking him as prisoner to Flint Castle (see Holinshed, II, 859).
36. Holinshed repeats the words recorded in parliament (*Rotuli Parliamentorum*, London, 1767–77, vol. iii, pp. 422–3).
37. See Saul, *Richard II*, p. 423.

Chapter 5

1. This chapter is a much expanded and revised version of what originally appeared as 'Honour, Debt, the Rejection and St Paul', in Ronald Knowles, *Henry IV Parts I & II*, 'The Critics Debate' (Basingstoke: Macmillan, 1992), pp. 73–86.

2. 'The Comic Element in Shakespeare's Histories', *Anglia*, 71 (1952–3), p. 96.
3. See Paul A. Jorgensen, *Shakespeare's Military World* (1956), pp. 130–43.
4. For the crusade as an instrument of English national policy and international politics, see John Barnie, *War in Medieval Society* (London: Weidenfeld and Nicolson, 1974), pp. 87–8.
5. See Percy Ernst Schramm, *A History of the English Coronation* (Oxford: The Clarendon Press, 1937), pp. 106–11, and chapter 4 above, *Richard II*, p. 61.
6. *Hall's Chronicle* (London, 1809: rep. New York: AMS Press, 1965), p. 27.
7. James Hamilton Wylie, *History of England under Henry the Fourth* (London: Longmans, Green, and Co., 1884), vol. 1, p. 294, summarises the record found in Thomas Rymer's *Foedera* (The Hague, 1745), vol. iv, pp. 35–6. M.H. Keen uses this instance to illustrate his argument that 'Important prisoners, as "great captains" and princes of an adversary's blood, were for this reason ["public interest"] at the disposal of the "head of war" without any reserve. He could indeed reserve to himself any prisoner for reasons of state, provided he was prepared to compensate his master for the loss of his ransom' (*The Laws of War in the Late Middle Ages*, London: Routledge & Kegan Paul, 1965, pp. 145–6).
8. *The Tree of Battles*, transl. and ed. G.W. Coopland (Liverpool: Liverpool University Press, 1949), pp. 134–5.
9. See Denys Hay, 'The Division of the Spoils of War in Fourteenth-Century England', *Transactions of the Royal Historical Society*, 5th series, 4 (1954), pp. 95–101. The argument here, drawn from the evidence of medieval authorities and modern historians, is directly opposite to that of Samuel Burdett Hemingway in his New Variorum edition (*Henry the Fourth. Part I.* Philadelphia and London: J.B. Lippincott Company, 1936, pp. 21–2), which is drawn on by the editors of the Arden (second series) and the New Cambridge editions. Hemingway repeats George Tollet's note from the Johnson–Steevens variorum edition of 1773 which claims that Henry had a right to Moredake only as a prince of the blood royal. E.A. Rauchet ('Hotspur's Prisoners and the Laws of War in *1 Henry IV*', *Shakespeare Quarterly*, 45 (1994), pp. 96–7) argues for the illegality of Henry's demands but the case rests on the demonstration that Henry flouts chivalric procedure (the formal transference of the captives' bond of faith from original captor) rather than breaks the law according to Bonet, who I quote, and according to early fifteenth-century indentures printed in Rymer's *Foedera*. These indentures indicate that the king reserved not only the right to princes of the blood but to any 'Lieutenant, ou d'autres Chieftains', as Keen argues (see above, n. 7).
10. The most helpful study remains Mervyn James, *English Politics and the Concept of Honour 1485–1642* (Oxford: The Past and Present Society, *Past and Present*, Supplement 3, 1978).
11. Compare Catherine Belsey, 'Richard's breach of the symbolic order has divorced the name of king from the power, laying bare a world of political struggle for possession of meaning, property and sovereignty', 'Making Histories', in Graham Holderness (ed.), *Shakespeare's History Plays: 'Richard II' to 'Henry V'* (Basingstoke: Macmillan, 1992), p. 113.
12. Paul A. Jorgensen, '"Redeeming Time" in *Henry IV*', in *Redeeming Shakespeare's Words* (Berkeley: University of California Press, 1962), pp. 52–69. For leading

critical positions on Hal's soliloquy, see Stephen Greenblatt's essay 'Invisible Bullets', *Shakespearean Negotiations: The Circulation of Social Energy in Renaissance England* (Oxford: The Clarendon Press, 1988), pp. 41–2, and Tom McAlindon's critique, 'Testing the New Historicism: "Invisible Bullets" Reconsidered', *Studies in Philology*, XCII, No. 4 (Fall 1995), p. 425.

13. See James, 'Honour and Lineage', in *English Politics and the Concept of Honour*, pp. 15–17.

14. Sukanta Chaudhuri, *Infirm Glory: Shakespeare and the Renaissance Image of Man* (Oxford: Oxford University Press, 1981); Walter Kaiser, *Praisers of Folly: Erasmus, Rabelais, Shakespeare* (London: Victor Gollancz, 1964); Roy Battenhouse, 'Falstaff as Parodist and Perhaps Holy Fool', *PMLA*, 90–1 (1975), pp. 32–52; John W. Draper, 'Sir John Falstaff', *Review of English Studies*, 8 (1932), pp. 414–24; Neil Rhodes, *Elizabethan Grotesque* (London: Routledge & Kegan Paul, 1980); John Dover Wilson, *The Fortunes of Falstaff* (Cambridge: Cambridge University Press, 1943); C.L. Barber, *Shakespeare's Festive Comedy* (Princeton, N.J.: Princeton University Press, 1959); David Wiles, *Shakespeare's Clown* (Cambridge; Cambridge University Press, 1987); J.I.M. Stewart, *Character and Motive in Shakespeare* (London: Longman Green and Co, 1949); Franz Alexander, 'A Note on Falstaff', *Psychoanalytic Quarterly*, 3 (1933), pp. 592–606; T.A. Jackson, 'Marx and Shakespeare', *Labour Monthly*, 46 (1964), pp. 165–73; Graham Holderness, *Shakespeare's History* (Dublin: Gill and Macmillan, 1985).

15. James L. Calderwood, *Metadrama in Shakespeare's Henriad* (Berkeley: University of California Press, 1979).

16. Paul A. Jorgensen, 'The "Dastardley Treachery" of Prince John of Lancaster', *PMLA*, 76–1 (1961), pp. 488–92. Yet in fact, Jorgensen can find nothing in medieval or Renaissance warfare which is so blatantly cynical as John's action.

17. *The Tudor Play of Mind* (Berkeley: University of California Press, 1978), p. 48.

18. Altman, *The Tudor Play of Mind*, pp. 35, 43. The Erasmus quote is from his debate with Luther on free will.

19. Ponet converts 'higher powers' to that of natural law which is above the prince (*A Short Treatise of Politic Power* [1556] (Menston: Scolar Press, 1970), pp. ciii^r–cvi^r). Peter Martyr, Ponet's fellow Marian exile in Strasbourg, interpreted 'higher powers' as the magistracy generally which should be deferred to with the proviso that if the magistrate 'commaund any thing, that is repugnant unto piety, and unto the law of God, we ought to obey God rather than men' (*Most Learned and fruitfull Commentaries . . . upon the Epistle of S. Paul to the Romanes* (London: transl. John Day, 1568), in Robert M. Kingdon (ed.), *The Political Thought of Peter Martyr Vermigli* (Genève: Libraire Droz, 1980), p. 3.) For Ponet, Peter Martyr and resistance theory, see Ronald Knowles, 'The Political Contexts of Deposition and Election in *Edward II', Medieval and Renaissance Drama in England*, 14 (2002). For *Romans* 13 and Catholic resistance theory, see J.H. Burns (ed.), *The Cambridge History of Political Thought 1450–1700* (Cambridge: Cambridge University Press, 1991), p. 238.

20. *A History of Political Thought in the Sixteenth Century* (London: Methuen, rep. 1961), p. 132.

21. *Certain Sermons or Homilies* (Oxford: Oxford University Press, 1844), p. 491.

Chapter 6

1. Unless otherwise stated, the Riverside edition of Shakespeare is quoted but several other editions are referred to, namely: John H. Walter (ed.), *King Henry V*, 'The Arden edition' (London: Methuen, 1954); Andrew Gurr (ed.), *King Henry V*, 'The New Cambridge Shakespeare' (Cambridge: Cambridge University Press, 1992); T.W. Craik (ed.), *King Henry V*, 'The Arden Third Series' (London and New York: Routledge, 1995); Stanley Wells and Gary Taylor (eds), William Shakespeare, *The Complete Works*, 'The Oxford Shakespeare' (Oxford: Clarendon Press, 1988).

2. See Richard Dutton, 'The Second Tetralogy' in Stanley Wells (ed.), *Shakespeare. A Bibliographical Guide* (Oxford: Clarendon Press, 1990), pp. 360–5, 377–80. T.W. Craik's introduction (see n. 1) includes 'Critical Opinions of the Play and its Hero', pp. 69–80. The standard bibliography is Joseph Candido and Charles R. Forker (eds), *Henry V: An Annotated Bibliography* (New York: Garland, 1983). A famous discussion is Norman Rabkin, 'Rabbits, Ducks and *Henry V*', *SQ* 28 (1977), pp. 279–96. An important lengthy critique, including the theoretical approaches of Cultural Materialism and New Historicism, is Graham Bradshaw, *Misrepresentations. Shakespeare and the Materialists* (Ithaca and London: Cornell University Press, 1993), pp. 34–124.

3. George Puttenham, *The Arte of English Poesie* [1589] (London: Constable and Co., 1906), p. 54.

4. David Riggs's 'The Rhetorical Basis of the Popular History' remains useful; see *Shakespeare's Heroical Histories: 'Henry VI' and its Literary Tradition* (Cambridge, Mass: Harvard University Press, 1971), pp. 34–31. For an up-to-date survey, 'Renaissance Historiography', see Ivo Kamps, *Historiography and Ideology in Stuart Drama* (Cambridge: Cambridge University Press, 1996), pp. 26–50.

5. 'Nor, indeed, is evidence to be found in the chronicles or annals of Kings of which our long history makes mention, that any King of England ever achieved so much in so short a time and returned home with so great and so glorious a triumph.' Frank Taylor and John S. Roskell (eds), *Gesta Henrici Quinti* (Oxford: Clarendon Press, 1975), p. 101.

6. 'Perspectivism' as an approach to the English histories has been suggested by other commentators; see Bradshaw, *Misrepresentations*, pp. 38–45, and Paola Pugliatti, *Shakespeare the Historian* (Basingstoke: Macmillan, 1996), pp. 42–57.

7. See Sister Ritamary Bradley, 'Backgrounds of the title *Speculum* in Mediaeval Literature', *Speculum*, 29 (1954), pp. 100–15.

8. A. Shickman, 'The "perspective glass" in Shakespeare's *Richard II*', *SEL*, 18 (1978), pp. 217–28, offers a useful survey, though he doesn't refer to the example in *Henry V*.

9. For this and the larger context of anamorphic painting, see Ernest B. Gilman, *The Curious Perspective. Literary and Pictorial Wit in the Seventeenth Century* (New Haven and London: Yale University Press, 1978), pp. 34–7.

10. Many critics have commented on this, see particularly W.L. Godshalk, 'Henry V's Politics of Non-responsibility', *Cahiers Elizabéthains*, 17 (1980), pp. 11–20.

11. See Gordon Ross Smith, 'Shakespeare's *Henry V*: Another Part of the Critical Forest', *Journal of the History of Ideas*, 37 (1976), p. 11.

12. Compare Canterbury's later 'honey-bee' speech (1.2.183–220) for variety of means *uniting* in one purpose to urge an absurdly disproportionate *division* of the English forces between France and the Scottish marches.

13. Theodor Meron provides an extensive chapter on Harfleur and the laws of siege warfare, in *Henry's Wars and Shakespeare's Laws* (Oxford: Clarendon Press, 1993), pp. 75–130.

14. Meron, *Henry's Wars*, pp. 89–90.

15. See M.H. Keen, *The Laws of War in the Middle Ages* (London: Routledge and Kegan Paul, 1965), pp. 63–81.

16. *The Tree of Battles*, ed. and transl. G.W. Coopland (Liverpool: Liverpool University Press, 1949), p. 156.

17. *Theater and World. The Problematics of Shakespeare's History* (Boston: North-eastern University Press, 1992), p. 193.

18. Bradshaw, *Misrepresentations*, p. 58, citing C.G. Cruikshank, *Elizabeth's Army* (Oxford: Oxford University Press, 2nd edn, 1968), and Lindsay Boynton, *The Elizabethan Militia* (London: Routledge and Kegan Paul, 1967).

19. 'The King Disguised. Shakespeare's *Henry V* and the Comical History', in Joseph G. Price (ed.), *The Triple Bond. Plays Mainly Shakespearean in Performance* (Pennsylvania: Pennsylvania State University Press, 1975), p. 99.

20. For opposed views see, for example, Paul Dean's critique of Richard Levin. In *The Multiple Plot in English Renaissance Drama* (Chicago: University of Chicago Press, 1971), p. 116, Levin argues that the subplot is a foil in contrast to the admirable exploits of Henry. Paul Dean, in 'Chronicle and Romance Modes in *Henry V*', *SQ* 32 (1981), pp. 18–27, shows how this view is arrived at by overlooking all that would call it into question.

21. See Meron, *Henry's Wars*, p. 115.

22. T.W. Baldwin, *William Shakspere's Small Latine and Lesse Greek* (Urbana: University of Illinois Press, 1944), vol. 2, pp. 72–6.

23. *Narrative and Dramatic Sources of Shakespeare* (London: Routledge and Kegan Paul, 1966), vol. IV, p. 364.

24. *King Henry V*, p. 309, fn 35–8.

25. Bullough, *Narrative and Dramatic Sources*, p. 365; Gurr (ed.), *King Henry V*, p. 28.

26. Meron, *Henry's Wars*, p. 158.

27. Meron, *Henry's Wars*, p. 161.

28. Meron, *Henry's Wars*, p. 161.

29. An interesting comparison is Ben Jonson's *Bartholomew Fair* (1614) in which he appears to have capitulated to the crude taste of the groundlings who had earlier cried down his *Catiline* (1611), yet by way of his 'special decorum' he provides a dramatised defence of his artistic principles.

Chapter 7

1. There is no adequate single summary of recent criticism of *Julius Caesar* even in the latest, otherwise ample, Arden edition (ed. David Daniell, Walton-on-Thames, Thomas Nelson, 1998). The following, put together, provide an

introduction: T.J.B. Spencer, 'Shakespeare and the Elizabethan Romans', *Shakespeare Survey*, 10 (1957), pp. 27–38: John W. Velz, 'The Ancient World in Shakespeare: Authenticity or Anachronism? A Retrospect', *Shakespeare Survey* 31 (1978), pp. 1–12: Robert S. Miola, 'Shakespeare and his Sources: Observations on the Critical History of *Julius Caesar*', *Shakespeare Survey*, 40 (1987), pp. 69–76. R.J.A. Weis, '*Julius Caesar* and *Antony and Cleopatra*', in Stanley Wells (ed.), *Shakespeare. A Bibliographical Guide* (Oxford: Clarendon Press, 1990), pp. 275–93. In their introduction to *Shakespeare: The Roman Plays* (London and New York: Longman, 1996), Graham Holderness, Bryan Loughrey and Andrew Murphy indicate the Cultural Materialist/New Historicist contribution to criticism of the Roman plays. For Roman values in Shakespeare, see Charles Wells, *The Wide Arch* (Bristol: Bristol Classical Press, 1993). Geoffrey Miles offers an excellent account of Stoicism in *Shakespeare and the Constant Romans* (Oxford: Clarendon Press, 1996).

2. See T.S. Dorsch (ed.), *Julius Caesar* (London: Methuen, 1965), p. 114.
3. Joseph W. Houppert argues that Decius' flattery of Caesar (2.1.203–11) offers a way of controlling tyrannical power which mediates between the disjunctive extremes of Brutus' argument here. But Decius uses flattery to ensure Caesar's assassination: sycophantic flattery abets tyranny. See 'Fatal Logic in *Julius Caesar*', *South Atlantic Bulletin*, 39 (1974), pp. 3–9.
4. For this point I am indebted to Camille Wells Slights, *The Casuistical Tradition in Shakespeare, Donne, Herbert and Milton* (Princeton, NY: Princeton University Press, 1981), pp. 86–91.
5. H.W.B. Joseph, *An Introduction to Logic* (Oxford: Clarendon Press, 1906), p. 523.
6. See Wayne A. Rebhorn, 'The Crisis of the Aristocracy in *Julius Caesar*', *Renaissance Quarterly*, 43 (1990), pp. 75–111.
7. See H.M. Ayres, 'Shakespeare's *Julius Caesar* in the Light of Some Other Versions', *PMLA*, 25 (1910), pp. 183–227.
8. Dorsch, *Julius Caesar*, p. 43, citing the 1902 Arden editor, M. Macmillan.
9. See Daniell, *Julius Caesar*, p. 208.
10. For the context of the Senecan ideal of constancy in the Stoic *sapiens*, see Geoffrey Miles, *Shakespeare and the Constant Romans*, pp. 129–30.
11. See Dorsch, *Julius Caesar*, p. 69.
12. See T.J.B. Spencer (ed.), *Shakespeare's Plutarch* (Harmondsworth: Penguin Books, 1968), p. 94.
13. See Leo Kirschbaum, 'Shakespeare's Stage Blood and its Critical Significance', *PMLA*, 64 (1949), pp. 517–29.
14. I use the commonly found terms, though the ascription of the laconic, Lacedemonian Attic style to Brutus has been criticised by Gayle Greene in '"The Power of Speech/To Stir Man's Blood": The Language of Tragedy in Shakespeare's *Julius Caesar*', *Renaissance Drama*, 11 (1980), pp. 67–93. Greene sees the assumption of Attic rationality as an illusion which has taken in some critics. My analysis supports Greene's demonstration of Brutus' creation of 'an illusion of irrefutable logic' (p. 84). For a thoroughly detailed examination, see Jean Fuzier, 'Rhetoric versus Rhetoric: A Study of Shakespeare's *Julius Caesar*, Act III, Scene 2', *Cahiers Elizabéthans*, 5 (1981), pp. 25–65. In contrast, Alessandro Serpieri reviews the Forum speeches in terms of modern semiotics: 'Reading the Signs: Towards a Semiotics of

Shakespearean Drama', in John Drakakis (ed.), *Alternative Shakespeare's* (London and New York: Methuen, 1985), pp. 119–43.

15. Between fourteenth-century philosophical nominalism associated with William of Ockham and the seventeenth-century experimental nominalism linked to Francis Bacon lies Shakespeare's theatre. To an extent Shakespeare's dramatic empiricism derives from the confluence of nominalism and Renaissance scepticism. See my '*Hamlet* and Counter-Humanism', *Renaissance Quarterly*, 52 (1999), pp. 1046–69. For a masterly summary of Ockham's nominalism, see Gordon Leff, *Medieval Thought* (Harmondsworth: Penguin Books, 1958), pp. 279–91. For the Baconian distrust of language as a vehicle for reality, see R.F. Jones, 'Science and Language in England of the Mid-Seventeenth Century', in Stanley E. Fish (ed.), *Seventeenth-Century Prose* (New York: Oxford University Press, 1971), pp. 94–111. Many years before the rise of modern theory Hiram Haydn put the case for the radical decentring of man brought about by the nominalist rejection of universals: 'It is no exaggeration to say that most of the germs of the Counter-Renaissance may be found in Ockham's epistemology' (*The Counter Renaissance*, New York, Charles Scribner & Sons, 1950, p. 88).

16. In 135 lines of dialogue Caesar addresses himself 17 times (i.e. approximately once every eight lines: see 2.2.41–8 in which 'Caesar' occurs four times). Caesar's dying word is 'Caesar'.

Chapter 8

1. *The Common Liar* (New Haven and London: Yale University Press, 1973), p. 30.
2. The most detailed survey is that of Marvin Spevack (ed.), *Antony and Cleopatra*, 'New Variorum Edition of Shakespeare' (The Modern Language Association of America, 1990), pp. 777–87. The reader of *Antony and Cleopatra* is fortunate indeed, not only in having Spevack's New Variorium Edition, but also in having the play available in the three leading series: see David Bevington (ed.), 'The New Cambridge Shakespeare' (Cambridge: Cambridge University Press, 1990); Michael Neill (ed.), 'The World's Classics. The Oxford Shakespeare' (Oxford: Oxford University Press, 1994); John Wilders (ed.), 'The Arden Shakespeare' (London and New York: Routledge, 1995). All give some attention to the staging of Antony hoist aloft to the monument.
3. Geoffrey Miles, *Shakespeare and the Constant Romans* (Oxford: Clarendon Press, 1996), pp. 42–3 discusses Elizabethan translations of Seneca's key phrase *unus idemque* for *constantia* as 'like himselfe'. Perhaps the most familiar occurrence in Shakespeare is, 'He will be found like Brutus, like himself' (*Julius Caesar*, 5.4.25).
4. See Marilyn L. Williamson, *Infinite Variety: Antony and Cleopatra in Renaissance Drama and Earlier Tradition* (Mystic, Conn.: Lawrence Verry Inc., 1974) where the following Senecans are discussed: Giambattista Giraldi Cinthio, *Cleopatra* (*c.* 1543); Cesare di Cesari, *Cleopatra* (1552); Etienne Jodelle, *Cleopatra Captive* (1552); Robert Garnier, *Marc-Antoine* (1578); Nicolas de Montreux, *Cleopatra Tragedie* (1595); Mary Herbert, Countess of Pembroke, *The Tragedie of Antonie* (1592); Samuel Daniel, *The Tragedy of Cleopatra* (1599). The exception is Don Celso Pistorelli, but his *Marcantonio e Cleopatra* (1576) appears to have been unknown to Shakespeare and his contemporaries.

5. My contextualisation, argument and conclusion differ from that of Russell Jackson's view, 'Caesar's triumph – like the other political questions of the play – is made the focus of Cleopatra's drive to self-expression and fulfilment', 'The Triumphs of *Antony and Cleopatra*', *Shakespeare Jahrbuch* (West) (1984), pp. 128–48.

6. T.J.B. Spencer (ed.), *Shakespeare's Plutarch* (Harmondsworth: Penguin Books, 1964), pp. 222, 248.

7. Spencer, *Shakespeare's Plutarch*, p. 282.

8. Spencer, *Shakespeare's Plutarch*, p. 290.

9. Robert Graves (transl.) (Harmondsworth: Penguin Books, 1957), p. 226.

10. Geoffrey Bullough (ed.), *Narrative and Dramatic Sources of Shakespeare*, vol. V, *The Roman Plays* (London: Routledge and Kegan Paul, 1964), p. 337.

11. D.D. Carnicelli (ed.), *Lord Morley's 'Tryumphes of Fraunces Petrarke'* (Cambridge, Mass.: Harvard University Press, 1971), p. 83.

12. Giovanni Boccaccio, *Concerning Famous Women*, transl. Guido A. Guarino, (New Brunswick: Rutgers University Press, 1963), p. 196.

13. *Not Wisely But Too Well: Shakespeare's Love Tragedies* (San Marino: Huntington Library, 1957), pp. 159–60.

14. Bullough, *Narrative and Dramatic Sources*, pp. 350, 354, 356.

15. The following details on di Cesari are taken from Williamson, *Infinite Variety*, pp. 87–92.

16. *Not Wisely But Too Well: Shakespeare's Love Tragedies*, p. 162.

17. Bullough, *Narrative and Dramatic Sources*, p. 228.

18. *Infinite Variety*, p. 163.

19. Bullough, *Narrative and Dramatic Sources*, p. 359. The following line references are to the text reprinted in this volume.

20. A full survey of the image of Cleopatra up to and including twentieth-century cinema is found in Lucy Hughes-Hallett, *Cleopatra: Histories, Dreams and Distortions* (London: Bloomsbury, 1990).

21. All line references are to the text indicated by Bullough, *Narrative and Dramatic Sources*.

22. *The Problem Plays of Shakespeare* (London: Routledge and Kegan Paul, 1963), p. 133.

23. The considerable literature on this subject is summarised by Spevack, *Antony and Cleopatra*, 'Staging the Monument Scenes at the Globe', pp. 777–93. Bevington's edition includes C. Walter Hodges' drawings of four reconstructions of the staging for 4.16. Most criticism glides over the problem, for example Janet Adelman writes, 'in the protected female space of her own monument, the memory of her womb can at last bring Antony forth whole and undivided, rendering him life' (*Suffocating Mothers. Fantasies of Maternal Origin in Shakespeare's Plays, Hamlet to the Tempest*, New York and London: Routledge, 1992, p. 187). My own approach agrees with Leslie Thomson, though our conclusions differ: 'The manner of the scene – the action – would be, should be physically awkward, but as elsewhere this awkwardness is juxtaposed with the language of genuine emotion, neither cancelling the other, each pulling at us simultaneously, asking us to judge the matter, to assess the value, the meaning of what we are seeing' ('*Antony and Cleopatra*, Act 4, Scene 16: "A heavy sight"', *Shakespeare Survey*, 41 (1988), p. 88).

24. Sir Thomas Wyatt, *The Complete Poems*, ed. R.A. Rebholz, (New Haven and London, Yale University Press, 1978), p. 87. *The Extravagant Shepherd* illustration is in Stephen Booth (ed.), *Shakespeare's Sonnets* (New Haven, Conn.: Yale University Press, 1977), p. 453. I am indebted to Elizabeth Heale for both references.

25. See Natalie Zemon Davies, 'Women on Top: Symbolic Sexual Inversion and Political Disorder in Early Modern Europe', in Barbara Babcock (ed.), *The Reversible World. Symbolic Inversion in Art and Society* (Ithaca and London: Cornell University Press, 1978), p. 147. For the humoural references, see also Neill's gloss, *Antony and Cleopatra*, p. 319. Geoffrey Miles writes very finely of the mesh of contradictions, 'constant in inconstancy', of Cleopatra's suicide (*Shakespeare and the Constant Romans*, pp. 186–88), but without emphasis on the carnivalesque element developed here.

26. For the extreme scepticism of a view which, in effect, reads the play as a companion piece to *Troilus and Cressida*, see Richard L. Nochimson, 'The End Crowns All: Shakespeare's Deflation of Tragic Possibility in *Antony and Cleopatra*', *English*, 26 (1977), pp. 99–132. Barbara J. Bono interprets Cleopatra in terms of neo-platonising Renaissance mythographers' speculation on Plutarch's 'Osiris and Isis' (*Literary Transvaluation. From Vergilian Epic to Shakesperean Tragicomedy* (Berkeley, University of California Press, 1984), pp. 191–213).

27. William P. Halstead, *Shakespeare as Spoken: A Collation of 5000 Acting Editions and Promptbooks of Shakespeare* (Ann Arbor, MI: 1979), vol. 12, p. 924b.

28. Spencer, *Shakespeare's Plutarch*, p. 219.

29. In his editorial introduction John Drakakis observes, 'This opposition of the rational, the logocentric, and the linguistic on the one hand, and the tactile, the irrational, the fecund, and the physical on the other identifies a structural motif in the play which effectively makes way for a carnivalesque reading of Egyptian excess' (*Antony and Cleopatra*, 'New Casebooks' (Basingstoke: Macmillan, 1994), p. 12).

30. See Tom McAlindon, *Shakespeare's Tragic Cosmos* (Cambridge: Cambridge University Press, 1991), pp. 230–1 and Bono, *Literary Transvaluation*, pp. 204–6, who both emphasise Plutarch's account of an impregnated Isis – Egypt. Terry Eagleton, *William Shakespeare* (Oxford: Basil Blackwell, 1986) writes, 'It is as though Cleopatra has the amplitude and spontaneity of Nature itself, containing all things within herself', p. 88.

31. Compare Barbara C. Vincent, 'Shakespeare's *Antony and Cleopatra* and the Rise of Comedy', in Drakakis (ed.), *Antony and Cleopatra*, pp. 212–47. For the modern response to carnivalesque theory, see Ronald Knowles (ed.), *Shakespeare and Carnival: After Bakhtin* (Basingstoke: Macmillan, 1998). Mikhail Bakhtin's idea of 'uncrowning' is found in *Rabelais and His World* (Bloomington: Indiana University Press, 1984), p. 11.

32. I refer to the famous letter of Sir Henry Wotton concerning the fire at the Globe during *King Henry VIII* (*All is true*) which depicted the 'many extraordinary circumstances of pomp and majesty' of the Order of the Garter, 'sufficient in truth within a while to make greatness very familiar, if not ridiculous' (Logan Pearsall Smith (ed.), *The Life and Letters of Sir Henry Wotton* (Oxford: Clarendon Press, 1966), vol. 2, pp. 32–3).

33. Spencer, *Shakespeare's Plutarch*, pp. 205–6.

34. Spencer, *Shakespeare's Plutarch*, p. 206.

35. My views here parallel those of Phyllis Rackin in her distinguished article, 'Shakespeare's Boy Cleopatra, the Decorum of Nature, and the Golden World of Poetry', in Drakakis (ed.), *Antony and Cleopatra*, pp. 78–100.
36. Neill suggests a debt to Samuel Daniel here (*Antony and Cleopatra*, p. 316).
37. Spencer, *Shakespeare's Plutarch*, p. 293.

Chapter 9

1. Throughout this chapter I shall refer to Caius Martius by his title, Coriolanus. Editors customarily use two speech prefixes in the course of the play: valuable modern editions consulted are by Philip Brockbank (ed.), 'The Arden Shakespeare' (London: Methuen, 1976); R.B. Parker (ed.), 'Oxford World's Classics' (Oxford, New York: Oxford University Press, 1994); Lee Bliss (ed.), 'The New Cambridge Shakespeare' (Cambridge: Cambridge University Press, 2000).
2. An established critical response assesses this topically looking at the Jacobean political reaction to the Midlands revolt of 1607: see E.C. Pettet, '*Coriolanus* and the Midlands Insurrection of 1607', *Shakespeare Survey*, 3 (1950), pp. 34–42; W. Gordon Zeeveld, '*Coriolanus* and Jacobean Politics', *Modern Language Review*, 57 (1962), pp. 321–34; Clifford Chalmers Huffman, '*Coriolanus*' in Context (Lewisburg: Bucknell University Press, 1971). My concern is also political, but in a much more structuralist way, examining the idea of Rome as it was promoted in humanist education. For a general introduction to criticism, see Bruce King, *Coriolanus*, 'The Critics Debate' series (Basingstoke: Macmillan, 1989).
3. Spencer, *Shakespeare's Plutarch*, pp. 301–3, 314–15.
4. One wonders about the contemporary notoriety of Marlowe's alleged remark reported in Baines' 'note', 'the first beginning of religion was only to keep men in awe'. See Charles Nicholl, *The Reckoning. The Murder of Christopher Marlowe* (London, Jonathan Cape, 1992), p. 46. Machiavelli on ancient Roman religion as a means of social control (*The Discourses of Niccolò Machiavelli* (London, Routledge and Kegan Paul, 1950), vol. 1, Bk 1, 11, pp. 240–3) is influenced by Polybius' view that 'superstitution' sustained the unity of the Roman state (*The Histories*, 'The Loeb Classical Library' (London: William Heinemann/New York: G.P. Putnam's Sons, 1923), vol. 3, Bk VI, 56, pp. 395–7).
5. *De republica. De legibus*, 'The Loeb Classical Library' (London: William Heinemann/Cambridge, Mass., Harvard University Press, 1948), Bk II, XII, pp. 407–9. In the early days of the republic only senior magistrates, often sharing both priestly and political functions of the patrician class, could read the auspices and consequently dismiss plebeian assemblies as against the omens. Even a contemporary augur declared that 'the auspices were merely got up for the interests of the state': see F.R. Cowell, *Cicero and the Roman Republic* (Harmondsworth: Penguin Books, 1967), pp. 347–8. See all of chapter 8 for religion as an instrument of state control.
6. 'Shakespeare gives the plebeians good arguments to answer back with' (*Brecht on Theatre* (New York: Hill and Wang/London: Eyre Methuen, 1979), 'Study of the First Scene of Shakespeare's *Coriolanus*', p. 253.

7. Geoffrey Rickman, *The Corn Supply of Ancient Rome* (Oxford: Clarendon Press, 1980), pp. 29–33 considers the problems of accepting Livy's suggestions on such matters.

8. My use of 'ventriloquialism' differs from that of Stephen Longstaffe's Bakhtinian approach ('A short-report and not otherwise: Jack Cade in *2 Henry VI*', in Ronald Knowles (ed.), *Shakespeare and Carnival: After Bakhtin* (Basingstoke: Macmillan, 1998), p. 16) and reverses that of Annabel Patterson (*Shakespeare and the Popular Voice* (Oxford: Basil Blackwell, 1989), pp. 41–50) who shows how the 'voice' of the lower orders finds expression in the reports of the authorities.

9. *Shakespeare's Rome* (Cambridge: Cambridge University Press, 1983), pp. 183–5.

10. Spencer, *Shakespeare's Plutarch*, p. 297.

11. Spencer, *Shakespeare's Plutarch*, p. 361.

12. See Joyce Van Dyke, 'Making a Scene: Language and Gesture in *Coriolanus*', *Shakespeare Survey*, 30 (1977), pp. 135–46.

13. *Coriolanus*, p. 297. '*Civitas et urbs in hoc differunt, quod incolae dicuntur civitas, urbs vero complectitur aedificia.*'

14. In 'The Comparison of Alcibiades with Martius Coriolanus' Plutarch records that both were 'wise and politike in the warres' (*Plutarch's Lives of the Noble Grecians and Romans Englished by Sir Thomas North* (London: David Nutt, 1895), vol. II, p. 190).

15. Mervyn James, *English Politics and the Concept of Honour 1485–1642* (Oxford: The Past and Present Society, 'Past and Present' Supplement 3, 1978), p. 30. Reprinted in *Society, Politics and Culture: Studies in Early Modern England* (Cambridge: Cambridge University Press, 1986), pp. 308–415.

16. See Tom McAlindon, 'Swearing and Forswearing in Shakespeare's Histories. The Playwright as Contra-Machiavel', *The Review of English Studies*, 51 (2000), pp. 208–29.

17. Presumably the extremely vicious words used at the siege of Harfleur in *Henry V*, the most famous siege in English drama, provide an ironic perspective here.

18. Julian Pitt-Rivers, 'Honour and Social Status', in J.G. Peristiany (ed.), *Honour and Shame* (London: Weidenfeld and Nicolson, 1965), p. 33.

19. For the significance of the concept of patriotism, see Ronald Knowles, 'The "All-attoning Name". The Word "Patriot" in Seventeenth-Century England', *Modern Language Review* (forthcoming).

20. See Howard Jones, *Master Tully. Cicero in Tudor England* (Nieuwkoop: De Graf Publishers, 1998), pp. 138–42, and T.W. Baldwin, *William Shakespere's Small Latine and Less Greeke* (Urbana: University of Illinois Press, 1944), vol. 2, pp. 575–616, particularly pp. 583–6. The edition of Grimald quoted here, *Marcus Tullius Ciceroes thre bokes of duties* (Washington: The Folger Shakespeare Library; London and Toronto: Associated University Presses, 1990) is edited by Gerald O'Gorman.

21. See Markku Peltonem, *Classical Humanism and Republicanism in English Political Thought 1570–1640* (Cambridge: Cambridge University Press, 1995), ch. 1, 'Classical humanism restated', pp. 18–53.

22. O'Gorman (ed.), *Master Tully*, p. 73. The Loeb Classical Library edition reference is I, 58 (p. 61).

23. O'Gorman (ed.), *Master Tully*, p. 110. Loeb I, 160 (p. 165).

24. O'Gorman (ed.), *Master Tully*, p. 180.
25. Loeb III, 90 (p. 367).
26. *De finibus bonorum et malorum*, transl. H. Rackham, The Loeb Classical Library (London: William Heinemann/New York: The Macmillan Co., 1914), III, 64, p. 285.
27. *De republica. De legibus*, transl. Clinton Walker Keyes, The Loeb Classical Library (London: William Heinemann/Cambridge, Mass.: Harvard University Press, 1948), II, 5 pp. 375–7.
28. The first entry for 'fatherland' in the *OED* is dated 1623.
29. *De finibus*, II, 45, p. 133. For the commonplace nature of this sentence in sixteenth-century England, see Peltonem, *Classical Humanism and Republicanism in English Political Thought 1570–1640*, pp. 24, 25, 45.
30. John J. Manning (ed.), *The First and Second Parts of John Hayward's The Life and Raigne of King Henrie IIII*. Camden 4th Series, vol. 42 (London: Royal Historical Society, 1991), p. 146. The passage is from the Bishop of Carlisle's lengthy exposition on the inalienability of Richard II's kingship.
31. *Shakespeare and the Popular Voice*, pp. 141–2.
32. Compare Louis Althusser, 'Ideology and Ideological State Apparatuses', in *Essays on Ideology* (London and New York: Verso, 1993), p. 29, on education and ideology in relation to the above remarks on Cicero in Tudor schooling.
33. See Parker (ed.), *Coriolanus*, p. 56, and Janette Dillon, *Shakespeare and the Solitary Man* (Basingstoke: Macmillan, 1981), p. 146.
34. For the concepts of autarky and pity, see John Ferguson, *Moral Values in the Ancient World* (London: Methuen, 1958), pp. 155–8.
35. Spencer, *Shakespeare's Plutarch*, p. 354.
36. See Bruce King, *Coriolanus*, pp. 24–31.
37. *Suffocating Mothers*: *Fantasies of Maternal Origin in Shakespeare's Plays, 'Hamlet' to 'The Tempest'* (London and New York: Routledge, 1992), pp. 147–64. As this section is the founding essay for the whole book Adelman's earlier article, 'Anger's My Meat: Feeding, Dependency, and Aggression in *Coriolanus*', 1980, is reprinted with some revisionary comments in the notes.
38. 'Annihilating Intimacy in *Coriolanus*' in Mary Beth Rose (ed.), *Women in the Middle Ages and the Renaissance* (New York: Syracuse University Press, 1986), pp. 89–111.
39. '"Say I play the man I am": Gender and Politics in *Coriolanus*', *Kenyon Review*, 8 (1986), pp. 86–95.
40. Compare the late Tudor observation, 'Moreover this ys also an argument that honor amongst most men ys of great estimation, that even from our infancie we do in a manner sucke this saying with the milke from our mothers breastes (which ys in everie bodies mouth) That yt ys much better to die with Honour then to liue with shame' (Robert Ashley, *Of Honour* (San Marino: The Huntington Library, 1947), p. 50).
41. *Suffocating Mothers*, pp. 150, 157.
42. As against *mamilla* or *mamma*. '*Mamma enim rumis, ut ante dicebant*' ('For people used to call the udder *rumis*', Varro, *De re rustica*). See Marcus Portius Cato, *On Agriculture*. Marcus Terentius Varro, *On Agriculture*, The Loeb Classical Library (London: William Heinemann/Cambridge, Mass.: Harvard University Press, 1934), II, XI, p. 415.

43. The fig tree was so named since the juice of the fig was used instead of animal rennet in the production of cheese from milk (see Varro, above).

44. Described thus in Pliny, *Natural History*, The Loeb Classical Library (London: William Heinemann/Cambridge, Mass.: Harvard University Press, 1945), vol. IV, Bk XV, XX, p. 341.

45. See the facsimile reprint of the 1595 Paris edition in Garland's 'The Renaissance and the Gods' series (New York and London: Garland, 1976). Varro and Pliny (see notes 40–2 above) are Stephanus' main sources.

46. See Ralph Berry, 'Sexual Imagery in *Coriolanus*', *Studies in English Literature*, 13 (1973), pp. 301–16.

47. See Christina Luckyi, 'Volumnia's Silence', *Studies in English Literature*, 31 (1991), pp. 327–42.

Chapter 10

1. For an excellent discussion of Lucian's exploitation of Homer's burlesque potential, particularly in his *Dialogues of the Gods*, see R. Bracht Branham, *Unruly Eloquence. Lucian and the Comedy of Traditions* (Cambridge, Mass.: Harvard University Press, 1989), pp. 136–47. The extended similes are the focus of Michael West, 'Homer's *Iliad* and the Genesis of Mock-Heroic', *Cithera*, 21 (1991), pp. 3–22.

2. Don Cameron Allen surveys the tradition of allegorising Homer, from the early figures of Eustathius, Proclus and Heraclitus of Pontus, to seventeenth-century commentators: see *Mysteriously Meant. The Rediscovery of Pagan Symbolism and Allegorial Interpretation in the Renaissance* (Baltimore and London: Johns Hopkins University Press, 1970), pp. 83–106, and p. 97 (of de Sponde) '[n]owhere could one find a better example of a virtuous man than Achilles.' For the dilemma of the Renaissance interpreter, see John M. Steadman, *Milton and the Paradoxes of Renaissance Heroism* (Baton Rouge and London: Louisiana State University Press, 1987), p. 44. Maurice B. McNamee, S.J. outlines the ethical development of valour, beginning with Greek autarky and Achilles, in *Honor and the Epic Hero. A Study of the Shifting Concept of Magnanimity in Philosophy and Epic Poetry* (New York: Holt, Rinehart and Winston, 1960).

3. '"Greeks" and "Merrygreeks": A Background to *Timon of Athens* and *Troilus and Cressida*', in Richard Hosley (ed.), *Essays in Shakespeare and Elizabethan Drama. In Honor of Hardin Craig* (Columbia: University of Missouri Press, 1962), pp. 223–33.

4. Quoted by H.T. Swedenberg, Jr., *The Theory of the Epic in England 1650–1800* (Berkeley and Los Angeles: University of Chicago Press, 1944), p. 30.

5. See Geoffrey Shepherd (ed.), *An Apology for Poetry* (Manchester: Manchester University Press, 1973), pp. 108, 114, 119, 127.

6. Sometimes Achilles was also remembered for his Platonic friendship (*sic*) with Patroclus, as H. David Brumble records in *Classical Myths and Legends in the Middle Ages and Renaissance* (Westport, Conn.: Greenwood Press, 1998), pp. 3–5.

7. Many commentators have gone over this ground as David Berington notes in his new edition, *Troilus and Cressida* 'The Arden Shakespeare' (Walton-on-Thames: Thomas Nelson and Sons, 1998), pp. 375–97. Earlier authorities are J.S.P. Tatlock, 'The Siege of Troy in Elizabethan Literature, Especially in

Shakespeare and Heywood', *PMLA*, 30 (1915), pp. 673–770, and Hyder E. Rollins, 'The Troilus–Cressida Story from Chaucer to Shakespeare', *PMLA*, 34 (1917), pp. 383–429. I am indebted to Robert K. Presson, *Shakespeare's 'Troilus and Cressida' and the Legends of Troy* (Madison: The University of Wisconsin Press, 1953) and Robert Kimbrough, *Shakespeare's 'Troilus and Cressida' and its Setting* (Cambridge, Mass.: Harvard University Press, 1964).

8. *Shakespeare's 'Troilus and Cressida' and its Setting*, p. 33. *The Recuyell* is a translation from Raoul Lefèvre's French which was, in turn, a translation from Guido Delle Colonne's Latin version of Benoît de Sainte-Maure's French combination and expansion of Dares and Dictys.

9. See Heather James, *Shakespeare's Troy. Drama, Politics and the Translation of Empire* (Cambridge: Cambridge University Press, 1997), p. 32.

10. Jill L. Levenson, 'Shakespeare's *Troilus and Cressida* and the Monumental Tradition in Tapestries and Literature', *Renaissance Drama*, VII (1976), pp. 62–3. The Tournai series comprised eleven tapestries measuring 15×30 feet, depicting some 500 figures.

11. See Presson, *Shakespeare's 'Troilus and Cressida' and the Legends of Troy, passim*; Bevington (ed.), *Troilus and Cressida*, pp. 376–8, and Geoffrey Bullough, *Narrative and Dramatic Sources of Shakespeare*, vol. VI (London and New York: Routledge & Kegan Paul, 1966), pp. 87–8. Scholars acknowledge indebtedness to the observations of J.S. Palmer in the *Transaction of the Royal Society of Literature*, 2nd series, 15 (1893), 64ff, and the seminal articles of Donald Smalley, 'The Ethical Bias of Chapman's Homer', *Studies in Philology*, 36 (1939), pp. 169–91 and Phyllis B. Bartlett, 'The Heroes of Chapman's Homer', *Review of English Studies*, 19 (1941), pp. 257–80.

12. *Possessed with Greatness. The Heroic Tragedies of Chapman and Shakespeare* (London: Scolar Press, 1980), p. 26.

13. Mildred Brand Munday draws attention to disparaging rhetorical devices used in the play including *tapinosis* (the derogatory epithet), *cacemphaton* (violent scurrility), *meiosis* (hyperbole reversed) and *diasyrmus* (depraving another's argument by ridiculous similitudes) in 'Pejorative Patterns in Shakespeare's *Troilus and Cressida*', *Bucknell Review*, 5 (1955), pp. 39–49.

14. See Linda Charnes, '"So Unsecret to Ourselves": Notorious Identity and the Material Subject', *Shakespeare Quarterley* 40 (1989), pp. 413–40.

15. The most substantial examination of this issue is W.R. Elton, *Shakespeare's 'Troilus and Cressida' and the Inns of Court Revels* (Aldershot: Ashgate, 2000) to which I am indebted, in spite of one qualm. Elton's expert scrutiny finds sufficient detailed evidence in *Troilus and Cressida* to indicate its suitability for an Inns of Court audience, yet much of the kind of detail – from law, logic, rhetoric and revels – would also be found in plays first performed in public playhouses.

16. B. Jowett, *The Dialogues of Plato*, vol. 2 (Oxford: Clarendon Press, 1875), p. 487.

17. Harold N. Hillebrand (ed.), *Troilus and Cressida* (Philadelphia & London: J.B. Lippincott Company, 1953), pp. 411–15.

18. Cambridge: Cambridge University Press, 1982. Cf. Rudolf Stamm, 'The Glass of Pandar's Praise', *Essays and Studies*, 17 (1964), pp. 55–77.

19. Yet, as Elton points out, Ulysses subverts his own arguments, 'If Achilles does return to combat, his deeds will shortly be forgotten. If he does not,

they will, in any case, be forgotten' (*Shakespeare's Troilus and Cressida and the Inns of Court Revels*), pp. 29–30.

20. See *OED*, Praise v.1.
21. *Troilus and Cressida*, Bk II, ll. 619, 1248–9, F.N. Robinson (ed.), *The Works of Geoffrey Chaucer* (Oxford: Oxford University Press, 1979), pp. 408, 415.
22. See J.W. Bennett, '*Nosce te Ipsum*: Some Medieval and Modern Interpretations', in Piero Boitani (ed.), *The Humane Medievalist* (Roma, 1982), pp. 143–4.
23. Elton summarises, 'Both Greek and Trojan council scenes follow conventionally deliberative topics, for example honour, advantage, safety and value' ('*Troilus and Cressida' and the Inns of Court Revels*, p. 78).
24. See Bevington (ed.), *Troilus and Cressida*, pp. 67–75. In a brilliant sequence (pp. 94–105) Elton provides a technical analysis of the dispute between Hector and Troilus, pointing out the latter's illogicality in such characteristics as circular argument (*petitio principii*), and fallacies (*ignorantio elenchi*), including fallacy of the consequent, false conversion of propositions and *secundem quid* (taking part for whole, hyperbole for the literal, etc.).
25. Bevington accepts Hanmer's reading of 'visible' as against the quarto and folio reading of 'inuisible'. Both equally travesty Platonic love language.
26. Jill Mann provides an analysis of 'worth' in the play in relation to medieval and classical economic theory, 'Chaucer and Shakespeare: "What is Criseyde Worth?"', in Piero Boitani (ed.), *The European Tragedy of Troilus* (Oxford: Oxford University Press, 1989), pp. 219–42.
27. See n. 7, above. For a more recent account of the criticism of Cressida, see E. Talbot Donaldson, *The Swan at the Well. Shakespeare Reading Chaucer* (New Haven and London: Yale University Press, 1985), pp. 149–51.
28. Hallett Smith, *Elizabethan Poetry* (Cambridge, Mass.: Harvard University Press, 1952), p. 292. For Harington, see p. 313. In Smith's view these Renaissance comments were following the recommendation of Plutarch in his *Moralia*. See also Pliny, *Natural History*, Bk XXI, sections xliv–xlv.
29. *The Arte of English Poesie* (London: A. Constable and Co., 1906), p. 41.
30. 'In play-summarizing terms, quarrel, argument, theme, *Troilus and Cressida* is thus a quarrel about a "quarrel" (Prologue, l.10); thematically, an argument about an argument. As argument is a basis of legal practice and advocacy, the play itself, like the war, is the argument that "is" the argument.' Elton, '*Troilus and Cressida' and the Inns of Court Revels*, p. 81.

Chapter 11

1. Compare the Puritan casuistry of William Ames, which duplicates Machiavelli's consequentialism:

> God can use the same instrument to produce divers and contrary effects, and these effects depend not upon the human instrument but upon God himself. This may serve to direct us in time of danger not to look so much upon the means which God uses, as to depend upon God Himself who can turn any means unto the Good of those that are His.

Quoted by Victoria Khan, *Machiavellian Rhetoric* (Princeton, N.J.: Princeton University Press, 1994), p. 91.

2. R.G. Collingwood, *The Idea of History* (Oxford: Oxford University Press, 1966), p. 41.

3. E.W. Sutton (transl.), 'The Loeb Classical Library' (London: William Heinemann/Cambridge, Mass.: Harvard University Press, 1942), pp. 224–5.

4. David Riggs' chapter, 'The Rhetorical Basis of the Popular History', in *Shakespeare's Heroical Histories: 'Henry VI' and its Literary Tradition* (Cambridge, Mass.: Harvard University Press, 1971), pp. 34–61 is very helpful.

5. George Nadel provides an excellent introduction to the theory of exemplarity, 'Philosophy of History before Historicism', *History and Theory*, III (1964), pp. 291–315. A more recent book-length study is Timothy Hampton, *Writing from History. The Rhetoric of Exemplarity in Renaissance Literature* (Ithaca and London: Cornell University Press, 1990), pp. 205–36 are given to *Julius Caesar*.

6. See David Riggs, *Shakespeare's Heroical Histories*, p. 50.

7. Quoted by F.J. Levy in his valuable article, 'Hayward, Daniel, and the Beginnings of Politic History in England', *Huntington Library Quarterley*, 50 (1987), p. 22.

8. See T.P. Wiseman, 'Practice and Theory in Roman Historiography', *History*, 66 (1981), pp. 388–9.

9. *Hall's Chronicle* [1809] (New York, AMS Press, 1965), pp. 245–48. Repeated in *Holinshed's Chronicles* (London: J. Johnson, 1808) III, pp. 262–64.

10. See Eric Cochrane, *Historians and Historiography in the Italian Renaissance* (Chicago and London: The University of Chicago Press, 1981), pp. 265–70.

11. T.J.B. Spencer (ed.), *Shakespeare's Plutarch* (Harmondsworth: Penguin Books, 1968), p. 300.

12. 'Truth and Fiction in Plutarch's *Lives*', in D.A. Russell (ed.), *Antonine Literature* (Oxford: Clarendon Press, 1990), p. 41.

13. See Collingwood, *The Idea of History*, p. 44.

14. Niccolò Machiavelli, *The Prince and the Discourses* (New York: The Modern Library, 1950), pp. 450–1.

15. Leslie J. Walker, *The Discourses of Niccolò Machiavelli* (London and Boston: Routledge and Kegan Paul, 1975), vol. 2, p. 173.

16. Niccolò Machiavelli, *The Prince*, transl. George Bull (Harmondsworth: Penguin Books, 1961), p. 91.

17. Allan H. Gilbert, *Machiavelli's 'Prince' and its Forerunners*, (Durham, NC.: Duke University Press, 1938), p. 78. This study takes the form of a detailed scholarly commentary on the whole of *The Prince*.

18. Sydney Anglo provides an excellent discussion of the limitations of Machiavelli's political thought with an extended analysis of the disjunctive mode, in *Machiavelli. A Dissection* (New York: Harcourt, Brace and World, 1969), pp. 243–53. For Machiavelli and consequentialist ethics, see Maureen Ramsay, 'Machiavelli's Political Philosophy in *The Prince*', in Martin Coyle (ed.), *Niccolò Machiavelli's 'The Prince'. New Interdisciplinary Essays* (Manchester: Manchester University Press, 1995), pp. 174–95.

19. A useful overview, 'Tacitism', is given by Peter Burke, in T.A. Dorey (ed.), *Tacitus* (London: Routledge and Kegan Paul, 1969), pp. 149–71. Book-length treatment is found in Kenneth C. Schellhase, *Tacitus in Renaissance Political Thought* (Chicago and London: Chicago University Press, 1976). This study focuses primarily on continental thought, for England see F.J. Levy, 'Hayward,

Daniel, and the Beginnings of Politic History in England', *Huntington Library Quarterly*, 50 (1987), pp. 1–34.

20. Greneway translated *The Annales of Cornelius Tacitus* and *The Description of Germanie*, Savile's contribution (first published in 1591), *Fower Bookes of the Histories of Cornelius Tacitus* and *The Life of Agricola*, plus his own work linking Tacitus' *Annals* and *History*, *The Ende of Nero and Beginning of Galba*. The edition was reprinted in 1604 and 1612.

21. See his chapter, 'Scepticism, Stoicism and *raison d'état*', in *Philosophy and Government 1572–1651* (Cambridge: Cambridge University Press, 1993), pp. 31–64.

22. See Ronald Knowles, '*Hamlet* and Counter-Humanism', *Renaissance Quarterley*, 52 (1999), pp. 1046–69.

23. See Burke, 'Tacitism', pp. 164–5 and Giorgio Spini, 'Historiography: The Art of History in the Italian Counter Reformation', in Eric Cochrane (ed.), *The Late Italian Renaissance 1525–1630* (London: Macmillan, 1970), pp. 91–133, particularly pp. 104–5.

24. 'The English Experience' (facsimile reprint), no. 287 (Amsterdam and New York: Da Capo Press and Theatrum Orbis Terrarum, 1970). Earlier criticism interested in stylistics was concerned with Lipsius as part of the anti-Ciceronian movement: see George Williamson, *the Senecan Amble* (Chicago: University of Chicago Press, 1966), pp. 121–49 and Morris W. Croll, 'Attic Prose: Lipsius, Montaigne, Bacon', in Stanley E. Fish (ed.), *Seventeenth-Century Prose* (New York: Oxford University Press, 1971), pp. 26–52.

25. Other commentators have drawn attention to this context, see, for example, Kahn, *Machiavellian Rhetoric*, p. 9.

26. See Quentin Skinner, *The Foundations of Modern Political Thought*, vol. I, 'The Renaissance' (Cambridge: Cambridge University Press, 1978), p. 253.

27. Anglo, *Machiavelli. A Dissection*, pp. 249–50, shows how Machiavelli misinterpreted the facts to agree with his theorum: Baglioni was already outmanoeuvred by the Pope and he gained by submission.

28. *Areopagitica*, in Ernest Sirluck (ed.), *Complete Prose Works of John Milton*, vol. II 1643–1648 (New Haven: Yale University Press/London: Oxford University Press, 1959), p. 501.

29. See Edward A. Berry, 'History and Rhetoric in Bacon's *Henry VII*', in Stanley E. Fish (ed.), *Seventeenth-Century Prose* (New York: Oxford University Press, 1971), pp. 281–308, particularly pp. 289–90.

30. See David Wootton, *Paolo Sarpi. Between Renaissance and Enlightenment* (Cambridge: Cambridge University Press, 1983). Tuck, *Philosophy and Government*, pp. 97–101, places Sarpi in relation to Tacitus and new humanism. Peter Burke has published an edition of Sarpi, *History of Benefices and Selections from the History of the Council of Trent* (New York: Washington Square Press, 1967). For Sarpi and Italian historiography, see Spini 'Historiography', p. 118.

31. *The Historie of the Civill Warres of France*, p. 421.

32. 'An Ode to James, Earl of Desmond' (*Underwoods*, XXV), see George Parfitt (ed.), Ben Jonson, *The Complete Poems* (Harmondsworth: Penguin Books, 1975), p. 162.

33. *The First Fowre Bookes of the ciuile wars between the two houses of Lancaster and Yorke* (1595), in Alexander B. Grosart (ed.), *The Complete Works in Verse and*

Prose of Samuel Daniel (London: The Spenser Society, 1885), vol. 2, p. 46. Peter Ure considers Bolingbroke's motivation in relation to Daniel but is unwilling to draw the Machiavellian conclusion which I find inevitable, see his *King Richard II*, 'The Arden Shakespeare' (London: Methuen, 1966), pp. lxxiii–iv.

34. *The Historie of the Civill Warres of France*, pp. 485–6.
35. See Blair Worden, 'Ben Jonson among the Historians', in Kevin Sharpe and Peter Lake (eds), *Culture and Politics in Early Stuart England* (Basingstoke: Macmillan, 1994), pp. 67–90.
36. John J. Manning (ed.), *The First and Second Parts of John Hayward's The Life and Raigne of King Henrie IIII* (London: Royal Historical Society, 1991), Camden Fourth Series, vol. 42, p. 2. This is the first publication of the second part of Hayward's work.
37. *Chronicles* III, p. 22.
38. Levy, 'Hayward, Daniel, and the Beginnings of Politic History in England', pp. 19, 20.
39. Manning (ed.), *The First and Second Parts of John Hayward's The Life and Raigne of King Henry IIII*, p. 229.
40. Manning (ed.), *The First and Second Parts of John Hayward's The Life and Raigne of King Henry IIII*, p. 239.
41. Collingwood, *The Idea of History*, pp. 25–8.
42. See Janet Coleman's section on 'The Legacy of the "Via Antiqua" and the "Via Moderna"', in her *Ancient and Medieval Memories. Studies in the Reconstruction of the Past* (Cambridge: Cambridge University Press, 1992), pp. 541–7.
43. *The Historie of the Civill Warres of France*, pp. 2–3.
44. 'Machiavelli's *via moderna*: medieval and Renaissance attitudes to history', in Martin Coyle (ed.), *Niccoló Machiavelli's 'The Prince'. New Interdisciplinary Essays* (Manchester: Manchester University Press, 1995), p. 44.
45. See Donald R. Kelley, 'The Theory of History', in Charles B. Schmitt *et al.*, *The Cambridge History of Renaissance Philosophy* (Cambridge: Cambridge University Press, 1988), p. 756.
46. *The First Fowre Bookes of the ciuile wars*, p. 7.
47. Compare the prologue of Ben Jonson's *The Alchemist* which invokes 'Judging Spectators' and 'justice', and the epilogue in which the audience is compared to a jury.
48. John Hayward, citing Philo, *A Treatise of Union* (London, 1604), sig. A3ᵛ.
49. 'The Second Coming', in *The Collected Poems of W.B. Yeats* (London: Macmillan, 1961), p. 211.

Bibliography

Adelman, Janet, *The Common Liar* (New Haven and London: Yale University Press, 1973).

Adelman, Janet, *Suffocating Mothers. Fantasies of Maternal Origin in Shakespeare's Plays, 'Hamlet' to 'The Tempest'* (New York and London: Routledge, 1992).

Alexander, Franz, 'A Note on Falstaff', *Psychanalytic Quarterly*, 3 (1933), pp. 592–606.

Allen, Don Cameron, *Mysteriously Meant. The Rediscovery of Pagan Symbolism and Allegorical Interpretation in the Renaissance* (Baltimore and London: Johns Hopkins University Press, 1970).

Allen, J.W., *A History of Political Thought in the Sixteenth Century* (London: Methuen, rep. 1962).

Althusser, Louis, *Essays on Ideology* (London and New York: Verso, 1993).

Altman, Joel B., *The Tudor Play of Mind. Rhetorical Enquiry and the Development of Elizabethan Drama* (Berkeley: University of California Press, 1978).

Anglo, Sydney, *Machiavelli. A Dissection* (New York: Harcourt, Brace and World, Inc., 1969).

Ashley, Robert, *Of Honour* (San Marino: The Huntington Library, 1947).

Augustine, St., *The City of God*, 2 vols, transl. John Healey (London: Dent, 1945).

Bakhtin, Mikhail, *Rabelais and His World* (Bloomington: Indiana University Press, 1984).

Baldwin, T.W., *William Shakespeare's Small Latine and Lesse Greeke*, 2 vols (Urbana: Illinois University Press, 1944).

Baldwin, T.W., 'Shakespeare's Aphthonian Man', *Modern Language Notes*, 65 (1950), pp. 111–12.

Baldwin, William, *A Treatise of Morall Philosophy*, ed. Robin Hood Bowers (Gainesville: Scholars Facsimiles and Reprints, 1967).

Barber, C.L., *Shakespeare's Festive Comedy* (Princeton, N.J.: Princeton University Press, 1959).

Barnie, John, *War in Medieval Society. Social Values and the Hundred Years War 1337–99* (London: Weidenfeld and Nicolson, 1974).

Bartlett, Phyllis B., 'The Heroes of Chapman's Homer', *Review of English Studies*, 19 (1941), pp. 257–80.

Barton, Anne, 'The King Disguised. Shakespeare's *Henry V* and the Comical History', in Joseph G. Price (ed.), *The Triple Bond. Plays Mainly Shakespearean in Performance* (Pennsylvania: Pennsylvania State University Press, 1975).

Battenhouse, Roy, 'Falstaff as Parodist and Perhaps Holy Fool', *PMLA*, 90–1 (1975), pp. 32–52.

Bellamy, J.G., *The Law of Treason in the Later Middle Ages* (Cambridge: Cambridge University Press, 1970).

Belsey, Catherine, 'Making Histories', in Graham Holderness (ed.), *Shakespeare's History Plays: 'Richard II' to 'Henry V'* (Basingstoke: Macmillan, 1992), pp. 103–20.

Bennett, J.W., '*Nosce te Ipsum*: Some Medieval and Modern Interpretations', in Piero Boitani (ed.), *The Humane Medievalist* (Roma, 1982).

Berry, Edward A., 'History and Rhetoric in Bacon's *Henry VII*', in Stanley E. Fish (ed.), *Seventeenth-Century Prose* (New York: Oxford University Press, 1971), pp. 281–308.

Berry, Ralph, 'Sexual Imagery in *Coriolanus*', *Studies in English Literature*, 13, (1973), pp. 301–16.

Berry, Ralph, *Shakespearean Structures* (London: Macmillan, 1981).

Bethell, S.L., 'The Comic Element in Shakespeare's Histories', *Anglia*, 71 (1952–3), pp. 82–101.

Bevington, David, *Action is Eloquence. Shakespeare's Language of Gesture* (Cambridge, Mass.: Harvard University Press, 1984).

Bevington, David, *see under* William Shakespeare.

Bliss, Lee, *see under* William Shakespeare.

Boccaccio, Giovanni, *Concerning Famous Women*, transl. Guido A. Guarino (New Brunswick: Rutgers University Press, 1963).

Bonet, Honoré, *The Tree of Battles*, transl. and ed. by G.W. Coopland (Liverpool: Liverpool University Press, 1949).

Bono, Barbara J., *Literary Transvaluation. From Vergilian Epic to Shakespearean Tragicomedy* (Berkeley: University of California Press, 1984).

Booth, Stephen (ed.), *Shakespeare's Sonnets* (New Haven: Yale University Press, 1977).

Boris, Edna Zwick, *Shakespeare's English Kings, the People, and the Law* (London: Associated University Presses, 1978).

Bourchier, Sir John (Lord Berners), *The Chronicle of Froissart*, 6 vols (London: David Nutt, 1903).

Boynton, Lindsay, *The Elizabethan Militia* (London: Routledge and Kegan Paul, 1967).

Bradford, John, *The Writings of John Bradford*, ed. Aubrey Townsend (Cambridge: The University Press, 1848).

Bradley, Sister Ritamaria, 'Backgrounds of the Title *Speculum* in Mediaeval Literature', *Speculum*, 29 (1954), pp. 100–15.

Bradshaw, Graham, *Misrepresentations. Shakespeare and the Materialists* (Ithaca and London: Cornell University Press, 1993).

Branham, R. Bracht, *Unruly Eloquence. Lucian and the Comedy of Traditions* (Cambridge, Mass.: Harvard University Press, 1989).

Braunmuller, A.R. (ed.), *The Life and Death of King John* (Oxford: Oxford University Press, 1994).

Braunmuller, A.R., *see under* William Shakespeare.

Brockbank, Philip, *see under* William Shakespeare.

Broughton, Bradford B., *Dictionary of Medieval Knighthood and Chivalry. Concepts and Terms* (New York: Greenwood Press, 1986).

Brumble, H. David, *Classical Myths and Legends in the Middle Ages and the Renaissance* (Westport, Conn.: Greenwood Press, 1998).

Bullinger, Henry, *The Decades of Henry Bullinger*, ed. Thomas Harding (Cambridge: The University Press, 1850).

Bullough, Geoffrey (ed.), *The Narrative and Dramatic Sources of Shakespeare*, 8 vols (London: Routledge and Kegan Paul, 1958–75).

Burgkmair, Hans, *The Triumph of Maximilian I*, ed. Stanley Appelbaum (New York: Dover Publications, 1964).

Burke, Peter, 'Tacitism', in T.A. Dorey (ed.), *Tacitus* (London: Routledge and Kegan Paul, 1969).

Burns, Edward, *see under* William Shakespeare.

Calderwood, James L., *Metadrama in Shakespeare's Henriad* (Berkeley: University of California Press, 1979).

Calvin, John, *Calvin's Institutes* (Grand Rapids, Michigan, n.d.).

Candido, Joseph and Charles R. Forker (eds), *Henry V: An Annotated Bibliography* (New York: Garland, 1983).

Caplan, Harry (ed.), *Rhetorica ad Herennium* (Cambridge, Mass.: Harvard University Press, 1954).

Carnicelli, D.D. (ed.), *Lord Morley's 'Tryumphes of Fraunces Petrarke'* (Cambridge, Mass.: Harvard University Press, 1971).

Carroll, D.A., 'Greene's "vpstart crow" Passage: A Survey of Commentary', *Research Opportunities in Renaissance Drama*, 28 (1985), pp. 111–27.

Cato, Marcus Portius, *On Agriculture*: Marcus Terentius Varro, *On Agriculture*, 'The Loeb Classical Library' (London: William Heinemann/Cambridge, Mass.: Harvard University Press, 1934).

Certain Sermons or Homilies (Oxford: The University Press, 1844).

Chauduri, Sukanta, *Infirm Glory: Shakespeare and the Renaissance Image of Man* (Oxford: Oxford University Press, 1981).

Cicero, Marcus Tullius, *De finibus bonorum et malorum*, 3 vols, 'The Loeb Classical Library' (London: William Heinemann: New York: The Macmillan Co., 1914).

Cicero, Marcus Tullius, *De oratore* 'The Loeb Classical Library' (London: William Heinemann/Cambridge, Mass.: Harvard University Press, 1942).

Cicero, Marcus Tullius, *De republica. De legibus*, 'The Loeb Classical Library' (London: William Heinemann/Cambridge, Mass.: Harvard University Press, 1948).

Clark, Donald Leman, *John Milton at St Paul's School* (New York: Columbia University Press, 1948).

Clark, Stuart, *Thinking With Demons. The Idea of Witchcraft in Early Modern England* (Oxford: The Clarendon Press, 1997).

Cochrane, Eric, *Historians and Historiography in the Italian Renaissance* (Chicago and London: The University of Chicago Press, 1981).

Coleman, Janet, *Ancient and Medieval Memories. Studies in the Reconstruction of the Past* (Cambridge: Cambridge University Press, 1992).

Coleman, Janet, 'Machiavelli's *via moderna*: Medieval and Renaissance Attitudes to History', in Martin Coyle (ed.), *Niccolò Machiavelli's 'The Prince'. New Interdisciplinary Essays* (Manchester: Manchester University Press, 1995).

Collingwood, R.G., *The Idea of History* (Oxford: Oxford University Press, 1966).

Colwell, F.R., *Cicero and the Roman Republic* (Harmondsworth: Penguin Books, 1967).

Cox, John D., *The Devil and the Sacred in English Drama 1350–1642* (Cambridge: Cambridge University Press, 2000).

Craig, Hardin, 'Shakespeare and Formal Logic', in Kemp Malone and Martin B. Ruud (eds), *Studies in English Philology: A Miscellany in Honour of Frederick Klaeber* (Minneapolis: Minnesota University Press, 1929), pp. 380–96.

Craig, Hardin, *The Enchanted Glass* (Oxford: Basil Blackwell, 1960).

Craik, T.W., *see under* William Shakespeare.

Crane, W.G., *Wit and Rhetoric in the Renaissance* (New York: Columbia University Press, 1937).

Croll, Morris W., 'Attic Prose: Lipsius, Montaigne, Bacon', in Stanley E. Fish (ed.), *Seventeenth-Century Prose* (New York: Oxford University Press, 1971).

Cruickshank, C.G., *Elizabeth's Army* (Oxford: Oxford University Press, 2nd edn, 1968).

Cushman, L.W., *The Devil and the Vice in English Dramatic Literature before Shakespeare* (London: Frank Cass, 1900).

Daniel, Samuel, *The First Fowre Bookes of the ciuile wars between the two houses of Lancaster and Yorke* (1595), in Alexander B. Grosart (ed.), *The Complete Works in Verse and Prose of Samuel Daniel*, 5 vols (London: The Spenser Society, 1885).

Daniell, David, *see under* William Shakespeare.

Davila, Arrigo Caterina, *The Historie of the Civill Warres of France*, transl. William Aylesbury (London, 1647).

Davies, Natalie Zemon, 'Women on Top: Sexual Inversion and Political Disorder in Early Modern Europe', in Barbara Babcock (ed.), *The Reversible World. Symbolic Inversion in Art and Society* (Ithaca and London: Cornell University Press, 1978).

Dean, Paul, 'Chronicle and Romance Modes in *Henry V*', *Shakespeare Quarterly*, 32 (1981), pp. 18–27.

Dessen, Alan C., *Elizabethan Drama and the Viewer's Eye* (Chapel Hill: University of North Carolina Press, 1977).

Dickey, Franklin M., *Not Wisely But Too Well. Shakespeare's Love Tragedies* (San Marino: Huntington Library, 1957).

Dictionary of National Biography, 2 vols (Oxford: Oxford University Press, 1975).

Dillon, Janette, *Shakespeare and the Solitary Man* (Basingstoke: Macmillan, 1981).

Dollarhide, Louis E., 'The Logic of Villainy: Shakespeare's Use of the Fallacies', *University of Missisipy Studies in English*, 10 (1969), pp. 49–57.

Donaldson, E. Talbot, *The Swan at the Well. Shakespeare Reading Chaucer* (New Haven and London: Yale University Press, 1985).

Doran, Madelaine, *Endeavours of Art: a Study of Form in Elizabethan Drama* (Madison: University of Wisconsin Press, 1954).

Dorsch, T.S., *see under* William Shakespeare.

Drakakis, John (ed.), *Antony and Cleopatra*, 'New Casebooks' (Basingstoke: Macmillan, 1994).

Draper, John W., 'Sir John Falstaff', *Review of English Studies*, 8 (1932), pp. 414–24.

Dugdale, Sir William, *The Baronage of England*, 2 vols (1675).

Duls, Louisa De Saussure, *Richard II in the Early Chronicles* (The Hague and Paris: Mouton, 1975).

Dunham, Jr, William Huse and Charles T. Wood, 'The Right to Rule in England: Depositions and the Kingdom's Authority, 1327–1485', *The American Historical Review*, 81 (1976), pp. 738–61.

Eagleton, Terry, *William Shakespeare* (Oxford: Basil Blackwell, 1986).

Erasmus, *The Collected Works of Erasmus. The Adages* (Toronto: University of Toronto Press, 1982–92), vols 31–4.

Evans, G. Blakemore, *see under* William Shakespeare.

Elton, William R., *King Lear and the Gods* (San Marino: The Huntington Library, 1966).

Elton, William R., *Shakespeare's 'Troilus and Cressida' and the Inns of Court Revels* (Aldershot: Ashgate, 2000).

Ferguson, A.B., *The Indian Summer of English Chivalry* (Durham: North Carolina University Press, 1965).

Ferguson, A.B., *The Chivalric Tradition in Renaissance England* (Washington: Folger Books, 1986).

Ferguson, John, *Moral Values in the Ancient World* (London: Methuen, 1958).

French, A.L., 'The Mills of God and Shakespeare's Early History Plays', *English Studies*, 55 (1974), pp. 313–24.

Fulke, William, *A Defence of the Sincere and the Translations of the Holy Scriptures into the English Tongue*, ed. Charles Henry Hartshorne (Cambridge: The University Press, 1843).

Fuzier, Jean, 'Rhetoric versus Rhetoric: A Study of Shakespeare's *Julius Caesar*, Act III, Scene 2', *Cahiers Elizabéthains*, 5 (1981), pp. 25–65.

Gabel, Leona C., *Benefit of Clergy in England in the Later Middle Ages*, Smith College Studies in History, 14, nos 1–4 (October 1928–July 1929, Northampton, Mass.).

Gaudet, Paul, 'Northumberland's "persuasion": Reflections on *Richard II* II.i. 224–300', *Upstart Crow*, 4 (Fall 1982), pp. 73–85.

Gierke, Otto, *Political Theories of the Middle Age* (Cambridge: Cambridge University Press, 1900).

Gilbert, Allan H., *Machiavelli's 'Prince' and its Forerunners* (Durham, N.C.: Duke University Press, 1938).

Gilman, Ernest B., *The Curious Perspective. Literary and Pictorial Wit in the Seventeenth Century* (New Haven and London: Yale University Press, 1918).

Godshalk, W.L., 'Henry V's Politics of Non-responsibility', *Cahiers Elizabéthains*, 17 (1980), pp. 11–20.

Grabes, Herbert, *The Mutable Glass* (Cambridge: Cambridge University Press, 1982).

Grafton's Chronicle, 1569, 2 vols (reprinted London: 1809).

Greenblatt, Stephen, *Shakespearean Negotiations: The Circulation of Social Energy in Renaissance England* (Oxford: Clarendon Press, 1988).

Greene, Gayle, '"The Power of Speech/To Stir Man's Blood": The Language of Tragedy in Shakespeare's *Julius Caesar*', *Renaissance Drama*, 11 (1980), pp. 67–93.

Gregory's Chronicle, in James Gairdner (ed.), *The Historical Collection of Á Citizen of London in the Fifteenth Century*, Camden Society New Series XVII (London: Camden Society, 1875).

Greneway, R., *see under* Cornelius Tacitus.

Grimald, Nicholas, *Marcus Tullius Ciceroes thre bokes of duties* (1556), ed. Gerald O'Gorman (Washington: The Folger Shakespeare Library: London and Toronto: Associated University Presses).

Gurr, Andrew, *see under* William Shakespeare.

Hall, Edward, *The Union of the Two Noble and Illustre Families of Lancaster and York*, 1548 (reprinted London: 1809).

Halstead, William P., *Shakespeare as Spoken: A Collation of 5000 Acting Editions and Promptbooks of Shakespeare* (Michigan: Ann Arbor, 1979).

Hammond, Antony, *see under* William Shakespeare.

Hampton, Timothy, *Writing from History. The Rhetoric of Exemplarity in Renaissance Literature* (Ithaca and London: Cornell University Press, 1990).

Hankey, Julie, *see under* William Shakespeare.

Hart, Jonathan, *Theater and World. The Problematics of Shakespeare's History* (Boston: Northeastern University Press, 1942).

Harte, N.B., 'State Control of Dress and Social Change in Pre-Industrial England', in D.C. Coleman and A.H. John (eds), *Trade, Government and Economy in Pre-Industrial England* (London: Weidenfeld and Nicolson, 1976).

Hattaway, Michael, *see under* William Shakespeare.

Hay, Denys, 'The Division of the Spoils of War in Fourteenth-Century England', *Transactions of the Royal Historical Society*, 5th Series, 4 (1954), pp. 91–110.

Haydn, Hiram, *The Counter Renaissance* (New York: Charles Scribner & Sons, 1950).

Hayward, John, *A Treatise of Union* (London, 1604).

Hemingway, Samuel Burdett, *see under* William Shakespeare.

Hillebrand, Harold N., *see under* William Shakespeare.

Hinton, R.W.K., 'English Constitutional Doctrines from the Fifteenth Century to the Seventeenth', I English Constitutional Theories from Sir John Fortescue to Sir John Eliot, *English Historical Review*, 75, no. 296 (1960) pp. 410–25.

Holinshed, Raphael, *The Chronicles of England, Scotland and Ireland*, 6 vols (2nd edn, 1587: reprinted London, 1808).

Holdsworth, W.S., *A History of English Law*, 17 vols (London: Methuen, 1903).

Holmes, Peter, *Resistance and Compromise. The Political Thought of the English Catholics* (Cambridge: Cambridge University Press, 1982).

Honigmann, E.A.J., *see under* William Shakespeare.

Houppert, Joseph W., 'Fatal Logic in *Julius Caesar*', *South Atlantic Bulletin*, 39 (1974), pp. 3–9.

Howard, Jean E. and Phyllis Rackin, *Engendering a Nation* (London and New York: Routledge, 1997).

Howell, W.S., *Logic and Rhetoric in England 1500–1700* (Princeton: Princeton University Press, 1956).

Holderness, Graham, *Shakespeare's History* (Dublin: Gill and Macmillan, 1985).

Holderness, Graham, Bryan Loughrey and Andrew Murphy (eds), *Shakespeare: The Roman Plays* (London and New York: Longman, 1996).

Huffman, Clifford Chalmers, *'Coriolanus' in Context* (Lewisburg: Bucknell University Press, 1971).

Hughes, Paul L. and James F. Larkin (eds), *The Tudor Royal Proclamations*, 3 vols (New Haven and London: Yale University Press, 1969).

Hughes-Hallett, Lucy, *Cleopatra: Histories, Dreams and Distortions* (London: Bloomsbury, 1990).

Huizinga, Johan, *The Waning of the Middle Ages* (originally 1924; rep. New York, Anchor Books, 1954).

Humphreys, A.R., *see under* William Shakespeare.

Ide, Richard S., *Possessed with Greatness. The Heroic Tragedies of Chapman and Shakespeare* (London: Scolar Press, 1980).

Jackson, Russell, 'The Triumphs of *Antony and Cleopatra*', *Shakespeare Jahrbuch* (West) (1984), pp. 128–48.

Jackson, T.A., 'Marx and Shakespeare', *Labour Monthly*, 46 (1964), pp. 165–73.

Jacobus, Lee A., *Shakespeare and the Dialectic of Certainty* (New York: St. Martin's Press, 1992).

James, Heather, *Shakespeare's Troy. Drama, Politics and the Translation of Empire* (Cambridge: Cambridge University Press, 1997).

James, Mervyn, *English Politics and the Concept of Honour 1485–1642* (Oxford: The Past and Present Society, 'Past and Present' Supplement 3, 1978).

James, Mervyn, *Society, Politics and Culture: Studies in Early Modern England* (Cambridge: Cambridge University Press, 1986).

Jardine, Lisa, *Francis Bacon. Discovery and the Art of Discourse* (Cambridge: Cambridge University Press, 1974).

Jardine, Lisa, 'Humanist Logic', in Charles B. Schmitt, Quentin Skinner, Ekhart Kesslar and Jill Kray (eds), *The Cambridge History of Renaissance Philosophy* (Cambridge: Cambridge University Press, 1988), pp. 178–98.

Jones, Howard, *Master Tully. Cicero in Tudor England* (Nieuwkoop: De Graf Publishers, 1998).

Jones, R.F., 'Science and Language in England of the Mid-Seventeenth Century', in Stanley E. Fish (ed.), *Seventeenth-Century Prose* (New York: Oxford University Press, 1971), pp. 94–111.

Jonson, Ben, *The Complete Poems*, ed. George Parfitt, (Harmondsworth: Penguin Books, 1975).

Jorgensen, Paul A., *Shakespeare's Military World* (Berkeley and Los Angeles: University of California Press, 1956).

Jorgensen, Paul A., 'The "Dastardly Treachery" of Prince John of Lancaster', *PMLA*, 76–1 (1961), pp. 488–92.

Jorgensen, Paul A., '"Redeeming Time" in *Henry IV*' in *Redeeming Shakespeare's Words* (Berkeley: University of California Press, 1962), pp. 52–69.

Joseph, H.W.B., *An Introduction to Logic* (Oxford: The Clarendon Press, 1906).

Joseph, Sister Miriam, *Shakespeare's Use of the Arts of Language* (New York: Columbia University Press, 1947).

Jowett, B., *The Dialogues of Plato*, 5 vols (Oxford: Clarendon Press, 1875).

Kahn, Victoria, *Machiavellian Rhetoric* (Princeton, N.J.: Princeton University Press, 1994).

Kaiser, Walter, *Praisers of Folly: Erasmus, Rabelais, Shakespeare* (London: Victor Gollancz, 1964).

Kamps, Ivo, *Historiography and Ideology in Stuart Drama* (Cambridge: Cambridge University Press, 1996).

Keen, M.H., 'Chivalry, Nobility, and the Man-at-Arms', in C.T. Allmond (ed.), *War, Literature and Politics in the Late Middle Ages* (Liverpool: Liverpool University Press, 1976), pp. 32–45.

Keen, M.H., *The Laws of War in the Late Middle Ages* (London: Routledge & Kegan Paul, 1965).

Keen, M.H., *Chivalry* (New Haven and London: Yale University Press, 1984).

Kelley, Donald R., 'The Theory of History', in Charles B. Schmitt *et al.*, *The Cambridge History of Renaissance Philosophy* (Cambridge: Cambridge University Press, 1988).

Kelley, Donald R., 'Ideas of Resistance before Elizabeth', in Gordon J. Schochet (ed.), *Law, Literature and the Settlement of Regimes*. Proceedings of the Folger Institute Centre for the History of British Political Thought, vol. 2 (Washington: The Folger Institute, 1990).

Kelley, Donald R., 'Law' in H.J. Burns (ed.), *The Cambridge History of Political Thought 1450–1700* (Cambridge: Cambridge University Press, 1991).

Kelly, H.A., *Divine Providence in the England of Shakespeare's Histories* (Cambridge, Mass.: Harvard University Press, 1970).

Kennedy, George A., *A New History of Classical Rhetoric* (Princeton: Princeton University Press, 1994).

Kimbrough, Robert, *Shakespeare's 'Troilus and Cressida' and its Setting* (Cambridge, Mass.: Harvard University Press, 1964).

King, Bruce, *Coriolanus*, 'The Critics Debate' (Basingstoke: Macmillan, 1989).

Kipling, Gordon, *The Triumph of Honour* (The Hague: Leiden University Press, 1977).

Kirschbaum, Leo, 'Shakespeare's Stage Blood and its Critical Significance', *PMLA*, 64 (1944), pp. 517–29.

Knowles, Ronald, 'The Political Contexts of Deposition and Election in *Edward II*', *Medieval and Renaissance Drama in England*, 14 (forthcoming).

Knowles, Ronald, 'The "All-attoning Name". The Word "Patriot" in Seventeenth-Century England', *Modern Language Review*, 96 (2001), pp. 624–43.

Knowles, Ronald, '*Hamlet* and Counter-Humanism', *Renaissance Quarterly*, 52 (1999), pp. 1046–69.

Knowles, Ronald (ed.), *Shakespeare and Carnival: After Bakhtin* (Basingstoke: Macmillan, 1998).

Knowles, Ronald, *Henry IV Parts I & II* 'The Critics Debate' (Basingstoke: Macmillan, 1992).

Knowles, Ronald, *see under* William Shakespeare.

Kunzle, David, 'World Upside Down: The Iconography of a European Broadsheet', in Barbara Babcock (ed.), *The Reversible World: Symbolic Inversion in Art and Society* (Ithaca and London: Cornell University Press, 1978), pp. 39–94.

Lechner, Sister Joan Marie, *Renaissance Concepts of the Commonplaces* (New York: Pageant Press, 1962).

Leech, Clifford, *Shakespeare: The Chronicles*, 'Writers and their Work', 146 (London: Longman Green & Co., 1962).

Leff, Gordon, *Medieval Thought* (Harmondsworth: Penguin Books, 1958).

Legg, Leopold G. Wickham, *English Coronation Records* (Westminster: Archibald Constable & Co. 1901).

Levenson, Jill L., 'Shakespeare's *Troilus and Cressida* and the Monumental Tradition in Tapestries and Literature', *Renaissance Drama*, VII (1976), pp. 43–84.

Levin, Richard. *The Multiple Plot in English Renaissance Drama* (Chicago: University of Chicago Press, 1971).

Levy, F.J., 'Hayward, Daniel, and the Beginnings of Politic History in England', *Huntington Library Quarterly*, 50 (1987), pp. 1–33.

Lipsius, Justus, *Six Bookes of Politickes or Civil Doctrine*, transl. William Jones, [1594] (Amsterdam and New York: Da Capo Press and Theatrum Orbis Terrarum, 1970).

Loganbill, Dean, 'The Contrast between the Chevalier Bayard, a Chivalric Knight, and Giovanni de Medici, a Pragmatic Captain', in Larry D. Benson and John Leyerle (eds), *Chivalric Literature. Essays on Relations between Literature and Life in the Later Middle Ages* (Kalamazoo: Medieval Institute Publications, Western Michigan University, 1980), pp. 117–30.

Longstaffe, Stephen, '"A short report and not otherwise": Jack Cade in *2 Henry VI*', in Ronald Knowles (ed.), *Shakespeare and Carnival: After Bakhtin* (Basingstoke: Macmillan, 1998), pp. 13–36.

Lowe, Lisa, '"Say I play the man I am": Gender and Politics in *Coriolanus*', *Kenyon Review*, 8 (1986), pp. 86–95.

Lucan, *Pharsalia*, transl. Robert Graves (Harmondsworth: Penguin Books, 1957).

Luckyi, Christina, 'Volumnia's Silence', *Studies in English Literature*, 31 (1991), pp. 327–42.

Mabbott, Thomas Ollive and J. Milton French (eds), *The Works of John Milton* 18 vols (New York: Columbia University Press, 1938).

McAlindon, Tom, 'Testing the New Historicism: "Invisible Bullets" Reconsidered', *Studies in Philology*, XCII, No. 4 (Fall 1995), pp. 411–38.

McAlindon, Tom, 'Swearing and Forswearing in Shakespeare's Histories. The Playwright as Contra-Machiavel', *The Review of English Studies*, 51 (2000), pp. 208–29.

McAlindon, Tom, *Shakespeare's Tragic Cosmos* (Cambridge: Cambridge University Press, 1991).

McCoy, Richard C., *The Rites of Knighthood. The Literature and Politics of Elizabethan Chivalry* (Berkeley: University of California Press, 1989).

McDonald, Charles Osborne, *The Rhetoric of Tragedy: Form in Stuart Drama* (Amherst, Mass.: University of Massachusetts Press, 1966).

McFarlane, K.B., *The Nobility of Later Medieval England* (Oxford: Clarendon Press, 1973).

Machiavelli, Niccolò, *The Discourses of Niccolò Machiavelli*, 2 vols (London: Routledge and Kegan Paul, 1950).

Machiavelli, Niccolò, *The Prince and the Discourses* (New York: The Modern Library, 1950).

Machiavelli, Niccolò, *The Prince*, transl. George Bull (Harmondsworth: Penguin Books, 1961).

Mack, Peter, *Renaissance Argument. Valla and Agricola in the Traditions of Rhetoric and Dialectic* (Leiden: E.J. Brill, 1993).

McNamee, Maurice B, S.J., *Honor and the Epic Hero. A Study in the Shifting Concept of Magnanimity in Philosophy and Epic Poetry* (New York: Holt, Rinehart and Winston, 1960).

Maitland, F.W., *The Constitutional History of England* (Cambridge: Cambridge University Press, 1926).

Mann, Jill, 'Chaucer and Shakespeare: "What is Criseyde Worth?"', in Piero Boitani (ed.), *The European Tragedy of Troilus* (Oxford: Oxford University Press, 1989).

Manning, John J. (ed.), *The First and Second Parts of John Hayward's The Life and Raigne of King Henrie IIII*, Camden 4th series, vol. 42 (London: Royal Historical Society, 1991).

Martyr, Peter, *Most Learned and fruitful Commentaries . . . upon the Epistle of S. Paul to the Romanes*, transl. John Day [1568], in Robert M. Kingdon (ed.), *The Political Thought of Peter Martyr Vermigli* (Genève: Libraire Droz, 1980), pp. 1–15.

Meron, Theodor, *Henry's Wars and Shakespeare's Laws* (Oxford: The Clarendon Press, 1993).

Meyrick, Sir Samuel Rush, *A Critical Enquiry into Antient Armour*, 3 vols (London: Henry G. Bohn, 1849).

Miles, Geoffrey, *Shakespeare and the Constant Romans* (Oxford: The Clarendon Press, 1996).

Miller, Perry, *The New England Mind: The Seventeenth Century* (New York: Macmillan, 1939).

Miola, Robert S., 'Shakespeare and His Sources: Observations on the Critical History of *Julius Caesar*', *Shakespeare Survey*, 40 (1987), pp. 69–76.

Miola, Robert S., *Shakespeare and Classical Tragedy* (Oxford: Oxford University Press, 1992).

Milton, John, *Areopagitica*, in Ernest Sirluck (ed.), *Complete Prose Works of John Milton*, vol. 2 (New Haven: Yale University Press; London: Oxford University Press, 1959).

Morgan, David, 'From a Death to a View: Louis Robessart, Johan Huizinga and the Political Significance of Chivalry', in Sydney Anglo (ed.), *Chivalry in the Renaissance* (Woodbridge: The Boydell Press, 1990), pp. 93–106.

Mousnier, Roland, *The Assassination of Henry IV* (London: Faber and Faber, 1973).

Munday, Mildred Brand, 'Pejorative Patterns in Shakespeare's *Troilus and Cressida*', *Bucknell Review*, 5 (1955), pp. 413–40.

Nadel, George, 'Philosophy of History before Historicism', *History and Theory*, III (1964), pp. 291–315.

Nashe, Thomas, *Works*, ed. R.B. McKerrow, 5 vols (London: A.H. Bullen, 1958).

Neill, Michael, *see* William Shakespeare.

Neilson, G., *Trial by Combat* (Glasgow: Hodge & Co., 1890).

Nicholl, Charles, *The Reckoning. The Murder of Christopher Marlowe* (London: Jonathan Cape, 1992).

Nichols, John, *Illustrations of the Manners and Expenses of Ancient Times in England, 1797* (New York: AMS Press, 1973).

Nochimson, Richard L., 'The End Crowns All: Shakespeare's Deflation of Tragic Possibility in *Antony and Cleopatra*', *English*, 26 (1977), pp. 99–132.

Patterson, Annabel, *Shakespeare and the Popular Voice* (Oxford: Basil Blackwell, 1989).

Parker, Patricia, *Shakespeare from the Margins* (Chicago and London: Chicago University Press, 1996).

Parker, R.B., *see under* William Shakespeare.

Pelling, C.B.R., 'Truth and Fiction in Plutarch's *Lives*', in D.A. Russell (ed.), *Antonine Literature* (Oxford: Clarendon Press, 1990).

Peltonem, Markku, *Classical Humanism and Republicanism in English Political Thought 1570–1640* (Cambridge: Cambridge University Press, 1995).

Peters, Edward, *The Shadow King. Rex Inutilis in Medieval Law and Literature 751–1327* (New Haven and London: Yale University Press, 1970).

Pettet, E.C., '*Coriolanus* and the Midlands insurrection of 1607', *Shakespeare Survey*, 3 (1950), pp. 34–42.

Pitt-Rivers, Julian, 'Honour and Social Status', in J.G. Peristiany (ed.), *Honour and Shame: The Values of Mediterranean Society* (London: Weidenfeld and Nicolson, 1965), pp. 19–78.

Pliny, *Natural History*, 'The Loeb Classical Library', 10 vols (London: William Heinemann / Cambridge, Mass.: Harvard University Press, 1945).

Pollard, A.J., *John Talbot and the War in France 1427–1453* (London: Royal Historical Society, 1983).

Polybius, *The Histories*, 'The Loeb Classical Library', 3 vols (London, William Heinemann / New York: G.P. Putnam's Sons, 1923).

Ponet, John, *A Short Treatise of Politic Power* [1556] (Menston: Scolar Press, 1970).

Potter, A.M., '*Troilus and Cressida*: Deconstructing the Middle Ages', *Theoria*, 72 (1988), pp. 23–35.

Pratt, Josiah (ed.), *The Acts and Monuments of John Foxe*, 8 vols (London: The Religious Tract Society, 1877).

Praz, Mario, '"The Politic Brain": Machiavelli and the Elizabethans', in *The Flaming Heart* (New York: Doubleday Anchor Books, 1958), pp. 90–145.

Presson, Robert K., *Shakespeare's 'Troilus and Cressida' and the Legends of Troy* (Madison: The University of Wisconsin Press, 1953).

Pugliatti, Paola, *Shakespeare the Historian* (Basingstoke: Macmillan, 1996).

Puttenham, George, *The Arte of English Poesie* [1589] (London: Constable and Co., 1906).

Rabkin, Norman, 'Rabbits, Ducks and *Henry V*', *Shakespeare Quarterly*, 28 (1977), pp. 279–96.

Rackin, Phyllis, 'Shakespeare's Boy Cleopatra, the Decorum of Nature, and the Golden World of Poetry', in John Drakakis (ed.), *Antony and Cleopatra* (Basingstoke: Macmillan, 1994), pp. 78–100.

Ramsay, Maureen, 'Machiavelli's Political Philosophy in *The Prince*', in Martin Coyle (ed.), *Niccolò Machiavelli's 'The Prince'. New Interdisciplinary Essays* (Manchester: Manchester University Press, 1995).

Rauchet, E.A., 'Hotspur's Prisoners and the Laws of War in *1 Henry IV*', *Shakespeare Quarterly*, 45 (1994), pp. 96–7.

Rebhorn, Wayne A., *Renaissance Debates on Rhetoric* (Ithaca and London: Cornell University Press, 2000).

Rebhorn, Wayne A., 'The Crisis of the Aristocracy in *Julius Caesar*', *Renaissance Quarterly*, 43 (1990), pp. 75–111.

Rhodes, Neil, 'The Controversial Plot: Declamation and the Concept of the "Problem Play"', *MLR*, 95 (2000), pp. 609–22.

Rhodes, Neil, *Elizabethan Grotesque* (London: Routledge & Kegan Paul, 1980).

Rickman, Geoffrey, *The Corn Supply of Ancient Rome* (Oxford: Clarendon Press, 1980).

Riggs, David, *Shakespeare's Heroical Histories: Henry VI and its Literary Tradition* (Cambridge, Mass.: Harvard University Press, 1971).

Robinson, F.N. (ed.), *The Works of Geoffrey Chaucer* (Oxford: Oxford University Press, 1979).

Rollins, Hyder E., 'The Troilus–Cressida Story from Chaucer to Shakespeare', *PMLA*, 34 (1917), pp. 383–429.

Rotuli Parliamentorum (London, 1767–77), vol. iii.

Rouse, Richard H. and Mary A. Rouse, 'John of Salisbury and the Doctrine of Tyrannicide', *Speculum*, 42 (1967), pp. 693–79.

Rymer, Thomas, *Foedera*, 10 vols (The Hague, 1745).

Savile, Sir Henry, *see under* Cornelius Tacitus.

Sarpi, Paolo, *The Historie of the Councel of Trent*, transl. Nathanael Brent (London 1640).

Sarpi, Paolo, *History of Benefices and Selections from the History of the Council of Trent*, ed. Peter Burke (New York: Washington Square Press, Inc., 1967).

Saul, Nigel, *Richard II* (New Haven and London: Yale University Press, 1997).

Schanzer, Ernest, *The Problem Plays of Shakespeare* (London: Routledge and Kegan Paul, 1963).

Schelhase, Kenneth C., *Tacitus in Renaissance Political Thought* (Chicago and London: Chicago University Press, 1976).

Schramm, Percy Ernst, *A History of the English Coronation* (Oxford: Clarendon Press, 1937).

Scragg, Leah, 'Iago – Vice or Devil', *Shakespeare Survey*, 21 (1968), pp. 53–65.

Segar, Sir William, *The Book of Honor and Arms (1590)* and *Honor Military and Civil (1602)*, ed. Diane Bornstein (New York: Scholars Facsimiles and Reprints).

Serpieri, Alessandro, 'Reading the Signs: Towards a Semiotics of Shakespearean Drama', in John Drakakis (ed.), *Alternative Shakespeare's* (London and New York: Methuen, 1985), pp. 119–43.

Shakespeare, William, *The Complete Works*, ed. Stanley Wells and Gary Taylor, 'The Oxford Shakespeare' (Oxford: The Clarendon Press, 1988).

—— *The Riverside Shakespeare*, ed. G. Blakemore Evans (Boston: Houghton Mifflin Company, 1974).

—— *Antony and Cleopatra*, ed. David Bevington, 'The New Cambridge Shakespeare' (Cambridge: Cambridge University Press, 1990).

—— *Antony and Cleopatra*, ed. Marvin Spevack, 'New Variorum Edition of Shakespeare' (The Modern Language Association of America, 1990).

—— *Antony and Cleopatra*, ed. Michael Neill, 'The World's Classics. The Oxford Shakespeare' (Oxford: Oxford University Press, 1994).

—— *Antony and Cleopatra*, ed. John Wilders, 'The Arden Shakespeare' (London: Routledge, 1995).

—— *Coriolanus*, ed. Philip Brockbank, 'The Arden Shakespeare' (London: Methuen, 1976).

—— *Coriolanus*, ed. R.B. Parker, 'The World's Classics' (Oxford, New York: Oxford University Press, 1994).

—— *Coriolanus*, ed. Lee Bliss, 'The New Cambridge Shakespeare' (Cambridge: Cambridge University Press, 2000).

—— *The First Part of King Henry VI*, ed. Andrew S. Cairncross, 'The Arden Shakespeare' (London: Methuen & Co., 1962).

—— *The First Part of King Henry VI*, ed. Michael Hattaway, 'The New Cambridge Shakespeare' (Cambridge: Cambridge University Press, 1990).

—— *King Henry VI, Part One*, ed. Edward Burns, 'The Arden Shakespeare' (Walton-on-Thames: The Arden Shakespeare, 2000).

—— *King Henry VI, Part Two*, ed. Ronald Knowles, 'The Arden Shakespeare' (Walton-on-Thames: Thomas Nelson and Sons, 1999).

—— *The Third Part of King Henry VI*, ed. Michael Hattaway, 'The New Cambridge Shakespeare' (Cambridge: Cambridge University Press, 1993).

—— *King Richard III*, ed. Antony Hammond, 'The Arden Shakespeare' (London: Methuen, 1981).

—— *Richard III*, ed. Julie Hankey, 'Plays in Performance' (Bristol: Bristol Classical Press, 1988).

—— *King Richard II*, ed. Peter Ure, 'The Arden Shakespeare' (London: Methuen, 1956).

—— *King Richard II*, ed. Andrew Gurr, 'The New Cambridge Shakespeare' (Cambridge: Cambridge University Press, 1984).

—— *Henry the Fourth. Part I*, ed. Samuel Burdett Hemingway, 'The Variorum Shakespeare' (Philadelphia and London: J.B. Lippincott Company, 1936).

—— *The First Part of King Henry IV*, ed. A.R. Humphreys, 'The Arden Shakespeare' (London: Methuen, 1960).

—— *The Second Part of King Henry IV*, ed. A.R. Humphreys, 'The Arden Shakespeare' (London: Methuen, 1966).

—— *King Henry V*, ed. John H. Walter, 'The Arden Shakespeare' (London: Methuen, 1954).

—— *King Henry V*, ed. Andrew Gurr, 'The New Cambridge Shakespeare' (Cambridge: Cambridge University Press, 1992).

—— *King Henry V*, ed. T.W. Craik, 'The Arden Shakespeare' (Walton-on-Thames: The Arden Shakespeare, 1995).

—— *King John*, ed. E.A.J. Honigmann, 'The Arden Shakespeare' (London: Methuen, 1954).

Shakespeare, William, *Julius Caesar*, ed. T.S. Dorsch, 'The Arden Shakespeare' (London: Methuen & Co Ltd, 1965).

—— *Julius Caesar*, ed. David Daniell, 'The Arden Shakespeare' (Walton-on-Thames: The Arden Shakespeare, 1998).

—— *The Merry Wives of Windsor*, ed. T.W. Craik, (Oxford: Oxford University Press, 1990).

—— *Troilus and Cressida*, ed. Harold N. Hillebrand, 'The Variorum Shakespeare' (Philadelphia and London: J.B. Lippincott Co., 1953).

—— *Troilus and Cressida*, ed. David Bevington, 'The Arden Shakespeare' (Walton-on-Thames: The Arden Shakespeare, 1998).

Shapiro, James, *Shakespeare and the Jews* (New York: Columbia University Press, 1996).

Shickman, A., 'The "Perspective Glass" in Shakespeare's *Richard II*', *Studies in English Literature*, 18 (1978), pp. 217–28.

Sidney, Sir Philip, *An Apology for Poetrie*, ed. Geoffrey Shepherd (Manchester: Manchester University Press, 1973).

Skinner, Quentin, *The Foundations of Modern Political Thought*, 2 vols (Cambridge: Cambridge University Press, 1978).

Slights, Camille Wells, *The Casuistical Tradition in Shakespeare, Donne, Herbert and Milton* (Princeton, NJ: Princeton University Press, 1981).

Smalley, Donald, 'The Ethical Bias of Chapman's Homer', *Studies in Philology*, 36 (1939), pp. 169–91.

Smith, Gordon Ross, 'Shakespeare's *Henry V*: Another Part of the Critical Forest', *Journal of the History of Ideas*, 37 (1976), pp. 3–26.

Smith, Hallett, *Elizabethan Poetry* (Cambridge, Mass.: Harvard University Press, 1952).

Smith, Logan Pearsall (ed.), *The Life and Letters of Sir Henry Wotton*, 2 vols (Oxford: Clarendon Press, 1966).

Spini, Giorgio, 'Historiography: The Art of History in the Italian Counter Reformation', in Eric Cochrane (ed.), *The Late Italian Renaissance 1525–1630* (London: Macmillan, 1970).

Spencer, T.J.B. (ed.), *Shakespeare's Plutarch* (Harmondsworth: Penguin Books, 1968).

Spencer, T.J.B. (ed.), "'Greeks' and 'Merrygreeks': A Background to *Timon of Athens* and *Troilus and Cressida*", in Richard Hosley (ed.), *Essays in Shakespeare and Elizabethan Drama. In Honor of Hardin Craig* (Columbia: University of Missouri Press, 1962).

Spencer, T.J.B. (ed.), 'Shakespeare and the Elizabethan Romans', *Shakespeare Survey*, 10 (1957), pp. 27–38.

Spevack, Marvin, *see under* William Shakespeare.

Sprengnether, Madelon, 'Annihilating Intimacy in *Coriolanus*; in Mary Beth Rose (ed.), *Women in the Middle Ages and the Renaissance* (New York: Syracuse University Press, 1986).

Stamm, Rudolf, 'The Glass of Pandar's Praise', *Essays and Studies*, 17 (1964), pp. 55–77.

Stephanus, Carolus, *Dictionarium Historicum,Geographicum, Poeticum* (New York and London: Garland Publishing, 1976).

Stewart, J.I.M., *Character and Motive in Shakespeare* (London: Longman Green and Co., 1949).

Stowe, John, *The Annales* (London, 1615).

Strong, Roy, *The Cult of Elizabeth* (London: Thames and Hudson, 1977).

Swedenberg, H.T., Jr., *The Theory of the Epic in England 1650–1800* (Berkeley and Los Angeles: University of Chicago Press, 1944).

Tacitus, Cornelius, *The Annales of Cornelius Tacitus. The Description of Germanie*, transl. R. Greenaway. *The Ende of Nero and Beginning of Galba. Fower Bookes of the Histories of Cornelius Tacitus. The Life of Agricola*, transl. Sir Henry Savile (1598).

Tatlock, J.S.P., 'The Siege of Troy in Elizabethan Literature, especially in Shakespeare and Heywood', *PMLA*, 30 (1915), pp. 673–770.

Taylor, Frank, and John S. Roskell (eds), *Gesta Henrici Quinti* (Oxford: Clarendon Press, 1975).

Thayer, C.G., *Shakespearean Politics. Government and Misgovernment in the Great Histories* (Athens and London: Ohio University Press, 1983).

Thomas, Keith, *Religion and the Decline of Magic* (London: Weidenfeld and Nicolson, 1971).

Thomson, Leslie, '*Antony and Cleopatra*, Act 4, Scene 16: "A heavy sight"', *Shakespeare Survey*, 41 (1988), pp. 77–90.

Tierney, M.A. (ed.), *Dodd's Church History of England*, 5 vols (London: Charles Dolman, 1840. Rep. Farnborough: Gregg International, 1972).

Tillyard, E.M.W., *Shakespeare's History Plays* (London: Chatto and Windus, 1944).

Trousdale, Marion, *Shakespeare and the Rhetoricians* (London: Scolar Press, 1982).

Tuck, Anthony. *Crown and Nobility 1272–1461* (London: Fontana, 1985).

Tuck, Anthony. *Richard II and the English Nobility* (London: Edward Arnold, 1973).

Tuck, Richard, *Philosophy and Government 1572–1651* (Cambridge: Cambridge University Press, 1991).

Tyndale, William, *The Obedience of a Christian Man*, in *Doctrinal Treatises, Works*, 3 vols, vol. 1, ed. Henry Walter, (Cambridge: The University Press, The Parker Society, 1848).

Ure, Peter, *see* William Shakespeare.

Vale, Malcolm, *War and Chivalry* (London: Duckworth, 1981).

Van Dyke, Joyce, 'Making a Scene: Language and Gesture in *Coriolanus*', *Shakespeare Survey*, 30 (1977), pp. 135–46.

Varro, Marcus Terentius, *see* Marcus Portius Cato.

Velz, John W., 'The Ancient World in Shakespeare: Authenticity or Anachronism? A Retrospect', *Shakespeare Survey*, 31 (1978), pp. 1–12.

Vincent, Barbara C., 'Shakespeare's *Antony and Cleopatra* and the Rise of Comedy', in John Drakakis (ed.), *Antony and Cleopatra* (Basingstoke: Macmillan, 1994).

Walker, Leslie J., *The Discourses of Niccolò Machiavelli*, 2 vols (London and Boston: Routledge and Kegan Paul, 1975).

Walter, John H., *see under* William Shakespeare.

Weis, R.J.A., '*Julius Caesar* and *Antony and Cleopatra*', in Stanley Wells (ed.), *Shakespeare. A Bibliographical Guide* (Oxford: Clarendon Press, 1990), pp. 275–93.

Wells, Charles, *The Wide Arch* (Bristol: Bristol Classical Press, 1993).

Wells, Robin Headlam, 'The Fortunes of Tillyard: Twentieth Century Critical Debate in Shakespeare's History Plays', *English Studies*, 66 (1985), pp. 391–403.

Wells, Stanley (ed.), *Shakespeare. A Bibliographical Guide* (Oxford: Clarendon Press, 1990).

Wells, Stanley and Gary Taylor, *see under* William Shakespeare.

West, Michael, 'Homer's *Iliad* and the Genesis of Mock-Heroic', *Cithera*, 21 (1991), pp. 3–22.

White, R.S., *Natural Law in English Renaissance Literature* (Cambridge: Cambridge University Press, 1996).

Wilders, John, *see under* William Shakespeare.

Wiles, David, *Shakespeare's Clown* (Cambridge: Cambridge University Press, 1987).

Wilkinson, B., *Constitutional History of Medieval England 1216–1399*, vol. 2 'Politics and the Constitution 1307–1399' (London: Longmans Green and Co., 1952).

Wilks, John S., *The Idea of Conscience in Renaissance Tragedy* (London and New York: Routledge, 1990).

Willett, John, *Brecht on Theatre* (New York: Hill and Wang/London: Eyre Methuen, 1979).

Williamson, George, *The Senecan Amble* (Chicago: University of Chicago Press, 1960).

Williamson, Marilyn, *Infinite Variety: Antony and Cleopatra in Renaissance Drama and Earlier Tradition* (Mystic, Conn.: Lawrence Verry, 1974).

Wilson, John Dover, *The Fortunes of Falstaff* (Cambridge: Cambridge University Press, 1943).

Wiseman, T.P., 'Practice and Theory in Roman Historiography', *History*, 66 (1981), pp. 375–93.

Wootton, David, *Paolo Sarpi. Between Renaissance and Enlightenment* (Cambridge: Cambridge University Press, 1983).

Worden, Blair, 'Ben Jonson among the Historians', in Kevin Sharpe and Peter Lake (eds), *Culture and Politics in Early Stuart England* (Basingstoke: Macmillan, 1994).

Wylie, James Hamilton, *History of England under Henry the Fourth* (London: Longmans Green and Co., 1884), 2 vols.

Wyatt, Sir Thomas, *The Complete Poems*, ed. R.A. Rebholz (New Haven and London: Yale University Press, 1978).

Yates, Frances, *Astraea. The Imperial Theme in the Sixteenth Century* (London and Boston: Routledge and Kegan Paul, 1975).

Yeats, W.B., *The Collected Poems of W.B. Yeats* (London: Macmillan, 1961).

Young, Alan, *Tudor and Jacobean Tournaments* (London: George Philip, 1987).

Zeeveld, Gordon, '*Coriolanus* and Jacobean Politics', *Modern Language Review*, 57 (1962), pp. 321–34.

Index